FABKGFT

C0-AVX-887

STARS

IN DE

ELEMENTS

A Study of Negro Folk Music
by Willis Laurence James

Edited by Jon Michael Spencer

Introduction by Rebecca T. Cureau

A Special Issue of Black Sacred Music: A Journal of Theomusicology

Volume 9   Numbers 1 and 2   1995

Published by Duke University Press

33188386

ML
3556
.J35
1995

With this issue, *Black Sacred Music*
will cease publication. A limited
numer of back issues are still
available from Duke University Press,
Box 90660, Durham, NC 27708.
Please see the inside back cover for a
listing of Special issues.

Black Sacred Music is indexed in
*Religion Index One, The Index to
Book Reviews in Religion,* and *The
Music Index.*

Photocopying Photocopies for course or research use that are supplied
to the end-user at no cost may be made without need for explicit
permission or fee. Photocopies that are provided to their end-users for
some photocopying fee may not be made without payment of permission fees to Duke University Press, at $1.50 per copy for each article
copied. Registered users may pay for photocopying via the Copyright
Clearance Center, using the code and price at the bottom of each
article-opening page.

Permissions Requests for permission to republish copyrighted material
from this journal should be addressed to Journals Permissions Editor,
Duke University Press, Brightleaf Square, 905 W. Main Street, 18-B,
Box 90660, Durham, NC 27708-0660.

Copyright © 1995 by Duke University Press.

ISSN 1043-9455
ISBN for this issue 0-8223-6432-8

Contents

T48

HOLY SPIRIT LIBRARY
96~0132
CABRINI COLLEGE, RADNOR, PA.

Chapter 14. The Great Fantasia

An epitome of contributors of both races to the progress of Negro music, whether writers, singers, composers, or other personalities.   230

Foreword

As of this year, 1995, this book is exactly fifty years old, and yet until now it has never been seen by the public. It might have been seen by a few publishers whom the author contacted after he completed the manuscript in 1945, but their responses might have been similar to mine when I first received a copy from Rebecca T. Cureau: The manuscript is a good first draft, but it is not yet ready for publication. But sensing the extraordinary information and insight resulting from the author's folkloric research, I decided to take the manuscript through two more carefully crafted drafts.[1]

First, at Cureau's suggestion, I incorporated into the original manuscript the improved version of chapter 2, which appeared in Atlanta University's *Phylon* in 1955 as "The Romance of the Negro Folk Cry in America." I should also point out that fifty-one pages are missing (or the author intentionally deleted them) from the collection of songs comprising the appendix. Nonetheless, the eighty remaining songs and the many musical examples throughout the book overshadow the loss.

Actually, the songs missing from the appendix were the least of my sorrows. Indeed, when I think back on the months of painstaking editing, the words of the old spiritual come to mind: "Nobody knows the trouble I've seen." The task of cautiously recrafting James's sentences and reworking his paragraphing was especially troublesome because before James's widow died in early 1994 I had made a promise to her. Through Cureau I had promised to maintain the overall integrity of James's scholarship, including his choice of lan-

---

1. Those drafts, along with the original manuscript, are housed in the Black Sacred Music Collection, Hampton University Archives, Hampton, Virginia.

guage and style of writing, both of which were affected by his having written the book so long ago, in 1945.

Sensing that I have kept my promise, I cannot suppress the feeling of edification that always accompanies the ethical act. Sensing that the promise has also resulted in a very satisfactory work, I also sense the thrill of what it must feel like to bring to one's native people a first translation of some immensely important work in a foreign language. With my "translation" now completed, the reader will wonder how for a half century we have managed to live without this phenomenal work of African American folklore. In any case, now it is here—glory, hallelujah!

Jon Michael Spencer

Introduction

At the time of his death in 1966, Willis Laurence James had lived to see a gradual turning of the tide in the direction of appreciation for the folk traditions that evolved in America during the era of African enslavement. Born at the turn of the century, when many of the oldest black traditions were still transmitted orally in rural areas throughout the South, James began to collect in his youthful memory songs that he later raised to the level of choral artistry. He was among that early group of well-educated and highly talented black musicians who undertook the study and preservation of a music widely considered the only indigenous American folk song next to that of the Native Americans.

There was hardly a time in his life when James was not drawn to the culture from which black folk song evolved. As a result of his work as a folklorist, folk song arranger, and original composer, his reputation as an authority on black folk life spread from the local and regional levels to the national arena during the 1950s, at which time he began receiving invitations to lecture throughout the country and abroad. In 1951 he was one of twenty-five musicians and music educators invited to a conference at the Library of Congress to consider the future of music in America. He also became a regular lecturer and panelist at the annual Newport Jazz Festival from its beginning in 1954, and at the Newport Folk Music Festival beginning in 1957. In 1961 he lectured at the opening of the Center for Negro Arts in Lagos, Nigeria. He also received prestigious honors for his work, such as the Honorary Superior Degree for Service in Music, which he was awarded in 1953 by the Department of Health, Education, and Welfare. Two years later, in 1955, he was awarded an honorary doctor of music degree from Wilberforce University in recognition of his efforts to preserve black folk song through collection, composition, and performance.

Willis Laurence James was born in Montgomery, Alabama, on September 18, 1900. As a child he was taken to Florida by his mother, Minnie James. They moved first to Pensacola and then to Jacksonville, where they settled down and attended the Bethel Institutional Baptist Church. For many years Bethel served as the setting in which the young James not only absorbed the tenets of his Baptist faith but also heard black concert artists and was exposed to the rich song tradition of the black spirituals.

James attended the Florida Baptist Academy (founded by Bethel Church), where he came under the tutelage of the individual who nurtured and encouraged his appreciation for the artistry of black folk song—the academy's music teacher, concert tenor Sidney Woodward.[1] James sang in the choral groups and male quartets trained at the academy by Woodward. Recognizing his young student's musical talent and particularly his potential as a violinist, Woodward took James to Atlanta in the summer of 1916 to play for concert violinist and Morehouse College professor Kemper Harreld.[2] The following fall James entered the tenth grade at Morehouse Academy and became Harreld's protégé. As his student there and subsequently at Morehouse College, James became an outstanding violinist and one of the leading tenor soloists in the Morehouse Glee Club and Quartet. He also became a member of the Morehouse Orchestra and later,

---

1. Maud Cuney Hare, "Musical Pioneers," *International Library of Negro Life and History* (1969). Born on a Georgia plantation, Woodward (1860–1924) was orphaned at an early age but overcame many hardships to obtain an education. Aided by a benefactor, he studied voice in Boston, concertized in the United States, and later toured many of the major capitals of Europe as a celebrated artist. Upon his return to the United States, he taught at the Florida Baptist Academy, Clark University in Nashville, and the Music School Settlement in New York.

2. Kemper Harreld (1885–1971) played a prominent role in the development of music at Morehouse College and in the Atlanta area. Trained at major American conservatories and in Europe, he performed widely throughout Europe and the United States and joined the music faculty of Morehouse College in 1911. He also became associated with Spelman College when the music departments of the two institutions merged in 1927.

during his college years, concertmaster and assistant conductor. During these latter years he began to demonstrate a talent for composing and arranging, often performing his own vocal compositions. His folk song arrangements were performed frequently by the Morehouse Glee Club and Quartet.

Following his studies at Morehouse College, James began his teaching career in 1923 at Leland College in Baker, Louisiana, where he remained until 1928. It was at Leland that he began his collection of black folk song, using the area surrounding the college (a former sugar plantation along the Mississippi River known as the Louisiana Sugar Bottoms) and the southeastern section of the state as the locales for his research. This period marks the beginning of James's fascination with the songs, cries, and hollers sung by the longshoremen, dockworkers, and laborers who work along the levees and in the fields. Several of the songs he collected during this period of fieldwork were arranged for the choral groups he directed at Leland. Four of them were recorded by the Paramount Record Company of Chicago in 1927; two were later published and are still performed.[3]

In 1928 James joined the faculty of Alabama State Normal College, in Montgomery, the city of his birth. He had recently married Theodora Joanna Fisher, a graduate of Spelman College, whom he had met during her year of teaching at Leland, 1926–27. James, a more mature teacher and seasoned musician as a result of his teaching experiences at Leland and his advanced training at the Chicago Conservatory of Music during the summers, began to make a positive impression during his first year as director of the choir and the small orchestra he started, and as instructor of a beginning class in violin.[4] During his second year at Alabama, James became director of the marching band and began working with jazz ensembles, a relatively new development at black colleges. James's interest in folk music now also embraced the tradition of quartet singing associated with the mining camps near Birmingham.

---

3. James himself wrote the music for these songs. The two later published were "Captain, Look-a Yonder" and "Cabin Boy Call."

4. *State Normal Journal* 2, no.1 (March 1929): 52–53.

In 1933, after five years at Alabama State Normal College, James joined the faculty of Spelman College in Atlanta, where he remained until his death in 1966. In the combined music department of Spelman and Morehouse he directed the Morehouse College Marching Band, taught a wide range of music courses, and occasionally, with Kemper Harreld, conducted the Morehouse-Spelman Orchestra and taught violin. One of James's principal duties was directing the Spelman College Glee Club, whose highly touted performances often included arrangements of James's collected black folk songs as well as standard classical works. While none of James's numerous arrangements of spirituals for the women's voices of the Spelman College Glee Club were ever published, some preserved in manuscript remain part of its repertoire, as do several of James's original compositions that are not based on folk sources. James also wrote arrangements and compositions for the male voices of the Morehouse Glee Club and Quartet; two of his songs remain popular in that ensemble's repertoire.[5] Beginning in 1935, the performance of James's arrangements and compositions based on his collected Christmas spirituals became a tradition at the annual Morehouse-Spelman Christmas carol concerts, initiated by Harreld in 1927.

Two events early in James's tenure at Spelman College were important to his career as a folklorist. First, in 1939 he received a General Education Board grant that enabled him to do extended fieldwork—the research for this book—during a period when folk traditions were still strong in many areas of the Deep South. Second, in 1941 he became involved with the Fort Valley State College Folk Music Festival, which for almost fifteen years gave him the opportunity to act on his belief that the folklorist should not only collect folk songs but encourage folk musicians to perform them.

From the start James intended this book to be a valuable contribution to the documentation of black folklore, which by now he was

---

5. The texts of these two songs, "Captain, Look-a Yonder" and "Roberta Lee," were published, along with two of James's collected work songs, in *Negro Caravan*, ed. Sterling A. Brown, Arthur Davis, and Ulysses Lee (New York: Dryden Press, 1941). An arrangement of "Roberta Lee" by the late Wendell P. Whalum, a former student of James, was published by Lawson-Gould in 1972 and attributed to James.

well equipped to undertake. "It is not enough merely to collect these songs," he wrote in his proposal to the General Education Board. "It is necessary to possess a first-hand knowledge of Negro customs, modes of expression, intimate domestic life and attitudes. . . . Great patience and understanding are required to win their [Negroes'] confidence and to have them sing with the naturalness and abandon with which they sing among themselves. . . . I believe that I am qualified to undertake the work because I am a Negro, a singer, and a composer."[6] James felt strongly that there needed to be made "a clear and authoritative statement" by a black scholar on the musical gifts evolving out of black folk life, since earlier works on black music by black scholars had concentrated on black contributions to the Western musical tradition.[7]

In September 1939 James began four months of fieldwork in the South Carolina Sea Islands (St. Helena, Port Royal, and James), the coal-mining regions of Alabama, the southern region of Georgia, and the coastal regions of Florida. He spent much of the remaining three months of his leave organizing his findings. He began to write this book in the early 1940s and completed it in 1945. In correspondence with publishers James described it as "a study of Negro folk music based upon first-hand observation, in the field and classroom, and covering a period of twenty years . . . arranged according to the unfolding of Negro music in America . . . to provide a source wherein one may acquire insight and comprehension regarding the true nature and meaning of all classes and types of Negro music." Whatever prevented James from finding a publisher for his manuscript, it was unquestionably an invaluable document of black folklore, as invaluable as the works of other pioneer black folklorists, such as Zora Neale Hurston. That it appears now, exactly fifty years after James completed it, makes it all the more important as a source of

6. Willis Laurence James, grant proposal submitted to the General Education Board, January 24, 1939. James had already done fieldwork on a Carnegie grant in the summer of 1935.

7. See, for example, James Monroe Trotter's *Music and Some Highly Musical People* (1878), Maud Cuney Hare's *Negro Musicians and Their Music* (1936), and Alain Locke's *The Negro and His Music* (1936).

insight into a folk culture of the Deep South that no longer exists as James knew it.

The publication of *Stars in de Elements* not only brings resolution to the extraordinary life of Willis Laurence James but also serves as a tribute to his mother, Minnie James Washington, who inspired and encouraged his early interest in his folk heritage, and to his widow, Theodora Fisher James (1905–94), who sought vigorously to find a publisher after his death. Although Mrs. James did not live to see the book in print, she did consent to have it edited and published with my introduction. From the outset of my work on James fifteen years ago, she was a staunch ally, supporter, and friend. Her generous assistance and cooperation in my use and organization of her husband's papers in the Spelman College archives figure largely in whatever success I have had in illuminating his place in American history. I gratefully dedicate this momentous fulfillment of our efforts to her memory.

Finally, this publication is a credit to Jon Michael Spencer, who was too young to know James while he lived but who recognized the importance of making this work available in published form. He has edited it carefully and thoughtfully, enhancing its clarity while preserving the integrity of James's thoughts and language. For his work and dedication I am profoundly grateful.

Rebecca T. Cureau

Dedication

To my mother
Minnie Ellis James Washington
who sang to me
before my ears knew the sounds

Willis Laurence James

Stars in de Elements

"Stars in de Elements": eternal torchbearers which lift the fog-
bound soul above the clouds, guide him upon the storm-tossed sea,
tune his soul with the infinite, and shine best when darkness is
deepest—given birth by the night.

Stars in de el - e - ments, ___ shine, shine, _ shine. _

Stars in de el - e - ments, ___ shine, shine, _ shine. _

Preface

This book has been written after a long period of investigation, participation, and instruction in the field of Negro music. There seems to be a need at this time for a treatise on the subject of Afro-American songs and singing from a Negro. Hence, this book represents an effort on my part to meet that need. There is no effort here to answer all questions regarding the subject. There is bound to be, as is always the case, room for improvement based upon latter-day considerations, observations, and convictions. Perhaps these can be expressed in due course. The main purpose of this work is to promote a clearer picture of the nature of Negro songs than is generally possessed today. It is my hope that the young as well as the adult person may find here a concise, friendly, stimulating source that may cause finer interest in a long-beloved subject.

If there are those who find occasion to disagree with certain statements made herein, this differing of opinion is considered a sacred right. It can be stimulating and beneficial if supported by sound premises. If this text can be an incentive for further investigation and bring inspiration to some composers, as well as make new friends for all folk music, our end has been reached.

Acknowledgments of help are best given to those who have sung the songs that have given me much of my knowledge. Many of their names, as well as the names of those who assisted me as guides and informants, are contained in the book proper. However, especial thanks must be extended to Mr. Curley Parrish of Birmingham, Alabama; to Percy Stone of Savannah, Georgia; to the Reverend Levi M. Terrill of Savannah and Atlanta, Georgia; to Principal Kennedy of Dixiana, Alabama; to Dr. Lorenzo Turner of Fisk University; and to Professor William Dinkins of Selma, Alabama. Also, mention should be made of the painstaking work done by Mrs. Lucille Fletcher Lee in copying much of the music as well as in typing and retyping the manuscript several times. Finally, thanks must be given to my colleagues, present and past: Kemper Harreld, Naomah Maise, Alma Stone, Portia Jenkins Crawford, and Sara Owsley Stivers, all of whom have given some of my findings a sympathetic hearing and performance in choral and solo form. Mr. Harreld's firsthand knowledge of early twentieth-century Negro singers, actors, and instrumentalists has been very helpful. The students of Spelman in particular, and of Morehouse in large measure, have—through their listening, singing, and general interest—provided me with a magnificent testing laboratory wherein I discovered the effect of my discussion and singing on "new ears" above the true folk level.

The late Dr. John Hope, President of Atlanta University, was the first person of high significance and influence to volunteer tangible assistance in my research. It was through his interest and solicitation that Atlanta University and Spelman College procured my first grant.

In recent years and indeed up to the present, Miss Florence M. Read, my own president at Spelman College, procured special assistance for my work from the General Education Board. Moreover, she has given added means and facilities of the college, which were helpful in my completing this book. Without their help this study could not have been realized in its present form.

Willis Laurence James

Chapter 1

Prelude

Negro music is the result of the ways and experiences of the Negro. However, since we are considering the Negro music found here in America—indeed, in so small an area as the southern United States—we are forced to consider a very special series of influences not like those of any other people in the world. It is therefore necessary for the reader to have a brief introduction that deals with the nature of folk music in general. This must be followed by a discussion about the singing ways and customs of Negroes in Africa as well as in America, and a consideration of both of these in relation to the progress of time, which is the great modifier of all of man's activities. Time itself is a rhythmical process. It is the orderly succession of time values which governs all of the vital functions of man's life and the universe. Music is also ordered by this great force. Let us, then, speak of the first half of music—rhythm.

The Rhythm Sphere

If one stops to consider the fact that he can be sure the sun will rise at a given instant in his locality on a given day, or that he can consult the calendar in his pocket for a date months ahead, he will be aware of the greatest force we have in the entire gamut of physical relations—movement according to natural principles.

Rhythm has two phases. The first and most fundamental is that which is provided by Providence and which gives us the movements of the tides—day, night, birth, growth, and so forth. The second phase is that kind which is produced by voluntary action on the part of man and lower animals. However, here we must have further division, for rhythm in lower animals seems to follow more of a set pattern of actions common to the species or class. On the other hand, man has the ability and the urge to use rhythm as a means of expression in art forms, to create definite symbols for the forms of rhythmic expression, and to assign these symbols to various devices he makes. It is from the latter phase of rhythm that music gets its power of movement, yet one must be aware that this latter phase is nothing more than a part of the great fundamental rhythm of the universe.

In order to make rhythm fit into our special understanding here, let us take the relationship of man to the rhythm in the universe and evaluate these considerations in a very elementary way. More than any other living thing, man has an awareness of ordered movement. He is in turn moved by it on a psychological level. Whenever the feeling of rhythm is established, man reacts to it in a personal and general way. The primitive races dance to the drum, or to the hand-clap, or to the striking of stones, wood, or metal, but the types of dances performed from country to country and from race to race are very different. Yet the awareness of rhythmic forces is always there and represented by the same principles. How marvelous it is that Negroes in Africa, Indians in America, and Chinese in Asia all used the drum principle at a time when none of them realized that the others existed in the world. It is equally amazing that the Negro and the white man, the yellow man and the red man, the brown man and the mixed man have all reacted to the urges of rhythm on a basis that meets at the common road leading to artistic expression in the various art forms, and that these forms are identical in all cases and may be generally classified as belonging to about six branches: music, literature, architecture, painting, dancing, and sculpture.

If a speaker or singer or instrumentalist does not have an awareness of the importance of rhythm, his listeners will remove him from their centers of concentration and get out of step with his procedure. One of the surest ways to be in possession of the controlling factors of art is to be in control of the rhythmic forces behind it. Hence, from this admittedly brief discussion, we can see that the force of rhythm is the prime mover in the realm of creation as well as in the realm of creativity.

Rhythm applied to the everyday commonplaceness in man's existence is equally fascinating to study. The beat of the heart, the stride in the walk, the movement of the breath, the movement of the peristalsis, and the processes of chewing and swallowing are all regulated on a definite and progressive series of time interruptions. It is also important to realize that any actions or sounds that are pleasing in themselves can be enhanced by the addition of a certain series of rhythmic factors. On the other hand, unpleasant factors have the opposite result when coupled with certain rhythmic factors—they can become more annoying. Take, for instance, a dripping hydrant, a screeching sound, or a rhythmic scraping. These prove that rhythm, as powerful as it is, may be employed disadvantageously or advantageously by man. This brings us to the handling of rhythm by the human mind.

The most natural use of rhythm by man may be found in speech. Here we have the variety of frequently used natural sounds emerging from the most perfect sound-producing instrument ever witnessed. Moreover, the use of the sounds is indispensable to the welfare of society. Therefore, the use of the sounds known as words is wrapped up with the very soul of the individual. It reflects his thoughts. The use of instruments of percussion is not alone the subject of consideration here, but we must realize that every instrument played by man is the servant of the rhythmic force in focus at the moment of playing.

Rhythm has two "demons." They are understood when the fact of their origin is shown to be a by-product of rhythmic functioning. The steady beat of a drum or other instrument produces a monotony, which is the first demon. The varying of these above-named beats will give variety up to a certain point, but if carried beyond this point will produce a complexity in keeping with only the most unusual rhythmic feeling, such as we find in certain primitive people. If taken beyond this, we have the second demon—confusion.

Primitive man learned that several things relieved the monotony produced in his early music efforts. (1) He could change the nature of the sounds making the pattern. (2) He could change the nature of the beat sequence. (3) He could consider dynamics with regard to the pattern by emphasizing certain beats and using crescendos and diminuendos. (4) Perhaps the most important feature of this whole development was when man found he could vary the pitch of the sounds producing the rhythms. This gives us the basis for melodic considerations and development.

However, before we go further, let us pause to summarize and give further explanation of the four developmental aspects of rhythmic functioning mentioned above. Rhythmic functioning (1) led to the development of new instruments with new sound-colors, (2) led to the development of new and more interesting rhythms and also a blending of these, (3) produced the first feeling for sound contrast in sequence and in free order, and (4) produced the rudiments of the scale and led to a definite song stage. The second demon need not be discussed since the matter of confusion can only be corrected by order. This merely means that the limits of complexity establish themselves by automatic check in the folk mind. Folk art is always at the level of the people's emotional needs at any given time. As the needs change, so does the particular art in question.

To make the situation clearer, the following figures demonstrate the principles given above:

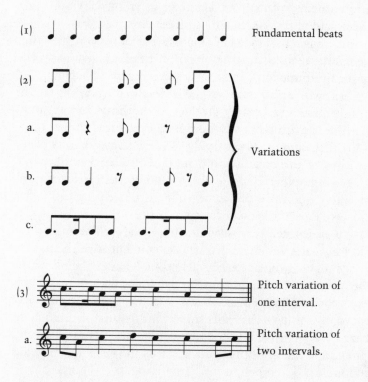

b. Pitch variation of six intervals.

(4) Dynamic considerations

(5) These tones were varied in color by using skins, stones, metal, baked earth, wood, and by all means the voice and hand-clap.

The Tone Sphere

Tone is a definite sound which differs from noise in that it can be produced and remembered on the basis of its relation to other sounds having its characteristics. For instance, a sound that has definite pitch is a tone, while a sound that does not have definite pitch is a noise. A hand-clap is a noise, whereas a vowel sound produced for a fraction of a second can be assigned a definite place in the pitch-relation center of the hearer. The latter may also be written down according to musical language symbols, therefore it may be made into an expressed thought. This is what is meant when some scholars have spoken of music as an art and a language. It should also be remembered, though, that the sheer projective quality of music is always the tone element, just as it is in speech. Speech is music insofar as it is produced by a musical instrument and has the governing influence of time values or rhythm present in its operation at all times. This brings us to the place of the voice in the development of tonal consciousness.

It is the opinion of musicologists and historians that the voice is the originator of the first music. It was, of course, not a usual speech procedure, but rather an unusual one based on emotional factors. It was through impassioned speech that man became aware of the quality in the voice known as tonal range. It was also through this same medium that he was made aware of the sustaining qualities of the voice. When he called someone or when he was frightened or happy, he discovered he no longer used the range and quality of voice that he did for common purposes. When man first found out about the possibilities of sustaining word formations or a single tone and about projecting the flow according to his emotional dictates rather than by a rigid rhythmic formula, he did a fundamental service for the development of song: He developed the chant.

Many theories have been developed in regard to the origin of man's use of the primitive scales. They do not belong here, since this book is not devoted to historical musical development in the broad sense. I prefer to present my own theory here. It is my opinion that the "scales" used by primitive peoples are not scales at all. The fact that certain preferences are shown for certain tones found in the scales of composers seems to be a result derived from choice based upon natural drives. The folk sang free of any considerations save the moment of inspiration, just as a bird sings in accordance with certain natural drives. Man in his earliest primitive state sang the same way. Of course, when he made his music functional, thereby using it as a formal means of expression, he modified the purely inspirational aspects. It was a matter of making sounds to fit a specific case, such as various ceremonies, dances, and so forth.

Scales are the products of a deliberate organization of notes into logical sequence. The fact that specialists had to do this shows that the folk had no such consideration. They were moved by what was most natural to them. They found it natural to sing in whole steps and skips, so they used these intervals. There was no feeling for the half step in a general way, so we could say that the half step bears a certain artificial character. Anyone who has led a group of average singers realizes their tendency to become confused in the management of half steps in the parts. It is for this reason, too, that the first vocal composers gave such careful consideration to the use of intervals that implied or used accidentals—sharps and flats.

There is no objection here to calling the primitive five-tone texture a "pentatonic scale." These tones were eventually understood by early man, as his instruments prove. What I am anxious to show is that man was not dependent on any such technical device as scales when he began singing. Man was his own law, composer, and instrument. The names of all tone orders are necessary in this day for clarity. Our complex systems of the past need ordering.

In speaking of the above, I have often been asked why it is that Negroes use the flat seventh if half steps are so unnatural. My explanation is simply this: When Negroes use the seventh tone with its strong leaning toward the tonic by half step, the tendency is to lower it in pitch and to approach it and leave it by step or by skip. The comparative infrequency of this device shows that the Negro does not like the trouble of doing this, despite the fact that it produces a charming effect. The same principle, I feel, was true of other peoples at the same level of musical development. Our choice of the stage of development in such discussions must be the determining factor in our conclusions as well as in our understanding. However, since our topic here deals with the Negro, let us see how these principles fit into what has taken place in Negro music in the United States.

The Negro in America is a transplant from Africa, with a maze of tribal, language, folk, and intellectual differences. These are now so blended as to represent a "New Negro." However, when we think back, a very different situation is apparent. American Negroes practiced the customs of their native lands and tribes for many years. Therefore, our next phase deals with the development of the Afro-American folk style in America.

Afro-American Folk Music

It so happens that the entire balance of this book deals with an understanding of American Negro music. However, we shall be better prepared if we show certain special aspects related to the very beginnings of our subject.

The American rhythms are all of a very dynamic and complex nature. When speaking of African rhythm, one must be aware of its nature as it is conceived and manifested by African peoples. A single rhythmic series does not satisfy the African feeling. There must be several rhythms going on at the same time. This sets up a type of rhythmic interference that produces fractional rhythmic divisions. Nicholas George Julius Ballanta, the African composer and musicologist, describes these interferences as vibrations. For musicians, perhaps "polyrhythmic" is the preferable term. For the layman "simultaneous rhythms" is a better name.

In order to produce these simultaneous rhythms, the African uses every means at his disposal, principally calling on drums and the hand-clap for the major portion of the effect. People who have visited

Africa and Brazil have been amazed at the command of the various drums developed by the natives. In fact, it is generally agreed that the African of certain regions is the greatest of all drummers in the world. Richard Wallenschek says the sending of messages by drums is peculiar to the African and that the process exceeds a mere code, representing the actual sounds of words. He explains that "varying the tones of the drums is done by pressure of the hands and the heels to the vibrating membrane, causing a change of pitch." Again, one can see that the African has resorted to the use of speech rhythms as a means of rhythmic expression. More than this, there is the use of the principles of variation we have previously considered. This is enough for our purpose here. If one wishes to know more of the African rhythmic combinations, he may read the introduction to *St. Helena Island Spirituals* by Nicholas George Julius Ballanta or Henry E. Krehbiel's book, *Afro-American Folksongs*.

Before we go into the main consideration of our story, something should be said regarding the more recent rhythmic practices, such as may be found today in certain rural sections of the South and even in a place like New York City's Harlem — indeed, wherever Negroes from the various places of the world have assembled. It is obvious that the Negro has accepted certain aspects of the Western rhythms. However, he always achieves polyrhythmic effects by singing in syncopes, patting the hands in various patterns, and using his feet as further accents to the rhythm. Whether or not Negroes do all these things at all times, the fact remains that they feel them. One of the most common manifestations of this urge is seen at the average Negro College football game in the South. When the people begin to sing or cheer together, they automatically go into a series of body rhythms against the music or cheer. In recent years it has been the practice of some schools to suppress this urge on the part of youngsters, because it all too frequently leads to dance representation not in keeping with certain behavioral standards.

As for the melodic consideration regarding the Negro and his American music output, it may be said that he has adopted certain Western idioms. For instance, there is greater formality in the Afro-American melody than one finds in the purely African song. This is due to Western influence in regard to the formal arrangement of note patterns. However, the actual structural form, from a stylistic point of view, places the American Negro song on an equivalent level with the African song. Both are antiphonal, being propelled by a leader who is entrusted with the progress of the song while a group sings the refrain or chorus—or the "burden," as the Negro aptly calls it. The chief difference between white song and Negro song in America is largely a rhythmical one. Yet there is a tendency on the part of the Negro to sing in wider intervals than does his white neighbor, and thereby to get greater dynamic force on the one hand and to obtain greater vocal elasticity on the other by using vocal inflection to close the gaps.

The following graphic examples are herewith used to give an idea of Negro rhythm and melody as applied in the United States.

1. Patterns of rhythms used by the varying Negro congregation on the folk level:

A. (4/4 meter throughout)

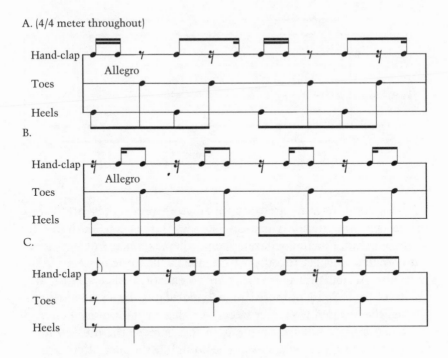

D.

E.

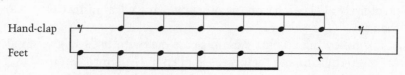

F.

These combinations are only meant to give a representation of rhythms most commonly used by Negroes in the deep South in religious worship. Imagine what happens when exponents of the different combinations get together by chance in the same meeting! Also note how difficult these patterns are to execute, especially for any length of time. Some of these can be handled only by a person who is sitting, thereby giving greater freedom to leg and foot movements.

The shout is a body movement in response to the music rather than a part of it, yet very often the sound of the feet offers a very interesting supporting pattern of rhythm.

An investigation of these series shows a strong kinship with the tango and habanera rhythms, which Negroes taught the Latin Americans and Europeans.

Herewith are examples of Negro singing characteristics showing embellishments, slides (portamentos), and rudimentary harmony. It is well to realize that rural Negroes sing rather contrapuntally, and whatever harmony results comes very spontaneously—springing from within the music.

2. A consideration of Negro folk harmony and melody.

A.

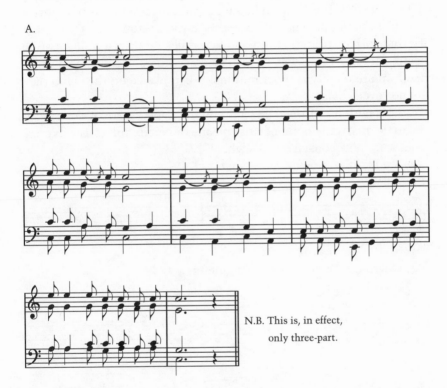

N.B. This is, in effect,
only three-part.

The above melody is one sung in Georgia to the text "Guide My Feet." The tune is made from three tones and two intervals, yet it has great power. The harmony is the strangest one could wish for, and yet it is produced by the voice leading—therefore, "counter-singin'."

The harmonic intervals show octaves, fourths, fifths, thirds, and sevenths used singly and in succession. There is no leading tone or fourth tone; therefore no B or F is found in the melody or harmony.

B.

The above wavy lines indicate slides (portamentos). No matter how fast the tempo, one yet hears the "curvin'" tones. It is this quality that forbids transcription and befuddles description. It must be heard, for only voices can do it. The grace notes used in the harmonization are merely approximations. When played on the piano they are not even that.

If no examples of male quartet singing appear here, it is because the male quartet is not a normal means of Negro folk music expression. It is to be considered elsewhere.

3. Standard version of an old meter.

4. Negro treatment of the same meter.

A comparison of the above examples shows a tendency on the part of the Negro to decorate the meters as sung by the white man and as invented by himself. This is the result of a feeling for rhythm and a certain type of melodic restlessness born largely of the Negro's inventive rhythmic impulse. Note that the embellishments are built around the so-called pentatonic scale.

None of the foregoing examples are to be taken as more than mere representations of so vast a thing as Negro folk tonal movement implies. These examples do show, in outline, what happens in the singing of Negro congregations.

As for dialect, it may well be considered an indispensable part of the Negro folk song. Its unique rhythms and tonal qualifications are ingredients of most vital effect. James Weldon Johnson limits dialect to two powers—pathos and humor. It seems that such a limitation deals only with the externals of dialect and misses its essences. Dialect has or generates form based upon rhythm. For instance:

> Dialect: I ain't go' steddy war no mo'.
> English: I am not going to study war anymore.

If one tried to sing these lines to the familiar tune, the form of the lines makes the first seem incomparably better.

A. Negro dialect   Example 3

I   ain't go'   sted-dy   war _   no   mo'.

B. English

I am not go-ing to   stud-y   war _   an - y more.

Reduced to poetic meter:

Reduced to word rhythms:

A. Negro dialect

A. Negro dialect

Ĭ ain't| gŏ' stĕddy| war| nŏ mo'.

B. English

B. English

Ĭ am| not going to studywar| anymore.

The sheer tonal aspect of dialect is a power unto itself, so that we mention tone color as a second power of dialect. When spoken it gives a series of sounds that have a tonal charm based on its peculiar liquid, flowing quality as well as the inflection. Music shows how important a conveyor of art-feeling tone is. The symphony orchestra demonstrates the force of color. It has always seemed to me that in the symphony of languages Negro dialect has the role of the cello. Most American English goes from clarinet to bassoon. The color of a sentence spoken in dialect and one spoken in English, if studied side by side, demonstrates the point.

The third power of dialect is perspective. When one hears or reads a sentence in dialect he not only hears words, he not only hears thoughts that may be expressed as meaningfully as they could be in any language, but he also hears a certain type of character. He sees a certain portion of the past. If he has imagination, he experiences a clarity of understanding in relation to all of the things that produced the dialect. He sees a specific art instance.

The fourth power is human interest. This realm exposes all of the things one may realize in a lifetime. When related to the Negro, it relates him to the world. The dialect is only a very specific, albeit necessary, instrument that brings the whole into quick and unmistakable focus.

The fifth power of dialect is spontaneity. It modifies the general manner of discourse in certain areas and offers to creative writers a freshness in figure and verse.

Of course, not all versions of Negro dialect are equally effective in singing. The Gullah speech, for instance, is not generally understood as well as the inland speech of the Negro living in closer contact with mainstream American culture. The changing of a word here and there has been done by several arrangers and singers with no detriment when the word substituted did not change the rhythm and remained Negro dialect. For instance:

1. Gullah: Pray is de key to de kingdom.
   Revision: Prayer is de key to de Kingdom.
2. Gullah: Nebuh me one.
   Revision: Ain't but me one.

These changes were made by the inland Negroes who learned these songs by way of Savannah, or perhaps Charleston or Brunswick.

No hard and fast rule can be set in regard to the exact dialect used by any group in singing a given spiritual. Different Negroes—in an area like middle Georgia, for instance—speak differently. Take a statement like "I am going to go," and change it into what one would hear among older and less developed Negroes in middle Georgia: (1) Ah'm gwine go, (2) Ah'm 'ine go, (3) I'm go' go, (4) I'm ganh go, (5) Ah'm gunno go, (6) Um 'o' go, (7) Um ino go, and (8) Um gwi' go. These are expressions that merely suggest to the reader the many possible shades of tone effected by dialect, as well as the necessity of adopting the best text of a song for general use.

Finally, it is to be hoped that the general principles set down herein are not looked upon as covering every instance in the realm of folk music. Our field is essentially a consideration of primitive folk music, and not all folk music is primitive. There are exceptions to most things. It is only important that they be looked upon as exceptions. For instance, if the tonal considerations of Jews, Magyars, Serbs, and Bulgarians are not in keeping with the five-tone, whole-step idiom that is the most widely dispersed and reputedly the oldest, then it is to be understood from a musical point of view that their development had passed from the very primitive aspect before their songs were traced out and brought before the world. Thus it is seen that our subject, Negro music, is a product of the ages, colored by the temperaments of the various Negro tribes that were brought to this country to live side by side with the races of the world and to be influenced by them.

Chapter 2
Cries in Speech and Song

I

Animals are capable of giving out sounds from their mouths that represent meanings and varying degrees of the powerful urge for expression. These sounds separate into two categories: those that man makes and those made by his lesser fellow inhabitants of this planet. Further, the sounds made by man fall into two categories—those that he learns how to make through instruction and experimentation, and those that arise seemingly from no plan or understood purpose but that persist in all races and in all conditions of society.

The cry is an instant reminder of the primitive. It is the oldest form of vocal expression. From it arise all of the things associated with speech and musical tone concepts. When the newly born babe utters its cry, it gives therewith the true indication of life itself. There is something mysterious about the cry as it affects all animals, whether it be articulate or not. There is a certain something in it that says more than mere words can express. In fact, it may be said that the cry is more reliable in its general inarticulateness than when it is used as a purveyor of a definite idea, as in connection with speech. Speech may be false, but a spontaneous cry is never false. Therefore, it is evident that the cry is an expression of nature or impulse through natural spontaneous sound.

When one hears the newsboy on the streets crying his sales line, the experience brings him to the brink of musical beginnings. If the age of man has saved any one thing in the realm of communication and kept it active unto this day as an unchanged factor in life, it is the cry in its several different manifestations. There is no need to wonder how the music of ancient man sounded in principle. Merely go into the streets where you live, the villages where vendors abide, the waterfronts of remote places, the fields, the churches, and wherever people dwell and act out the patterns of life.

There are cries that are articulate in regard to speech and inarticulate in regard to musical expression. These are the types that can only be given the barest approximation in notation. They are the very primitive agents of expression that are yet heard in myriad ways—notably at contests, parades, disasters, and various cases involving individuals.

Cries that are articulate from the standpoint of music, but not from the standpoint of words, represent the type that is heard less in urban areas. Perhaps they are older than song, if we are to consider song as the wedding of words to notes. It was those cries that Negroes made famous in the old South. Being direct and therefore authentic importations from Africa, the cries baffled the white man. Because of their wordless nature, they sounded savage, wild, depraved, and unworthy of civilized attention. The names for these plaintive and, I say, beautiful fragments and phrases were used in derision. Famous among those yet-surviving names are "corn field holler," "nigger squall," "piney-woods whoop," "roustabout drunk-yell," and "loud mouthing." Many Negroes took to using these names for their cries and no doubt made up some of the names used here. The last one seems to belong to this class:

Wordless cry:

Yüh _____

The meter here is merely for convenience. A cry like this is the source of a series of startling variations done in the freest manner imaginable—depending, of course, upon the gifts of the crier.

Sometimes Negroes would give out a cry that was articulate in both speech and music. When this was done, the groundwork for a song cry had been laid. Very often this led to the creation of a song akin to the "Water Boy" type, in which the cry and the song are joined together. One of the most lovely examples of this grouping is "I'm Gwine to Alabamy," found in *Slave Songs of the United States*, by William Francis Allen, Charles Pickard Ware, and Lucy McKim Garrison. Here is an illustration that points to the fact, often not seen by most people, that the Negro used his cry as a definite expression of feeling, even though the cry itself may have no words. There are variations of this old cry that carry beautiful verse as a part of the song:

> When I see my ma in de mawnin',
> Oh won't dat time be sweet!
> Gwine to put my money in her welcome hand,
> An' pretty little shoes on her feet.

It is obvious that this cry, which precedes and links the verse to the main musical idea, has sprung from no wild, base emotion. There are musical cries that use no verse but simply cry out a short and oft-times irregular musical statement, giving it variety by the addition or omission of a word here and there. For instance:

For the convenience of the reader I have divided the cry into seven basic divisions. Most common among these is the "call," an example of which was just seen above. Frequently the man who gives the orders to a group of men at work, such as a section gang, is referred to as the "caller." The train caller is familiar to all, and the car caller in parking lots is also a familiar figure. The cry, which asks for something for or from someone else or which pronounces judgment, is thus referred to as a call. When a man is thirsty and calls the water boy, or if he is tired and "calls on de boss," or if he is working and calls the procedure for getting the job done, these things will affect his mood and are reflected in his voice. The color, range, and dynamics of his cry will be different for each. The Negro has a warmth that causes him to be one of the world's greatest callers.

These sounds have been observed to be connected in varying degrees of intensity and frequency with the following: joy, sorrow, love, hate, pain, pleasure, comfort, and distress. These emotions are related to life in a pattern of great mixture and uncontrolled occurrence so that the factor of sound in their varying manifestations and types is synonymous with living itself.

The places, customs, mores, and occupations of man do have deep-seated effects upon his nature and do fashion the kind of person he will in general become. So we can say that people who live differently use sounds differently, but that the basic sound reservoir that has been referred to previously is unchangeably present in all men and is in all ways similar. This applies likewise to the lower species.

During World War II a large number of Negro soldiers were stationed in the Atlanta University dormitory, which is directly in front of my house. White officers and Negro noncommissioned officers drilled and inspected these soldiers alternately. It was always possible to tell when the Negroes were in charge, even though I was in the house. The white officers gave the commands, while the Negro officers called them. For comparison:

> White officers: Atten-n-tion!
> Negro officers: Atten-n-sho-wan-n!!

This difference ran throughout the entire procedure of maneuvers.

If one could go to a Negro baseball game of the old type—existing prior to the last war—the point would be brought to focus in a very different situation. At that time it was the custom for the umpire to give his decisions in a more dramatic manner than is now the case. The Negro umpire in the small Negro town felt himself called upon to be more than adjudicator. He was a performer. He used his hands, feet, and face as indicators. He called, or sang, if you please, his decisions: Baw-oo-well! (Ball!).

Though not a Negro cry, it is good for illustration to speak of one call as presently practiced on the radio. The call, or chant, of the tobacco auctioneer is one of the most distinctive examples in the world. It is musical and, as far as language goes, may be said to be partly articulate and partly inarticulate. This call is among the most authoritative of the cries and the most generally useful, although it is not as beautiful as many of the others. Generally it is not a selling cry, for it is used mainly to assemble the buyers and terminate the sale. The tobacco really sells itself.

In the latter part of the last century and during the first decade of the present one, Negroes adopted the square dance of the white man (more in principle than in policy). As is well known, it is necessary to have someone call the figures. Right here is where the Negro's social heritage—musical, oratorical, and histrionic powers—got a chance to develop through a new medium. There were scores of Negroes throughout the South who achieved lasting reputations as "set-callers." In fact, their popularity rose to such heights that they were in many cases professionals who were paid a fee to bring color and entertainment to the dance. They invented an entirely new system of "callin' sets." As they would call the figures, frequently they would dance original solo steps and give out their calls in the pattern of a musical phrase. Their original sayings may be represented here by two specimens that were sure to "draw fire."

> If you like the way she look
> Hand de lady your pocketbook.
> Swing her fancy
> Come to de middle,
> But be careful
> Don't bust de fiddle.[1]

The next one seems to imply some connivance with the refreshment vendor:

> Sody water fine
> Wid de cakes just brown,
> Better buy yo' gal some

---

1. A worthy example of the excitement found in this dance is also shown in the delightfully humorous poem by Paul Laurence Dunbar, "The Party."

Fo' she put you down.
Lemonade cool
And de glasses tall,
Yo' better buy yo' gal some
Fo' de others git it all.

It may appear at first sight that this call is a "dance cry." It is not considered such for the reason that it belongs to an individual calling the dance sets rather than to the dancers themselves. It is an appendage to the spirit of the dance and does not necessarily fit into the dance rhythm or music. It is more of an aside.

From the standpoint of sheer human interest, the most significant of all cries are those that comprise our second group. These are referred to as street cries. I have chosen selling cries for the reason that all cries heard in the streets are not selling cries and vice versa. This cry is the most familiar, most often heard, and the most self-respecting of all cries. No matter how humble the crier is, even if he possesses only a basket of frowsy collard greens, he represents what all businessmen aspire to be—a man who fashions and operates his own business. It should be noted that the selling cry denotes an independence that would be the envy of many a more prosperous merchant, if he but knew it. If business is not good in one spot, he can move at a moment's notice to another, more desirable place.

Selling cries are personal expressions that belong to the maker, singer, or crier. No one need ask where a particular cry came from, as is so often done in regard to other folk material. For audacity and resourcefulness the selling cry stands alone as the finest single expression coming out of this segment of Negro folklore. There is often more imagination in one cry than would be expected in a dozen stanzas or phrases. As is obvious, this cry is a species of the work song, being among its predecessors.

Religious cries are used principally by the Negro preacher in dispensing the "gravy" type of sermon. This is a phase of oratory that is peculiar to Negro life and culture. It is not merely fiery, frenzied declaiming, but a subtle, musical use of the voice that defies description. All of us have heard in person or on the radio Negroes praying or preaching in this manner. The voice moves in short phrases preceded by a sort of buzzing, roaring sound that blends with the words and seems a part of them. However, the words themselves take on a clarion tone quality that moves through a chromate of sound so as to emerge in unsuspecting blends and shapes. When a Negro preacher reaches the point where he feels the audience is ready to change the service into an informal feast of spontaneous rejoicing, he will often lay aside any pretense of text and enter into a picturesque, oratorical cadenza embellished with a very deftly controlled pantomime. This action will produce a religious excitement that in turn produces vocal "shouts" among the congregation. A favorite device of some Negro preachers is to select a strange word or phrase and cry it over and over with variations of tone and inflection. Prayers that use cries are hauntingly beautiful. They seem to come more from the heart than from mere formal supplications. The prayer-maker is too full for any utterance that is not colored tonally by his emotions. This is called "zooning."

Field cries or "corn field whoops" either signify a loneliness of spirit due to the isolation of the worker, or serve as a signal to someone nearby or merely as a bit of self-indulgence (like singing to oneself). These cries are usually of an inarticulate nature as regards the language and music factors. Briefer than most of the others, they yet often achieve a fascinating effect because they are frequently heard in silent, open country by persons who are not expecting them. A field cry almost always proves an ideal motif that could bear rich fruit in the hands of a real composer.

The night cry, curiously enough, is exactly what it sounds like it would be. Negroes working on farms in the day have, as do all men of similar occupation, a desire for relaxation and self-expression; and they have the urge to go visiting at night on nearby plantations. Such a visit is usually undertaken to see someone of interest. Since it takes time to visit and return, the man will give out his night cry as he journeys along. He will also do the same thing when returning to his home. This prevents the visitor from being entirely separated from other human beings during any part of the visiting process. Also, the cry may serve as a signal in the night to a friend or, as I stated above, it may be a personal, disjointed serenade. At times, beautiful hunting cries are used to find the dogs and fellow possum huntsmen. The

Negro's individuality, however, is not so well expressed in these stereotyped hunting versions as in the others. For sheer charm and mystic potency, no musical utterance can be more arresting than the cry of a gifted Negro moving in the night unseen, unknown. The degraded "whiskey squall" does not deserve consideration here, since it is an abnormal manifestation without rational dependability. Yet it is a cry and has its roots in the others mentioned here.

Dance cries, as I have pointed out, are among the oldest and most vital of all cries known to man. When on the folk level the dance reached a pitch of excitement where the dancers lost themselves in the joy of it all, the voice naturally gave out a response, which was also a form of rhythmic accompaniment to the movement of the feet. Since the main consideration was always the movement of the body, the cry imitated, in sound, some aspect of primitive dance movements. Also, the words more often than not turned out to be mere sounds. Some of these were as follows: (1) Da, da, da, (2) Da, da, da-de-o, (3) Dum, a-lum, lum, (4) Ha-dee, lo, la, (5) Hi-dee, hi-dee-hoo (after Cab Calloway), and (6) Doo-dah, doo-dah. These same cries are used today in various places with about the same energy as in the past. Children use some of these in playing games and dancing to hand-claps, just as their elders do.

For our interests, however, these dances show themselves to best advantage when looked at through the vista of present-day dance development. The persons responsible for this are Louis Armstrong and Cab Calloway. Somehow Armstrong and Calloway found the trick of using old folk-cry principles to supplement the normal means of singing. This is a principle already shown as being a folk one. Being gifted in voice projection, Calloway invented or adopted a series of nonsense syllables and fitted them into his songs based on jazz rhythms. When this was done, people realized the thing as a part of themselves, but they did not know why. They did not realize they were listening to the cries of their vegetable man, their train caller, their charcoal vendor, their primitive ancestors, heated in the hot crucible of jazz by the folk genius of Calloway and Armstrong until they turned into a new American alloy. It is possible that neither Calloway nor Armstrong realized what had taken place. If that is the case, then it is all the more remarkable. The response of the orchestra in imitating the cries of Armstrong and Calloway carried the cry into the orchestra itself. These rhythms and inflections have been picked up by orchestras in general during the last two decades. This has caused a vital development in dance music.

Water cries belong to all nations and peoples. There is a peculiar charm about the water and being borne upon its ever-changing bosom. This experience takes man into a sphere where he is not equipped naturally to dwell and makes him feel himself the adventurer. To journey upon the water gives one a feeling akin to loneliness, even when in the company of others. It brings into sharp relief the things that go into making land and home important. However, the need for variety and the love of travel and discovery have also made man love the water and build up a lore associated with it. Life upon the water is a different life, created by man for himself. Thus it is very natural that this situation would beget a type of folk-art expression all its own.

Negroes in America have served on the rivers and their shores as workers—boatmen, roustabouts, longshoremen, raft-haulers, and fishermen. Out of the lives of these men have come cries that are perhaps more plaintive than any others, especially those from the old Mississippi River boatmen. These cries seem to possess the echo of the water in them. They are filled with a peculiar nostalgia. For some reason, too, they are very technical vocal pieces. Their brevity finds exception in a few calls of several broken measures in length. Most Negro water cries are sheer music, having no words. For this reason it is difficult to identify them alone. Fortunately, many of these cries have been joined to songs that deal with life on the river.

Now, consider briefly twenty of the elemental sounds produced in animals and see how many overlap in use by man and beast. Note the great variety. The mere naming of the sounds demonstrates the point: laugh, snort, roar, hiss, whistle, song (hum), scream, moan, groan, grunt, coo, yell, yodel, growl, bark, bleat, mew, neigh, bay, whinnie. It is very important and interesting to note that the lower species and man are identified by sounds common to them. However, man has a rather unlimited range of sound formations based upon his ability to take any of the elemental sounds and combine them into new sound types, such as words; for it is true that the languages of man do rely heavily on the twenty sounds listed above.

All of the aforesaid has been in support of the thesis that sounds are basic in animal nature and that man has more need for sounds, a greater ability with sounds, and a wider variety of sounds than any other living thing. Inarticulate sounds have greater meaning than ordinarily believed.

II

The word "cry" is mainly to be defined here as the most elemental song sound regardless of how or where one experiences it. Therefore, we must consider that certain sounds produced through the mouth and the nose are not sung since these sounds do not emanate directly and essentially as a functional product of the larynx or voice box. Such sounds as vowels and their modifications are the main concern here, but there are other important types of sounds that must be considered. For instance, the laugh is the best known and most used of all inarticulate cries. The giggle is a close second. The vocal yawn and the scream are less common but equally familiar forms of the cry. It is also notable that these sounds are closely wrapped up with deep human feelings.

When man or a lesser animal is thrown off normal physical and/or emotional balance by a sudden crisis, he utters the primeval basic cries that spring from his innermost depths. It would seem that these sounds have laid dormant, awaiting their truest and best need for manifestation. Thus, they spring forth with fresh, startling, never-failing vitality at the given moment, causing those who hear them to realize more vividly than they could with coherent language the distress or joy or surprise of the individual.

Certain types of crises seem to rob man of his cultural veneer and the rational use of vocal sounds. The main point here is that they exist at given moments. There are also cries that are slightly less spontaneous and not caused by immediate crises, cries that are more songlike or musical in that they cling to definite pitch movements. Both of these cries are brought together in Negro folk music expression—work songs, blues, spirituals, jubilees, dance songs, and so forth. These song cries are the main ingredients in all Negro folk music. Indeed, the cry is basic to determining the distinguishable characteristic so highly prized and imitated in our present-day American music.

The song cries of Negroes are divided into three categories: (1) plain cries, which are the simplest in form and structure, including some street cries and many of the so-called whoops and hollers; (2) florid cries, which are the type most prevalent and the most favored—folk preaching, blues, spirituals, jazz, and the work songs are greatly indebted to this species, which is not at all possible to set down in our present system of music; and (3) coloratura cries, which are among the most amazing and remarkable vocal feats in folk music. (Certain highly specialized and unusual feats as those accomplished by, for instance, Yma Sumac, are not typical of her race and are therefore considered as exceptional and inapplicable in this particular instance. However, they are very applicable in the general principle.) These cries are not as easily heard as the others, and they are restricted in application because of their great complexity. Some of the best illustrations today can be found in some of the recordings of the Ward Sisters, Mahalia Jackson, Cab Calloway, Louis Armstrong and on some of the preaching records of the 1920s era. The plain and florid cries are really heard at all times when Negro music is sung or played in the authentic styles.

The greatest activity in the employment of the Negro folk cry in present-day music is to be found in the amazing rise of gospel singing in every state west of the Mississippi River and across the sea in Europe. As Negro churches became more European in decorum and program, the great mass of less Europeanized Negroes began to look elsewhere for full-vented religious expressions in music and preaching. So a great urge arose to use the Negro folk cry in connection with the religious antidote for segregation and all of the ills that bred it and were bred by it—poverty, sickness, social abuse, and spiritual pain.

Although more advanced Negroes at first resented these gospel songs as well as their creators and purveyors, they have gradually (very gradually) become more tolerant. Some churches where they were initially outlawed have carefully and quietly let down the bars to both the gospel song and gospel singers. Leading Negro newspapers speak in praise of Mahalia Jackson, the Ward Sisters, Rosetta Tharpe, Thomas Dorsey, and several others as outstanding artists. These artists perform at Carnegie Hall, and they have a tremendous hold on the record industry and therefore on radio and television. More important, these gospel songs and singers are more numerous than any other active Negro music and musicians.

When one hears these songs, he is conscious of a type of voice production that is strange and primitive but seems to exhaust the innermost recesses of the singer's heart, mind, voice, and soul. The folk listeners are similarly affected. Many faint, break forth in shouts, leap out of their seats, or scream incoherently. Thus, anyone who takes the time can easily see that the Negro has taken his cries—whoops, hollers, calls—and grafted them onto present-day song patterns whose practice goes back hundreds of years. This, and this alone, accounts for the great pull the gospel songs exert on Negroes and white men of all classes here and in Europe. Rhythm is secondary but vital.

White men, in the South particularly, are imitating the Negro gospel singer—even in his physical activities while singing. This is vocal jazz in practice and in principle. I have seen numerous jazz audiences of Negroes and white men (even in New England) driven to hand-clapping participation with Mahalia Jackson as singer. Commercialization has drained all of the real spiritual value off and left gospel singing anemic in terms of real, true, basic Negro religious fervor. Very often gospel music creates this religious fervor, but it differs from the spiritual in that it takes anything musical from any source and is governed in its uses by financial considerations and the white businessman. However, the fact remains that the gospel song seems irresistibly here to stay; and as long as it is based upon Negro cries, it will remain. Furthermore, like jazz, it will be generally learned by white men.

This principle of grafting the cry onto present-day music is also noticed in another field—the present-day popular song and the crooner and stylist. The styles of singing in America have felt the indelible imprint of the Negro song cry to the extent that every popular white singer owes much to the Negro singer. The crooner would be impossible without the Negro vocal influence; and, of course, every Negro song stylist today, especially the woman, is a living expression of the plain, florid, and coloratura song cry of Negro origin. Without these sounds we would not have American music in its present vigorous form.

American music is making our performers and composers unique. Whether one likes it or not, a new type of vocal art is in the process of development in this country. Its roots have long been accepted here and abroad by the great mass of average listeners, and the constant flood of sound is bound to create a new type of listener in the course of fifty or one hundred years. What the vocal amalgam will be like is a fascinating consideration. We must realize that our present European standard is the result of the confluence of the singing of the folk, the church, and the theater. We have these same forces vigorously at work in Negro song, and we are transferring their essences into the mainstream of American song. How these cries affect the instrumental music of our day is to be shown in a later section of this chapter. Suffice it to say for now that man has not always sung as he does now, and he certainly will not do so in the future in America. The constant change is pouring out of every radio and phonograph. Listen to any popular recording of thirty years ago and listen to those by today's stars of either race and sex: The contrast is startling.

When one hears a screaming bevy of bobby-soxers in the throes of ecstasy at concerts or programs featuring some famous crooner or stylist, one is listening to the cry answering the cry. How much more natural could it be? We are amazed at these outbursts because we do not realize that the bobby-soxers are far less inhibited than we of older origin and that their ears have been adjusted to these cry sounds from birth. Moreover, these cry sounds are less veneered and have much more direct contact with the spirits of these listeners than does the song itself. In the not-too-distant past it was the songwriter—Victor Herbert, Irving Berlin, Charles Rudolf Friml, William Ball, Jerome Kern—who was famous. Today it is the popular singer who is famous. He uses the composer for a foil and places his vocal inventions in the foreground, using elements of (if not whole) Negro cries.

For these reasons I have never thought that Negro folk music was a logical sequence of developments—cry, work song, spiritual, blues, jazz—for the Negro has always possessed the fundamental ingredient for all these in his cries. It was a mere grafting of these cries onto different needs, impulses, and borrowed tunes and songs, just as is being done today. So much has been said about the twelve-bar blues, whereas in fact the structure is based upon a series of Negro cries. So is all Negro folk music in this country. The bars of the blues are a result of the Negro cry and dance in conjunction with one another. The "silent bars" continue to be used by professional blues singers for the insertion of dance effects and "jive."

Because Negro cries have hitherto been so neglected from an analytical viewpoint, a concentrated list is given for clarity and reemphasis: (1) calls, (2) selling (street cries), (3) religious, (4) field, (5) night, (6) dance, and (7) water. These divisions are all subject to further divisions in terms of music and speech and their various modifications. It should be borne in mind that our consideration here, being a musical one, does not take into account all of the cries, such as those growing out of fear, distress, and grief in the purest sense.

In presenting the following examples, it becomes necessary to set some of the cries as "spoken" ones, since no system of notation is able to convey the sound impressions created through them. These types are definitely musical, but they are also less than music in the accepted sense of the term. Then, too, the uses of them are so likely to change the inflections several times during the course of a day that it becomes unfair to the reader to give them too definite a tonal setting. Therefore, in reading these spoken cries one should imagine hearing them in terms of more familiar examples gleaned from past experiences or from the lips of Negroes in their own localities. This hit-or-miss procedure is the best that can be offered.

Where the music could be set—and fortunately it frequently could be—great pains were taken to arrive at correct representations.

Call

Plain

All dem dat goin Norf an' Eas' git re'd - y.

Speech Cries (Indefinite tonality)

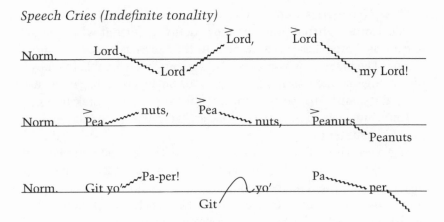

Old Man River keeps rolling along in art as well as in water. The connection between water and Negro folk music is permanent in this country. New Orleans was the southern terminal point for the palatial riverboats, and Negroes were the musicians for them. The famous Strekfus Line was the main source of living for many Negro musicians and workmen. Long before, during, and after slavery the Negro river singer was creating lonesome, strange, florid, and coloratura cries about the river, women, towns, money, saloons, boats, white men, and black men. However, it must be repeated that many of these cries had no words at all. The voice was used as an instrument—as a horn, if you please, pure and simple.

It is certainly true that man's music comes from within and that his instrument plays what is within him. He will always be moved by his relationship to his environment. So as the boats were worked by musicians, the Negro laborers felt some of the same things that caused them to create the water cries. Moreover, the musicians heard these sounds from Negro boatmen and shoremen as early as 1811 and worked them into jazz patterns and carried them inland after they left the boats.

It is no accident that the names St. Louis and New Orleans are connected with the greatest traditions in Negro folk instrumental music. Neither is it mere chance that the most famous blues is called "St. Louis" and that the most famous jazz is called "New Orleans": Both cities are water towns.

These Negro cries were played in true form at times and were, as in vocal music, fitted onto the more definite, formal white music selections. Later these cries came into their own as seed for compositions. The brazen instruments (not clarinets) were unable to convey the strange sounds as normally played. So Negroes began to use derby hats, sink stoppers, plungers, handkerchiefs, whisk brooms, and anything else to modify the tone and give a more throaty quality to the instruments.

Negro cries have to this day continued to be the chief ingredient of all true jazz. The more Negro and white musicians become aware of this, the greater will be their understanding and ability as players and singers of Negro music. Even when a jazz cornetist, trumpeter, clarinetist, or saxophonist plays chords of the white man's origin based upon the European third and second—augmented, diminished, major, or minor—he colors these with a certain oily, sliding, melancholy character that is obviously the result of the Negro cry impulse or, as often as not, the cry itself. Jazz is largely Negro cries sung or played or both.

The waterports of Charleston, Mobile, Jacksonville, Pensacola, Savannah, and other cities had remarkable influence on Negro folk music and should be given credit for it. For example, the influence of James Reese Europe of Mobile and Eugene Mars Mikel of Charleston was of great importance in the assembling of Negro musicians, literate and illiterate, as well as singers. These men brought the cry into use on the eastern seaboard as a powerful force in popular and ragtime music.

The Negro cries were and are so natural to Negro musicians that they do not see the cry as an integral part of their nature. In fact, during my studies I learned that certain Negroes have been wont to ridicule Negro cries on the one hand and to find great pleasure in playing them on the other. Others have been greatly moved by these cries whenever and wherever they were heard.

In August 1953 Eubie Blake, the famous composer of "Shuffle Along" and many other famous hits, was at Music Inn. Blake has gone through ragtime, jazz, and classical music. He is now more than seventy and plays the piano wonderfully well. At the age of sixty-odd years, he graduated from New York University in the Schillinger system of composition. He has known all levels of Negro musicians personally and intimately, having played with them.

One morning at a lecture I presented on Negro cries, at a conference on Negro folk music presided over by Marshall Stearns, I sang a florid Negro cry. Eubie Blake leaped halfway from his seat and yelled, "Oh, professor, professor, you hit me, you hit me." He placed both hands over his heart and continued with great emotion: "You make me think of my dear mother. She always sang like that. I can hear her now. That's the stuff I was raised on." He sat down quietly, except for a deep sigh that had no audible competition from anyone. It was reverently quiet. I was forced to continue—unnecessarily. Blake was a living testimony to the influences that had made him musically unique even without formal training (which he did not acquire until he was old and famous and did not really need it). He knew all along that it was the cry that had guided him.[2]

The young gospel singer Roy Hamilton, who brings his natural and acquired song styles into the popular field, was born in Georgia. He has lived in the East, singing a combination of cries, blues, and European song styles. He is suddenly a sensation. Why? The question is answered already. Listen to his singing of "You'll Never Walk Alone," "Ebb Tide," or "Beware," and you will discover the unique application of African colors to the European song fabric. Having done this, spirituals, work songs, jazz, gospel songs, and popular songs should be listened to and noted for the influence of the cry, vocally and instrumentally. If this thesis is sound, it should apply in general. It will. Only look for substances instead of identities, sounds instead of melodies, manner of tone projection rather than from what it is projected. A cry on an instrument is as real and as meaningful as the cry from the human throat. It too is life suspended briefly in vibrant sound cast up from the innermost human depths— the source of all musical art.

2. It is herewith suggested that the reader hear the following recordings in the order named: Ethnic Folkways Library 1484A, 1481B; Savoy 4023A, 4023B; Ethnic Folkways Library 1488B. These few records will reveal a lot. The Folkways records are sung by many old Negroes, the Savoy by young. Note the transference back and forth of cry patterns—plain, florid, coloratura.

Olin Downes, writing of eighty-seven-year-old Arturo Toscanini in the *New York Times* (February 7, 1954) and expressing his wonder at Toscanini's artistry, said: "Man is more than an animal. . . . the art which he has created is greater than man himself, and the guide to grander horizons than the race has yet known." Presently it would seem that the Negro is supplying an important ingredient in this gradual process. The white man has been busy trying to find the cause of Negro musical uniqueness somewhere in Africa, when the cause was always present by his side with the Negro, who was suffering and struggling for existence and pouring out his tension, despair, love, and, yes, hate in his strange native cries, which in turn fascinated his white tormentor and made him his willing student, disciple, and musical confrere. Perhaps, as it seems, the Negro spoke the transcendent language of races through his flexible spiritual nature, whereas the white man only discovered his own true nature in the folk cry as it grasped and shook him in its power. Unique and powerful as the Negro's native musical urge is, it would not be of value as a thing apart from his fellowman, for it is truly a language of life.

To return once more to the greatest musician of our time, Toscanini, let us say that when the incomparable master stands before his orchestra and pleads, "Canta! Canta! Canta! Preciso! Canta!" (Sing! Sing! Sing! Truly! Sing!), he is asking for the most profound, poignant musical expression found on Earth, and he knows his men comprehend instinctively. At this point in his lofty artistic height, he links himself with all classes of musicians—players, singers, conductors, composers—who work from within and seek truth in mere sound. One may also state this conversely and say that the simplest, humblest singer or player who reveals his soul is akin to the greatest. It only remains for his fellowman to comprehend and to place his contribution in the right cultural position by constant use, refinement, and selection.

Chapter 3
Dances, Blues, and Ballads

I

One may well consider the dance song to be synonymous with the Negro song in general. At one time or another the Negro has used all classes of his songs for dancing. This is very likely due to the fact that the Negro has such a tremendous drive behind his singing. The urge to keep time and the great enjoyment derived from making music force the Negro into an irresistible desire for body movement. This has also been characteristic of many other peoples. The various dances of races that are bound up with various customs and celebrations give proof of this, such as the rituals of the American Indian and of the various religious sects and denominations of the white man in America, from the Shakers of New England to the various Holiness groups of the present.

In the case of the folk Negro, a distinction is made between dance that is "sinful" and dance that is "holy." Sinful dance is looked upon as being associated with mere pleasure. No matter how discreetly the dancers may deport themselves, the charge that dancing for mere pleasure is sinful is rigidly held to. Nonetheless, there is bound to be a group of people who are in sympathy with both sides and who practice both forms of dancing. This has never been studied on our part, but the principle is too evident to deny. Besides, there are many people above reproach as church members who do not dance for pleasure but who do not feel too strongly against the practice.

Thus, all through the years we have had a rather determined effort on the part of the church Negro to kill off the social dance. There has been a desire on his part to force dance music out of existence, regardless of its merits or nature. Until recently, the fiddle and the banjo have been looked upon as being products of the Devil himself.

There was a time not so long ago when all musical instruments were looked upon as being evil or sinful and were not to be found in the church. The best and most reliable church members were certainly not to have any instruments in their possession. Hence, the social dance was left entirely to the care of the "worldly" people.

The nature of the "shout" or "holy dance" has been known in the South for years. It is the most generally accepted dance ever created by Negroes in this country. I use the term "created" in the sense of the dance being an outgrowth of new surroundings as opposed to it being a new rhythmic conception. The shout is not a uniform thing, for it varies in step and style. As the music goes, so does the shout.

Generally speaking, the shout is no longer done in the way that it was during the early nineteenth century. During this period there were in certain parts of the South two phases of the shout. One was indulged in by the youth during the week more for amusement than for worship. An eyewitness account of both phases, which appeared in the *Nation* on May 30, 1867, may help us understand them:

> There is a ceremony which the white clergymen are inclined to discountenance, and even of the colored elders some of the more discreet try sometimes to put on a face of discouragement; and, although if pressed for Biblical warrant for the "Shout," they generally seem to think "he in de Book," or "he dere-da in Matchew," still it is not considered blasphemous or improper if "de chillen" and "dem young gal" carry it on in the evening for amusement's sake, and with no well-defined intention of "praise." But the true "Shout" takes place on Sundays, or on "praise" nights through the week, and either in the praise-house or in some cabin in which a regular religious meeting has been held. Very likely more than half the population of a plantation is gathered together. Let it be the evening, and a light wood fire burns red before the door of the house and on the hearth. For some time one can hear, though at a good distance, the vociferous exhortation or prayer of the presiding elder or of the brother who has a gift that way and is not "on the back seat"—a phrase the interpretation of which is "under the censure of the church authorities for bad behavior"—and at regular intervals one hears

the elder "deaconing" a hymnbook hymn, which is sung two lines at a time and whose wailing cadences, borne on the night air, are indescribably melancholy.

But the benches are pushed back to the wall when the formal meeting is over, the old and young, men and women, sprucely dressed young men, grotesquely half-clad field hands—the women generally with gay handkerchiefs twisted about their heads and with short skirts—boys with tattered shirts and men's trousers, young girls bare-footed, all stand up in the middle of the floor, and when the "sperichil" is struck up begin first walking and by and by shuffling around, one after the other, in a ring. The foot is hardly taken from the floor, and the progression is mainly due to a jerking, hitching motion which agitates the entire shouter and soon brings out streams of perspiration. Sometimes they sing the chorus of the spiritual, and sometimes the song itself is also sung by the dancers. But more frequently a band, composed of some of the best singers and of tired shouters, stand at the side of the room to "base" the others, singing the body of the song and clapping their hands together or on the knees. Song and dance are alike extremely energetic, and often, when the shout lasts into the middle of the night, the monotonous thud, thud of the feet prevents sleep within half a mile of the praise-house.

It is necessary to return to the consideration of the secular dances of the Negro in order to gain a true conception of what was considered sinful but was at the same time the expression of the more ordinary, everyday feelings of the people. These early dances of the Negro, fresh from Africa, were certainly startling to the European from a sensuous point of view, if not from an aesthetic one. The savage brutal dances of the Voodoo cultists were certainly a revolting and amazing spectacle. However, there were other, less savage dances that were looked upon by white people as totally hideous, dances that were neither as violent nor as unorthodox as the modern jitterbug or even the late Charleston. These otherwise vital, picturesque dances, which were to later affect the entire dance pattern of this continent, were ahead of the stiff ballroom conservatism of the times. However, the fact that these dances were looked upon as sinful did not help them to survive in their best form, since, as has been pointed out, the people who were given the custody of the dances were looked down upon as social degenerates. Being considered such did not allow them to ennoble what they practiced, to say the least.

Hence, we have a series of dances in Negro music that come all the way from Africa to Georgia, Florida, Alabama, Louisiana, Tennessee, Arkansas, Texas, and Mississippi, and pass through their dark, forbidding backstreets and move through their social gutters, finally to emerge in Harlem, where they are seized upon and taken into "high society." Under more tender names and modified body motions—unless one pursues them in the various nightclubs—these dances come into American life as new choreographies, verse, song-hits, and shows.

One of the oldest of the Negro dances is the counjai. This dance was developed from an African dance called "condjo." There was a Creole dance coming from this called Criole Candjo. It was a triple-meter dance and was done in a fairly moderate tempo. There is no description of this dance at my disposal, but judging from the general nature of Creole dances, it may be said to have been vivacious and free-form. An example is given in *Afro-American Folksongs*, by Henry Krehbiel. It is probable that "conjai" was an African name, but the use of it in connection with a French proper name gives credence to the idea that it was a development of the black Creoles.[1] The conjai is a dance in two-four or four-four meter. It is graceful and rather like a minuet, which is another factor favoring the French derivation of the word. "Conjai Babete" is here given as an example.

Conjai Babéte

Allegretto moderato

Con - jai   Ba-béte con - jai   con - jai   Ba-béte con - jai!

1. According to Lorenzo Turner, eminent authority on African language survivals in America, the word *kanja* means "ginger" in Gullah. Perhaps the ginger is reflected in the spice of the dance.

This is very reminiscent of a part of "La Paloma," which is based on the Negro tangana rhythm. This dance was very popular, and the Negroes who were not of French mixture took it up with enthusiasm. Not being able to pronounce the patois, they called their dances "coonjine." They also sang "Coonjine Baby," instead of the Creole "Conjai Babete." Herewith was born the most famous American dance name in music. For some reason Negroes all over the South loved to dance the Coonjine Baby. It was the one musical piece everyone tried to play on the piano and that everyone does play even to this day. I was amazed to hear both of my children playing the tune when they were not of more than kindergarten age. When one could not play "Coonjine Baby" on the piano, he was no player at all. Hence, the folk expression: "Yo' caint eb'm play Coonjine Baby!"

The mid-South Negro used more rhythmic feeling than did his Creole cousin. He gave us a version of the Charleston rhythm:

Coonjine Baby

Coon-jine Ba - by   coon-jine. _   Coon-jine Ba - by   coon-jine. _

So great was the popularity of this piece that it was soon made facetious. The words to it rapidly sank beneath the level of decency, but the rhythm that had captured everyone was to come forth again in the Charleston, which was the forerunner of the modern jitterbug.

The rhythm is a combination of the African tangana and the congo (conga), which form the basis for the tango and the Cuban form of the malaguena, even though the latter is in a different meter. This simple dance movement has found its way into the most unsuspected usages. It evidently was felt and used long before it received specific recognition in "Coonjine Baby." For instance:

Violin   Accompaniment

This is a variation of the coonjine rhythm and if reduced to two-four meter will be found to represent the exact number of beats, as does the coonjine.

Reduced to 2/4 meter

(Leopold Auer says this is the "most folk-like of all the movements.") The above example is from the last movement of French composer Edouard Lalo's *Symphonie espagnole*, which was written for his Spanish friend, violinist Pablo de Sarasate. Sarasate was fond of Cuban music and wrote this music for his violin. It is very likely that he heard Cuban music during his journey or perhaps even in Spain, where it is well known. Spain has long been artistically influenced by the African temperament.

Also, one may hear variants of this same rhythm in any jazz piece of note, especially orchestrated jazz pieces. Many of these are too subtle to be picked out by the uninitiated:

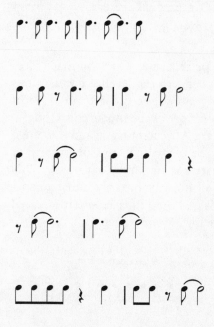

These fundamentals can be used to create scores of other sequences. No effort is made here to assign overdue importance to coonjine rhythm. It is merely important to show its fundamental roots in Negro dance rhythms and therefore in American dance as a whole. This simple dance has been one of the greatest motivating forces in the entire range of Negro music. It is no wonder that every adult Negro has sung or whistled it at least once and that most have tried it as a one-finger piece on the piano. Almost everyone smiles when the name coonjine is said in his presence. This is probably due to the happiness he has received from the little song during his childhood. Perhaps it is due to the peculiar magic of the sound of the word itself. However, the coonjine is laughed at and loved intermittently by almost all Americans. It has been performed all the way from the barnyard, through minstrelsy, to Carnegie Hall.

Negro dances are very numerous and have a unique nomenclature. The names of some of the dances furnish elemental pictures of Negro life or even life in the United States as a whole. The dances seem to be named after places, incidents, animals, customs, and persons. A description of some will provide a note of human interest as well as develop a fuller appreciation for the folk nature of the dances themselves.

In the days when freight was heavy on the lower Mississippi River, the goods were mostly packed in barrels so the roustabouts could handle them with less trouble. These barrels were kept in warehouses along the shore. Negroes called these "barrel-houses." When the shipping season was almost over and the barrel-houses were about empty, the river Negroes were permitted to have dances in them. Of course, the Negroes who frequented them (men and women) were rough and were generally looked down upon by other Negroes. Hence "barrelhouse dance" was a synonym for low-level dancing. As would be expected, though, Negroes developed a special dance and called it "barrelhouse." The coonjine was popular and was done at the barrelhouse.

Gwine to de barrel-house,
To see my baby jine. (coonjine)

She ain't good lookin',
But Lawd, she dress so fine;

Gwine to de barrel-house,
On Sat'day night.
If my gal messin' 'round,
Go' break de dam dance up in a fight.

"Boogy woogy" is a name that was originally used by Negroes to describe a very loose, ill-fitting, cheap suit. It finally came to apply mainly to overalls and jumpers worn by roustabouts. Especially during the season when lent would cover the workers, "boogy woogy" meant a dance where overalled men and gingham-aproned women sought sex and relaxation. The dance was very much like the barrel-house in character. Negro piano and guitar players would play a rhythmic sequence over and over. One of these, which I have heard all of my life, took New York by storm only fifteen years ago. It goes as follows:

We shall soon see in another section how this and another dance figure influenced the modern blues:

Git my box-back coat,
My Stetson hat,
Take off my boogy woogy,
Catch a train, Lawd, bound for Chattanoogy.

See my brownskin gal
Dey call Coree,
When I take off my boogy woogy,
Leave dat train, Lawd, bound for Chattanoogy.

The dance called the "bumbo-shay" is the product of the Negro's observation and creative adaptation. In certain situations boats called "bum-boats" were used to transfer articles and persons to larger boats or vessels lying out in deeper water. These boats sometimes carried in tow smaller boats that were called shays. When the water was rough the boats cut funny and fantastic patterns. The dance was derived from this. There is another old American dance that sounds like this in name, but the two are very different in character.

"Snake hips" is perhaps the most imaginative name given to any Negro dance. Anyone who has seen a snake in motion will realize the uniqueness of the name. However, the matter of one's taking artistic inspiration from such an ordinarily unwelcome spectacle as the snake is rather perplexing.

"Jump Jim Crow" is the most surviving of all the dance names. With regard to its origin, the most plausible theory is that a one-legged Negro acquired such great skill as a dancer that his name was given to the dance he created. From this dance a series was developed which was known as the "Jim Crow dances." Many of these exist in substance today. However, the name of the dance became so bound up with Negro life that the term has become a symbol of segregation and the ills bred of it. It is doubtful that a similar paradox may be found in the dances of any other race.

R. Nathaniel Dett wrote a suite that he entitled *In the Bottoms.* The name "bottoms" is taken from the fact that certain parts of Mississippi and Louisiana are very low country. Negroes refer to the Louisiana lowlands as "cane bottoms" and "sugar bottoms," and the rich soil of the Mississippi lowlands around the Delta is referred to as the "black bottoms." Negroes living here had a wonderful opportunity to develop their own dances as well as other folklore. The region is still comparatively out-of-the-way and rural. One of the dances was set by Dett and called "juba." The dance is not a folk one, but the character is folk-like. In fact, the tune of the piece is so folklike that one may accept it as being very typical. This dance style was modernized slowly. The Negroes of Georgia and South Carolina seem to have held on to the old form the longest. The Creoles in some places know the juba yet pronounce it "giouba." During the modernizing phase the Negro aptly renamed the derivative in keeping with its locale—"blackbottom."

The reason for the current scarcity of these dances in their original form is simple. The Negro has never felt called upon to preserve any one dance over a long period of time. His urge to create new ones has always been his drive where the dance is concerned. This is also true of his songs. As James Craig once told me, "When we git tired of one, we jes let it go."

Negroes of middle age (say from fifty to sixty) are aware of the rapid changes always going on in the dances of any Negro community. Some of these dances are held on to in substance for a much longer time than are others. The essential fact remains that all of them show signs of being changed in keeping with folk desire. It is only necessary to see a jitterbug exhibition to realize that practically every American dance finds its moment of glory in the executions done by various dancers. This is indeed the real Negro dance composite—a tribute to the Negro's consummate creative ability in the realm of movement. From the point of view of the musician, the jitterbug seems to have choreographic powers of a high order. Here the purpose is not merely a response to personal feeling, but a tremendous release of the Negro's entire life cycle in America. When one has seen it in a Harlem ballroom, he has seen the Negro folk dances in outline and through the ages. He has also seen the turbulent Negro spirit in a moment of feigned relaxation. Though the tempo may be faster or slower, the fundamentals remain obvious to the person who has seen Negroes in the South dance for twenty-five years or more.

As fond as Negroes are of melody, they are fonder of rhythm. However, they always find it desirable to use the two together, with emphasis on the latter. Thus, in the days of slavery, and since, we see Negro dance instruments made of the simplest materials. The jawbone of an animal was played with a key that was rubbed over the teeth in imitation of some African instrument, possibly the "casuto" spoken of by David Livingstone and others who have written of Africa. (This same principle is kept alive today by the use of the common washboard, which is played with a seamstress's thimbles on the finger and thumb.) Many uses were found for dry goods, soap, and packing boxes. These were beaten upon with sticks, stamped upon when large enough to support a man, and used as amplifiers for other sounds, such as wire and taut twine. Jugs, bottles, and even the blade of a hoe or plow would be used. In keeping with the African feeling, several of these instruments would be used simultaneously with different rhythms. Of course, the drum was the main dance instrument at the beginning. It remained for all time the best timekeeper known to man. These drums were made from small and half-size barrels. The Creole Negroes had a drum made from the quarter barrel. The same was true of the Negroes of the West Indies, according to Lafcadio Hearn, as Henry Krehbiel notes in *Afro-American Folksongs*.

As Negroes in America took on the ways of the white man, European instruments were taken on, too. For a long time the violin was popular. So was the banjo, which was named and used by Negroes from Bandore. It was all but discontinued after the guitar became popular. After a while the piano became more available to urban Negroes and was used as the principal means of dance music expression. In theaters the drum and piano usually formed the "orchestra." At the more well-to-do dances and theaters, combinations of players—either string players or mixed—furnished the music. This gave rise to the Negro dance orchestra. These Negro combinations took up the popular airs of the day and put their own racial stamp upon them. From this circumstance a new type of dance music began its development in the southern United States.

There were orchestras that played almost exclusively for white people and orchestras that played for Negroes. The latter group was the keeper of the Negro taste and dance style. Although they were not looked upon as being in the same social and economic class as the more prosperous groups, they were usually richer creatively and musically. Strictly speaking, they were the folk players. Often they could not read a note of music, but rather played "f'om de head." I venture to say that they also played from the heart. Stimulated by this type of playing, Negroes began to pay more attention to formal dancing and to bring racial dance steps into the ballroom dance styles.

The Negro orchestra of today, while not a part of folk music in the strict sense, must be thought of in connection with the Negro folk dances, for it is from this source of rhythmic expression that these orchestras gain their fascinating rhythms. The rhythmic feeling of the players, which would otherwise find expression in the dance, is expressed through the instruments. The Negro orchestra player is noted in America for dancing to his own music while engaged as a part of the performance unit. The Negro dancer is equally famous for his dynamic inventions. Thus their exuberant spirits have come to be the principal ingredient in dance as it is known in America. Bojangles Robinson is the rhythmic summation of a way of life. Noble Sissle, Duke Ellington, Fletcher Henderson, Cab Calloway, Florence Mills, Josephine Baker, George Walker, Katherine Dunham, and Jimmy Lunceford represent the footprints of African dance motion upon the European tonal plane. Will Marion Cook used dance material in *Clorindy, the Origin of the Cakewalk, In Dahomey, Abyssinia*, and *Bandanna Land*. Perhaps no one ever used Negro folklore in dance forms and rhythms quite so elegantly as did Cook. A review of some of his work would be stimulating to the present musical generation.

Finally, if nothing has been said of Negro children's games, songs, and dances, it is for the reason that, in my opinion, these are only reflections of adult conceptions. The Negro child is taught his games and songs as other children are taught theirs. Observation has convinced me that the Negro child imitates the dances of his elders. As he becomes an adult, he puts his games aside and includes in his adult dances what he has learned in his childhood dance. When one sees Negro adults dance, one has also seen the children. The music of one is often used for the other and with complete agreement. Nonetheless, a few children's songs are placed in the music section of this book.

Following is a table representing some typical American Negro dances over a period of at least 150 years.

Name	Meter	Characteristics	Activity in the United States
Conjai	2/4	Rhythmic, not very fast.	Common in Louisiana before and after the Civil War; of African origin.
Coonjine	2/4; 4/4	Sensuous, intense, rhythmic.	Spread all over the United States until the middle of the twentieth century.
Bumbo-Shay	2/4; 4/4	Loose-jointed, rather fast.	Old, obsolete; of African origin.
Bamboola	2/4	Wild and exotic.	Obsolete in this country. Still found in the West Indies.
Juba	2/4; 4/4	Joyous and rough.	Sometimes found at present in the rural South.
Buck	4/4; 2/4	Leaping, free-footed.	Still active. Now referred to as tap dancing; however, was more vigorous.
Rabbit	4/4	Partly standing and on hands and knees. Very funny.	Common in Georgia, Alabama, and Florida during the nineteenth century.
Barrelhouse	4/4	Slow, common, suggestive.	Popular in Louisiana and the lower South after the Civil War.
Jim Crow	2/4; 4/4	Saucy and comic.	Before and shortly after the Civil War.
Pigeon Wing	2/4; 4/4	Akin to Buck, with arms moving winglike.	Vestiges still found among present-day dances.
Breakdown	4/4	Heavy-footed, rough and lugubrious.	Used in rural areas, under more modern names.
Slowdrag	4/4	Seductive, lazy.	Very old and still practiced, sometimes unknowingly.
Ball de Jack	2/4; 4/4	Violent swaying of legs, held together closely.	General in the South.
Jook (Boogy Woogy)	4/4	Shuffling, slow.	Common in the urban South and still active in some places, for instance, the coastal region of the South.

N.B. Boogy Woogy has recently spread all over the U.S. This is not to be confused with the dance.

Name	Meter	Characteristics	Activity in the United States
Blackbottom	4/4	Sometimes hand clasping, sometimes embracing, or both. Animated but not wild.	Active in general, shortly after World War I.
Shimmy 1. Shim-Sham 2. Shawobble	4/4; alla breve	Convulsive, highly suggestive, sensuous.	General from about 1914 to 1920. Less active since.
Charleston	2/4; alla breve	Limber-kneed, twisting, improvisational.	General from 1920 to 1930. Rarely seen at present.
Cake Walk	2/4	Fancy promenade. Steps improvised.	Very old and popular in the deep, rural South until around 1920. May still be found in rare cases.
Snake Hips	4/4; 2/4	Lithe, undulating, informal.	Very briefly in use around 1920.
Peck	2/4; alla breve	Violent movement of the shoulders, neck, and head.	Popular mainly on the stage during the early twenties.
Grape-Pick	2/4	Mainly movement of the arms; agitated	Popular around 1930, mostly on the stage.
Big Apple	Alla breve	Picturesque, colorful, and requires skill; vivacious.	Used mostly for entertainment from 1933 to 1935.
Truck	4/4	Shuffling.	General after World War I. Now obsolete.
Jump	Alla breve	Characteristic of many other dances, especially the Buck, the Tap, and the Juba.	General and consistently in use.
Jitterbug	Alla breve	Wild, skilled, acrobatic, sometimes primitive.	Used generally. One of the most popular dances.
Zokie	Alla breve	A variant of the Charleston and Truck.	Very recent, not widely used.

Typical Negro Dance Music Groups

A
Boxes, jawbones and key, hoe, stones, drums (slavery)

B
One or two banjos
Jawbone and key (obsolete, very old)
Pans (one or more)

C
Drums
Bones
Sand blocks
Banjo (sometimes)

D
Fiddle and rhythm (or solo) (banjo obsolete)
The name fiddle is used traditionally.

E
Fiddle (sometimes omitted)
Mandolin
Guitar (two guitars alone; very rare)

F
Fiddle
Mandolin
Guitar
Bass fiddle

G
Fiddle (one or two)
Mandolin (one or two)
Guitar

Harmonica
Washboard
Bass viol

H
Fiddle
Mandolin
Guitar (one or two)
Harmonicas
Jug (sometimes with washboard)
Bass viol

More Advanced Levels

I
Piano and trap drums (sometimes solo)

J
Piano
Trap drums
Violin (name "violin" has been accepted)

K
Piano
Violin (one or two)
Trap drums
Cornet

L
Piano
Violin (one or two)
Cornet
Trombone (sometimes clarinet)
Trap drums

M
Tailgate band (so named because the band played from the rear of a moving wagon advertising a dance show or picnic):
Trombone
Cornet
Trap drums

N
Various combination of modern instruments played by non–note readers in small places for profit.

II
The word "blues" has the power of an entire folk fantasia. No one word in our language conveys such musical definiteness and personal meaning to the Negro as does "blues." Not every Negro can distinguish a spiritual from some other Negro music, but he can tell a blues from a spiritual at all times. No other creation of the Negro has the tragic force found in blues, if the name is understood to mean "trouble." There is a frankness here that at times is more than the listener is prepared to accept. No scene is too personal, no thought too private, no act too base to find expression in this strange, crying folk drama epitomized in song form.

Were it not for the sake of satisfying a general curiosity, this paragraph might just as well be dismissed. However, lately so much has been attached to the Negro meaning of the name "blues" that a brief discussion of it is unavoidable. One theory has it that the word came into use as a synonym for "evil," the belief being that any very blue thing was evil. Another theory is that the Union soldiers were called "the Blues," and their presence in the South caused so much sorrow that "blues" became for Negroes and whites a synonym for "trouble and grief." One more theory says that the old Blue Laws gave so much gloom to the regions where they were in force that the word "blues" was used in describing them as a whole. At any rate, the fact is that blues are songs that are made with a tear on the cheek and sung to the movement of dancing feet. In our day the blues represent the truest form of active Negro dance music.

A moment of reflection causes us to realize that blues are a series of cries strung together in the form of a song. After the Negro had developed the Afro-American musical cry, he naturally felt the impulse to carry it a step further. He wanted to express a complete idea. Following the dictates of an unusual musical endowment, the phrases were strung together in a manner that created a musical sentence. It must be remembered at this point that the custom is to pause briefly after each utterance of the cry. This feeling was continued in the development of the blues. When the consideration of a song was undertaken, some means had to be used to give order to the procedure of singing and pausing alternately, just as was done in the perfecting of the old chorale singing. This end was reached by using the great ordering force of the universe—rhythm.

The mere statement of this fact is not sufficient for clarity, so let us see how the process worked itself out. In the case of the pure blues—blues that were made without the idea of commercialization or the aid of an instrument—the pauses were bridged by merely joining the cries together in accordance with the feeling created by the rhythm of the first phrase. Hence the oldest of the blues (pure blues) do not conform to the general principle of having a break between the phrases, as does our present-day form. They form a continuous song expression, much in the same way as the other Negro songs. Here is an example of a very old blues that has this principle in its best form.

Down de Line

The musical rest indicates what would ordinarily be a pause in the primitive cry, or a break in the present-day form of blues. The feeling for the pause is evident, but the time value has been definitely settled by the eighth rest. Let us continue by using another old pure blues example:

Spanish an' 'Merican War Blues

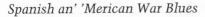

Some folks got de blues 'bout de Span-ish an' 'Mer-i-can war. Some

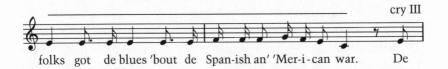

folks got de blues 'bout de Span-ish an' 'Mer-i-can war. De

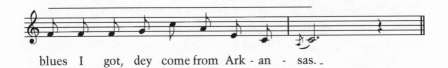

blues I got, dey come from Ark - an - sas. _

For yet another illustration, consider the blues with only two cries:

Woman, Woman

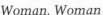
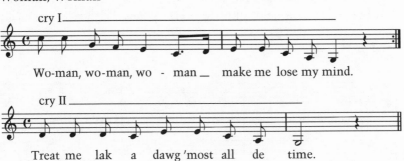

Wo-man, wo-man, wo - man _ make me lose my mind.

Treat me lak a dawg 'most all de time.

The above examples show something more than the blues as musical expression that originated from cries. They also give a very definite hint as to the age of these songs as a form of expression. The second verse of "Woman, Woman" goes:

> Baby, baby, hear me at yo' door,
> Done work for yo' since eighteen-eighty four.

When the blues were joined to the use of a musical instrument— like the banjo and, by all means, the guitar—another development in the blues form took place. So long as the singer used no instrument, he was a comparative law unto himself. When he began the use of instrumental accompaniment, he was forced to keep a definite pitch. He was also forced to bring his voice and the instrument into rhythmic agreement. When he took his pitch, the singer-player was forced by natural feeling to play a phrase so as to establish a pitch and a tempo. This introduction was considered an organic part of the piece, as has been the case time and time again in formal music. When the phrase ended and was given over to the metrical rest, the introductory instrumental phrase was repeated. This was also done at the end of the piece. These accompaniments were very rhythmic and very simple, following the principle of the melodic line and implying, at the most, tonic, subdominant, and dominant harmonies. During my research two of these rather stock accompaniments have come to light, one of which is popular today as boogy woogy. However, let it be said that this name is almost ancient among southern Negroes.

Now, let us combine a blues with this rhythm, and it will be seen that the accompaniment, plus the cry, provides the form of the piece.

Ball an' Chain

N.B. The F clef is used for convenience.

In this case it may be seen that the piece is made of fifteen measures and that the two cries are three measures. The folk accompaniment is five measures longer than the vocal part. This answers the question of how the form of the blues came into being. It is necessary to remember that the blues, being solo vocal music, were wedded to the instrument. Blues and ballads are therefore very closely akin to one another, whereas spirituals and blues are far apart due to their different natures, one being chorally antiphonal and the other being soloistic with an organic accompaniment.

Before going further, it is best to give a melodic conception of the other folk-blues accompaniment in wide use about forty years ago:

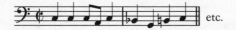 etc.

This is merely one possible instance of this pattern.

The conclusions given above have been arrived at through years of investigation and study. Indeed, they are the product of firsthand experiences and the handling of scores of folk musicians of varying ages and types, many at the folk festivals I have conducted. Perhaps this is the first time these approaches have been described. If so, the credit for them must go to the folk who produced them.

In the last music figure shown above, there seems to be a certain tendency toward chromatics. This again is the result of the instrumental influence of the blues. When the blues singer plays his guitar, his fingers slip over the frets and produce unintended tone colors. He is fascinated, and since he is a good musician, he remembers these effects and uses them again. How many times does one hear a guitarist making his "box" weep by the sliding of his hand up and down the neck or by rolling the joints of the fingers?

But this was nothing when the gifted Negro "pianna picker" started his method of playing. Here is a gifted Negro with an instrument that is primitive enough to be percussive and at the same time refined enough to express the musical mind of Johann Sebastian Bach, Ludwig van Beethoven, Frédéric François Chopin, and Franz Liszt. Here he has a musical feast spread before him. He experiments and finds new things. His fancy takes wing and he creates a new type of piano-playing. The foot would rather stamp out the rhythm on the floor. The left hand drums a heavy descant, a novel, offbeat song, while his voice cries the blues—weary, ugly, happy, beautifully impromptu. The Negro blues "pianna picker" is therefore the real moving spirit behind the blues. Ma Rainey, Bessie Smith, Ethel Waters—all are subservient to his genius. Without his genius they can do nothing but silhouette the spirit of the blues. But this one-man orchestra can give a comprehensive rendition all by himself. He makes the blues no longer a mere song but a vital dance music, a mold for the American musical conception for years to come—jazz!

The next important phase of this discussion is the rise of the blues and a simultaneous consideration of the various classes of blues. The pure blues have been given sufficient attention for the reader to be on a fairly good footing where this phase of the blues is concerned. However, there are several developmental stages that one should consider in order to have a clear picture of blues in our time.

The first performers of blues were singers who were eager to accept what was given to them. The white listeners were as moved by their strange music as the Negroes who lived with it. They were in a position to pay for it and were willing to do so at all times. Since the blues were not always "polite," blues singers were usually given to performing to men only, at saloons, barbershops, and on street corners. As time passed, Negro singers were used to "drum up trade." These black minstrels would be paid to perform at certain saloons on Saturdays. It is probable that some medicine "doctor" heard a concert of this nature and decided to use the principle on a larger scale. This gave rise to the once-popular medicine show. These cure-all circuses traveled throughout the South and set up gaslit stages outdoors in vacant lots. The community was invariably a Negro one; therefore the music that sounded best to them was their own. Of all Negro music, the blues were best suited for the audience. There was a note about the blues that would catch the fancy of the more conservative in the audience, if care was taken not to make the verse too open in its suggestivity. These songs formed the core of these shows, supported by male dancers and "jokers." Women sang the blues at home.

Women were eventually introduced into the group as singers and dancers. When this happened, a new day was born for the further development of the blues. Whereas the men sang blues in just as forceful and original a manner as anyone could, it seemed more natural for a woman to sing about her disappointments and sorrows. Negro women had little protection from their men, due largely to the unhappy lot of the Negro man in the South. She was frustrated at every turn, so that the badge of grief was symbolized by her mere presence. It was reality in the first degree when she sang:

> A woman's born fo' trouble jes as sho' as you born;
> When she need somebody to help her,
> De man she favored done gone!

It was also reality in the first degree when she advised:

> Don't trust no one man, git you a easy job;
> Rather keep on workin'
> Dan live wid a man dat's so hard.

It is natural that where men and women have differences, the largest share of sympathy usually goes (and rightly so) to the women. When others heard songs like these and beheld the possible living example before them, they joined in the song in spirit and frequently in body.

It was natural for these women to move in rhythmic response to their own singing. When they reached the breaks in the blues, they went into various impromptu folk-dance steps or used sensuous body movements. This proved so effective that the form became standardized. Thereafter when one thought of the blues singer, the individual was always a woman singing hoarsely and doing dance cadenzas in the breaks. From this point onward, blues have been a composite of voice, dance, and instrument—that is, blues in the professional sense, which is the only type now generally known. (For convenience let us henceforth refer to them as voice-instrument blues. This name is suggestive of the absolute interdependence existing in the familiar "St. Louis Blues," for instance, which is the ideal of all modern blues-makers.) These breaks were not overlooked by the instrumentalist. When the singer did her steps, the piano encouraged her by sending her a vigorous offbeat innovation. At this point a masterpiece of showmanship prevailed. The singer and player carried the audience back and forth between the spirits of their own "house-rent" dances and the professional stage with such rapidity that they were overwhelmed on the emotional shuffleboard. As a small boy, I sat in the old Globe and Air-Dome theaters in Jacksonville, Florida, and saw Negroes all but dash onto the stage in their excitement when Ma Rainey would take them on one of these folk-drama excursions supported by Eugene Mikel and his four musical counterparts.

From all this activity it has been seen that the blues moved rapidly indoors, that they were bound to pick up chromatic color from the instruments, and that they were moving along a path that would only lead to some sort of formal recognition. The force was so great in this direction that the more respectful Negroes cagily ventured into socially forbidden places "to see what was making folks act like that." Many required rather extended visits in order to acquire their information. Soon the better class of dance combinations were forced to play blues but discreetly refrained from singing them. The vogue was growing, but there were two distinct camps among Negroes. The white people accepted the religious and dance songs and the adaptations of Stephen Foster but knew little of the blues. These songs the Negroes had hitherto sung for themselves, so the time was ripe for a radical development.

William C. Handy was equipped by nature to work with the blues. It is known that Handy took note of these songs in 1903. To my mind this must refer to the vocal-instrument type rather than to the old folk type. These songs appealed to Handy as a musician and as a man. He lived the hard way, tramping about with men far beneath his genius in an effort to eke out a life in his first love—music. He knew firsthand all of the sorrows blues spoke of. He realized the great value of the music and gave to the world his conception of how it should be treated. His methods were correct and simple.

Handy did what no respectable person had dared do prior to his time. He gave the blues a place of respectability by expressing the spirit of blues without giving the coarse, obscene expressions of the blues a place in his texts. At a time when the tango was the fashion, Handy took its rhythm and put it in Negro blues. By sheer genius he recognized that the tangana rhythm belonged to him by nature. At the time only scholars knew that the tango was based on African rhythm. So, without knowing anything about the tangana, Handy seemed to identify its nature. It is for reasons like this that music scholars in this country and some parts of Europe have taken such exceptional note of Handy. Indeed, he is the "Father of the Blues" (the blues as we have it today). His influence has been felt in most recent phases of Negro and white musical development. Sure, he did not create the blues, but he did create a place for them. It is also of interest to note that Handy, being no singer, is the most famous person connected with the blues. It may be said that the late Ma Rainey and Handy represent the true character of blues today—vocal and instrumental. Handy's place is more secure and enduring, due to his ability as a composer. Rainey composed blues every time she sang. She also lost them on each occasion, for her remarkable improvisations were never recorded.

The phonograph companies began a new blues epoch around 1917–18 with the advent of Mammie Smith. Prior to this time, the best-known blues singer on records was Marian Harris. She was a white woman who sang blues so well that many Negroes thought she was a Negro. Her records were very good and very authentic, but when Mammie Smith came along there was a note of racial color and understanding that moved Negroes to action. Every small furniture store seemed to have Mammie Smith records playing daily at full blast. The sales went great. Of course, other companies and other singers took the cue, and soon the deluge was on. Bessie Smith, Trixie Smith, Ida Cox, Ethel Waters—all had scores of blues records. The rush was so great that new blues were appearing overnight. Bessie Smith and Ethel Waters held top positions in the final stages. By this time Ma Rainey was showing signs of tiring.

These records produced a new and unsuspected position for blues singers. Whereas the singer had been able to create an impression by "taking the dancebreaks" in the songs, she was now forced to surrender this spot to the instrumentalist or the orchestra. This situation did not last long, however, for the singers began to improvise short statements to take the place of their dancing. This was given the name "jive."

The records also gave the singers and players a chance to hear themselves and to hear and learn from their rivals. This situation caused the blues to become stereotyped and repetitive. The spontaneity began to wane. Too many blues sung by Ida Cox sounded as if they had been learned from Bessie Smith, who sounded so much like Ma Rainey that most people could swear it was an Ethel Waters version. The public also began to know the blues by heart and to tire of the sameness. The great stimulus coming from this was to create a new acceptance for blues and to cause the entire American population to become acquainted with the music that was to modify all dance music for the next generation. As Handy points out, the breaks gave birth to jazz. The improvisation that closed these gaps also opened a new vista. These records furnished the school whence the men in the orchestra gained the freshness and folk impulse necessary to create the new medium.

Some men besides Handy must be mentioned in the early development of the "concert blues." Fletcher Henderson was one of the first educated Negro pianists to be identified with blues. He was the musical director of Black Swan Record Company. In this capacity he came into contact with blues singers and developed accompaniments for their songs. He was the accompanist for Ethel Waters and Bessie Smith. His style was imitated by almost every other blues accompanist of his time. The effect of his playing shone through his orchestra and built up a new idiom which was fashioned on a blues base but supported a most original superstructure in tone and rhythm sequences. Spencer Williams was one of the founders of this new blues era. His compositions have a rather unfolkish tinge at times, insofar as the text is concerned. Yet the music is almost always good. As a blues composer he seems closest to Handy, who has seen fit to become the publisher of his works.

Duke Ellington, a lyric genius, has infused his whole personality with the blues, but he is such a consummate master of mood that this is not always revealed in his music. The blues must be sought out in the definite sense, and they are always felt. His style is more synchronized than that of Henderson, who developed the "shouting brass." He lacks the pianistic skill of Henderson, so that he is forced to ask more from his men in the orchestra. He composes most of what he asks for. The peculiar wailing, riding quality found in Ellington's music is perhaps the most subtle use yet made of the blues essence. It is blues, and yet it is not. It is new music from old means.

At present, blues are in two separate trends. We will discuss each of these separately. The blues have moved into the church, insofar as the musical idiom is concerned (it must be clear that blues texts have not been taken into the church). Such persons as singer-guitarist Sister Rosetta Tharpe, singer-guitarist Sister Creecy McKissack, singer-pianist Arizona Drane, and the "Six-Wing Angel" Utah Smith have had a great influence in this connection in the South during recent years. So, the religious songs one hears from the church singer give a definite suggestion of the blues. This is not pure folk creation, of course, but rather a result of the blues pressure from radio and records. Many would-be composers give blues idioms to the church in ballads and arrangements. There is a definite likeness, too, in the preaching of the Negro "zooning" preacher and blues music. Perhaps the blues music had been hidden in the Negro church all along and is just lately being aired or recognized in definite form. Again, let us emphasize that blues as music is one thing and that blues as language is quite another.

In speaking of blues in connection with preaching on the folk level, reference is made to tonal considerations and idiomatic concepts. If one hears sounds from a minister, the gospel quartet, or the deacon, which at times are very much like some sounds heard from the blues singer, one should not be shocked at all. Blues are musical cries, while Negro folk sermons are musical cries in extended form, and the gospel quartet is a combination of these. Both the blues and folk preaching are of the same musical nature. The difference is that one connects itself with the spiritual realm and the other connects itself to the carnal realm—indeed, often to the basest element in the whole scheme of carnality. With this comparison made, we may go to the next consideration—"dirty blues," "lowdown blues." Negroes created these names, so they are not unaware of their opposites. In other words, "respectable blues" are known. The sordid blues are daily gaining in favor. Their chief stronghold is a certain type of nightclub.

It so happens that when some people cross the thresholds of these clubs, they are willing to accept the cheapest and often rawest kind of sensual entertainment. The intellectual and the playboy, the society matron and the party-girl, seem to find here a common ground and blend into a rather wide-range, unpretending, take-what-comes grouping. They take the "dirty blues" as the main source of vocal satisfaction. The singers who specialize in this song type go to deliberate pains to make their lines as raw as possible under existing standards. These songs no longer express the feelings of distraught souls speaking in the only language that has meaning to them. They are now the means to an end, conceived on the bases of sex, money, alcohol, narcotics, and the animalistic. It is plain that blues are going back to the gutter. However, this time they are retreating, whereas before they were advancing from an unavoidable stage of existence in Negro life. It may be that some blues, as sung on records now, give another impression. These are frequently milder versions of what the singer often gives out in the nightclub. The place where the blues is not influenced by records and radio is not to be found in this country. The city has become the master beyond question.

Perhaps in years to come only the beautiful music of some modern blues may be generally heard and remembered, where otherwise the entire song, music, and words would have been used to represent this peculiar Negro music. All races have sex songs of this nature. So far as I can tell at this writing, the music and the words of these songs are of about equal value. In the case of most modern blues, the music is superior to the words in lasting artistic value. The music of Handy and Henderson, the sophisticated swing of Ellington, and the formative creations of George Gershwin may send other rarely gifted dance composers into this rich melodic realm. This could mean a new development in American music based on natural, preconceived folk idioms rather than on theoretical formulae. Blues would have then passed technically from the high point of the vocal-instrument genre into the newer, more expansive area of purely artistic instrumental music. *Rhapsody in Blue*, by Gershwin, has already demonstrated this possibility.

It is not fitting that a discussion of blues should close on a prophetic and personal note. The spirit should return to the folk. To that end, two blues verses come to mind. When the Negro woman sings "Blues ain't nothin' but a woman want to see her man," she is certainly too personal. She forgets for the moment that blues are also beautiful music. She has never known that blues represent what is perhaps her most purely racial musical utterance. The summary of all that is in blues—good, bad, noble, and poetic—is expressed in what is perhaps one of the finest lines in secular music:

De blues is a mean, dirty, lowdown thing,
When you can't help yo'self,
Don't cry, jes walk an' sing.

III

Negro ballads are so close to blues and work songs in nature that it is well-nigh impossible to separate them. He who understands blues has a very reliable knowledge of ballads and is right on the threshold of the work songs. If a folk blues tune is set to words that tell a story in ballad form, the result is, of course, a ballad. It is true, however, that some modern blues forms are used to tell stories. Examples of this are found in many blues. Too often the sound of the music confuses us as to what is taking place in the text. For instance:

John Henry was a man didn't 'bey no law.
Didn't need no gun,
Could whip an' man he cross.

De white man say, John Henry, do lak yo' please.
Done hear 'bout yo',
All de way f'om Tennessee.

This is a well-known example of what has been said. Negro ballads are more a matter of words than music. The above stanzas are obviously in the realm of the ballad, but the music would have to be in blues form, and it is:

John Henry (Blues-Ballad)

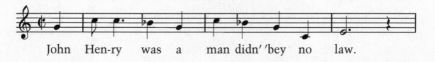

John   Hen-ry   was   a   man didn' 'bey no   law.

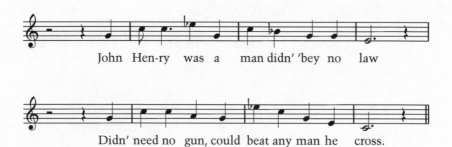

John Hen-ry was a   man didn' 'bey no   law

Didn' need no gun, could beat any man he   cross.

Bus Ezell, of Fort Valley, Georgia, is fond of this type of song. The one given here is not one of his, but it does belong to Georgia.

Chapter 4
The Rise of the Work Songs

The philosophy, beauty, and grandeur of the Negro work song has been largely overlooked until very recently. This is the result of neglect, on the one hand, and circumstances inherent in the system producing the work song, on the other. In the first place, those who came south to help the Negro out of his blighted depths were very religious people who were anxious to see the very best and noblest virtues in their charges and to show these virtues to the world in a manner intended to impress others who would be willing to let down a ladder upon which the Negro might begin his climb upward. Consequently, the religious songs received all of the attention from these early benefactors. To say that these fine people were correct in establishing the spirituals and jubilees as the forefront of the Negro's musical creation is to deal in platitudes. They are generally agreed to be the best and noblest of the many Negro folk songs (a point not agreed to by all), but they were and are not the only true, significant, and important of the songs emanating from the Negro. In fact, there are certain elements of the Negro and his existence which one is able to find only in the songs of labor.

The work songs are the oldest Negro folk songs and may be said to have their functional origin in Africa. It is obvious that the slave was forced to live in the environment of the white man's civilization for a period of indefinite length in order to become sufficiently imbued with the Christian religion and to warrant making that religion a personal medium of expression and salvation in the immediate as well as the immortal sense. The pagan faiths of past centuries had to be renounced and forgotten in order to make way for the more sublime and enduring tenets of Christianity. However, when the spiritual did begin to develop, it went apace because of what it meant to an oppressed people. The momentum was very much accentuated by the fact that after the war the Negro received such aforesaid dynamic encouragement in the province of the spiritual and jubilee.

While the Negro was in Africa, the work song was known and practiced very much in the sense that it is today. The work he did in Africa was as intimately bound up with his perceptual consciousness as the work he later was called upon to perform in America. Then, too, slavery existed for the Negro in Africa before it did in America. Surely no one would say that the Negro was unable to transfer his African work songs to his new environment on exceedingly short notice so that they would meet his new needs.

Many of these African work songs were sung for a time in the native tongue on plantations where censorship did not deprive the early slave of this last possession of his. The same capacity to create work songs, as far as it includes the race as a whole, may be said to dwell universally in the Negro. The only determinant as to the product of this capacity is one of an environmental nature. Where environments offer situations that are akin, there is more possibility for a proportionate similarity in the product. A. L. Speight, in his article titled "Notes on African Music," in the July 1934 issue of the *Musical Quarterly*, has this to say in regard to the work songs of the African natives: "These songs describe the work underground and introduce such subjects as drilling and breaking up the rock, accidents, the treatment received from European miners, and what the singers intend to do with their pay."

A like attitude is represented in the songs portrayed in *Songs and Tales from the Dark Continent*, by the late Natalie Curtis-Burlin. A comparison of the situations expressed in these songs is in many respects identical to those found in the American Negro work songs. From a musical point of view, the similarity is in many cases even more striking. It is to be seriously regretted that the first work songs of the Negro slave and ex-slave were lost to the world. A comparison of these early songs with those that are being produced today would take us further along the road to a better understanding of Negro musical development. From a sociological as well as musical point of view, such an understanding could produce a picture of the Negro's mind during slavery which is different from that shown through the spiritual.

If one sets out during this age to provide himself with a collection of work songs taken from the Negro, he is embarking upon a much more difficult venture than he would have experienced even ten years ago. The rapid economic and industrial changes are wreaking havoc with the system that produced the work songs. Of course, considering some of the changes, one must be aware of certain benefits to the Negro in an ethical sense, for the deplorable conditions under which some of the work songs were made rivals the rigors of slavery in the fullest sense of the word.

On the other hand, some peculiar change is taking place in the attitude of the Negro which causes him not to react to his job in a singing mood. Having to compete with the industrial machine has made him feel somewhat like an industrial outcast. The group spirit formerly found at every turn where the Negro laborers were engaged has been stunned. A man works largely as a servant for some machine that cannot share his feelings or react in any way to his emotional urges. Only in certain places where the Negro is permitted to work in gangs on roads, docks, and large agricultural enterprises does one find the work song surviving. Unfortunately, the prison camp is becoming the last firm "standing ground" for fine art expression. I say "unfortunately" because too often when a man becomes a prisoner, a part of his creative urge is directed in a concentrated way toward the sordid phase of his existence.

On the other hand, a study has shown that there are many songs that break the prison bonds and fly above the local into the broader ways of life. There are also many cases where songs have been preserved in prisons by men who entered twenty or even thirty years ago. (John A. Lomax and Alan Lomax bring this fact out admirably in their book *American Ballads and Folk Songs*.) That the prison camp is unique in its capacity to evoke the strongest of group feeling is not denied; that many splendid work songs have been salvaged there is to be acknowledged. However, in the near future the names "prison songs" and "work songs" may become synonymous if other sources are not found by the student of folk music through the most diligent and painstaking effort. This method involves contacting those men who worked in various situations in past years where these songs were sung. The student must also find and exploit the few remaining sources in civil life.

Certainly no effort has been made here to taboo the work song that is created in prison. The beautiful and beloved "Water Boy," which was introduced in so timely a manner by Avery Robinson, is solely the product of the Georgia chain gang.[1] The point here is to show in a very definite way the direction in which the work song is receding and to emphasize the somewhat neglected opportunity to find them in less stereotyped cases.

There are other reasons for the comparative scarcity of the work song. Work songs, as I use the term, were created by men. Women and children have not contributed to the repertoire as they have in the cases of the religious songs and other folk songs. The fact that women did the same work as men in the days of slavery has not been overlooked here. As has been pointed out, with a few exceptions we are forced to deal with work songs of comparatively recent date. All of the many true work songs that have come under my notice bear the unmistakable stamp of having been born through the minds of men. This would reduce the source of output in comparison with that of the other Negro folk songs, with the possible exception of the desperado type. These songs were created not only by men, but by a certain type of man who was engaged in the sort of work conducive to the creation of the songs. Contrary to much current opinion, then, not all Negroes are endowed with the ability to create worthwhile folk songs. This would decrease the number of work songs that come from the Negro. Finally, in most cases the work song is sung in places that are not frequented by the class of people who are capable of preserving them. All of these factors working together undoubtedly have been responsible for the present difficulty one has in locating this material, as compared to the relative ease of locating spirituals, jubilees, and other folk songs.

The work song is more singular in its application than most of the Negro songs, in that it developed out of a phase of life that is in large

---

1. It is significant to note that "Water Boy," which was the first work song to gain a place in the programs of discriminating artists or to enjoy national artistic prestige, is a song from the lips of a Negro in prison. Of course, this proves nothing, but the coincidence is more striking.

measure a subdivision of the overall life experiences of Negroes. The religious songs evolved out of the universal feeling of the need for help and reassurance, whereas the work songs evolved out of a more particularistic world. This is why the work song is not always understood as easily as the other songs. For instance, there is a rather constant use of words that belong to a world unfamiliar to the layman. On the other hand, the religious songs, built upon the tenets of Christianity and texts taken from the Bible, speak a language that is more readily understood. Meanings in work songs are of necessity very subtle in places where a more open statement may mean disaster for the singer. There are also instances where the most threatening and contemptuous language is to be found in the work song, thus illustrating the range of circumstances and personalities in regard to the creators and their locations.

To say that no songs are sung by the Negro at work except those that are avowedly work songs is to be wholly wrong. There are certainly times when one hears all of the various song types from the lips of Negro workmen, yet the place of the work song must not be misunderstood because of this. No one should feel that these various songs represent a type of work song, for there is no fast rule that can be made as regards the matter of singing certain songs at certain times. In *Slave Songs of the United States* mention is made of certain spirituals used for rowing or doing other kinds of work. This may be the case, as stated, for indeed we have heard Negroes in widely separated cases sing a spiritual while working. So allowance must be made for one's state of mind at a given time, which may cause one to violate a custom or principle that is generally adhered to.

The Negro created both the work songs and the religious songs. He recognized his need for both; otherwise they would never have been produced. The same may be said of the other songs that are sung during the process of labor but make no reference to actual participation. The only songs that may be said truly to represent the Negro at work are the songs growing out of his toil. Highly religious groups of workmen here and there may at times prefer to use a spiritual or jubilee as encouragement for their hard toil, but if this is done, the spirit of worship has taken hold above the spirit of labor. Many times have I seen Negro women, including my mother, reach a plane of religious worship while doing housework and singing a Negro hymn. This same condition is sometimes found among men. However, when it comes to the case of women, it is more common, because, as I have said, women do not have work songs. It is good always to consider the fact that the Negro is in certain cases unwilling to sing any song that is not religious, but these cases have always been comparatively few, to my knowledge.

Looking at the subject from a musical point of view, there is much that is powerful and beautiful in the work song. The weird calls and the powerful swings between major and minor modes create a feeling of singular artistic participation. There is less here that seems to have been developed under the influence of the white man's singing. It is when one turns to the words of the songs found among these people of labor that the greatest individualism and power is felt. In fact, it may be said that the music truly exists for the words. All of the things that have developed in the routine of his occupation seem to be turned to pure gold in the mind of the black troubadour of toil. The most compelling humor, philosophy, determination, indignation, remorse, love, hope, despair, pride, recklessness, and loyalty find expression through the emotional gamut of the work song. Almost at will one may call gems from the casual perusal of a group of work verses.

Sometimes it is necessary for the layman to seek the aid of the singer in order to unravel the meaning of the highly figurative language of the work song. It is the subtle meanings couched in the wording of these songs that cause many to lose interest in what to them appears to be the frankest of nonsense. At times it has been my experience to find such an attitude of disinterest on the part of people who have good opportunity for the development of an understanding of the word pictures of the uneducated Negro. It is necessary for one to have frequent contact with the source and to be taught by the Negro if he would be at home with him in his "various language."

For instance, listen to these words: "Smoke in de stack / Scared ter come out." These words mean that on the river it gets so bitterly cold that the smoke is scared to leave the protection of the stack, or that on the railroad the section boss or foreman is so mean that when he comes around even the smoke runs for cover. It may also mean that the Negro is afraid to show signs of his feelings. So the figure is used variously but always the same theme predominates— fear and a refuge.

Now consider these words: "Jack Frost eben doin' 'roun'-about." Here is another case of the river being cold, so cold that the very person of Jack Frost will become frozen if he does not dance the "'roun'-about" to add warmth to his body.

Now consider this phrase: "Can't git a toe-holt." This is a phrase borrowed from the lingo of the mule driver. Often when the earth is wet, the mules cannot pull the "wheeler" (a big shovel carried upon two wheels) because of a lack of sufficient footing to brace themselves. This is referred to by the Negroes as "not gittin' a toe-holt." Hence, when the Negro is unable to get himself out of his difficulties, he "can't git a toe-holt."

Let us look further at another piece of text: "De cap'm got a rock quarry / In de way back o' his head." No, the captain is not necessarily a dumb man in every case, but rather he is viewed as unable to think of a kind word or do a good deed for the men who work under him. As they say, "He don't never think nothing but hell!" Indeed, the figures about "de cap'm" are some of the most striking, for the cap'm is the Negro's nemesis.

Another text about "de cap'm" goes: "Gonna do lak dynamite fuse / Ef de cap'm don' mind." The dynamite fuse is of long patience, this song is saying. It burns slowly and withholds the explosion as long as it can. However, just before the explosion, it stops its sputtering, complaining: "Ef I had mah weight in line / I'd whip dis cap'm / Twell his clothes start fryin'." A mule driver uses his line in his right hand to flog the mules as well as to direct them, so this song is saying that if the driver had a line that was as heavy as he is, he would be pleased to use it on "de cap'm." Here the mule driver, by wishing for an impossible weapon, has excused his failure to commit the suicidal act that burns in his soul—flogging the white man.

The job of the mule driver is said to be a difficult one in this song: "I'm the lead mule / I'm de swing." The wheelers are usually hauled by four mules on heavy jobs. The mules are two abreast. The right-front mule is the "lead mule," and the rear mule is the "swing mule."

Here the singer complains that the mules work less than he does and that there is no one to help him.

Now consider this phrase from a work song: "Ah got a rainbow rollin' 'roun' mah shoulder." This is a gem of many facets, for this figure is used by different Negroes in different ways: (1) Like a rainbow, no one knows whence I came or where I am going. (2) I have good luck to protect me. (3) I have no way of knowing how long I'm going to stay after I come here. (4) I can always get some money (based on the old story that a pot of gold hangs at one end of the rainbow).

Another phrase in the work song is: "Been here f'om can't ter can't." At many camps the men go to work when it is too dark to see and work until it is too dark to see—hence, "can't ter can't."

The phrase "Lawd, boy, I done rivered" is interesting, too. It means one has worked and sweated as long as one is able to stand it for the present. A worker might also sing, "I'm washed up," or "I'm too damn tired to sweat!"

Now consider these words: "Ef yo' head's under water, boy / Don't swell yo' chest." Here a very sound principle of physics is made to apply to equally sound common sense—a rather terse but comprehensive example of the Negro laborer's mental makeup. It is impossible to "swell yo' chest" without breathing. Hence, the lesson is that one should do nothing at the wrong time. In other words, wait for "yo' changin' " day.

There are many other words whose meaning would be unclear to the layman, such as: "I got a hook team / Layin' in de pay car do'." The hook team is used to help the various teams pull out of hard places, invariably at the beginning of a "scoop." The hook team, in this case, is the pay envelope. The worker's reliance on it to pull him out of his situation is far out of proportion to the meager contents.

Now consider the words: "Tired o' being a headlight mole." This means the worker is tired of digging in the earth for a living. "Headlight," meaning "eyes," is the mark of differentiation between the man and the blind mole.

Let us continue with this passage: "Some things here, I can't see / Hay fer de mule, but hell fer me." The state of the mule is one to be pitied, for the mule is galled, beaten, and worked to death. Yet, this driver seems willing to change places.

These words also have interesting meaning: "I got a min', Lawd / Lak de top o' de mountain." There is no possibility of superciliousness here. This is merely rising above whatever situation is at hand, a freeing of oneself in the kingdom of fancy. Here we see a spirit that will not be broken. So we also hear these words: "I got a min', Lawd / Lak de top o' de mountain, / It won't break down, / Won't break down."

The foregoing verses were picked at random from my collection. The analyses were obtained from various sources at the time of collection. The explanations given by the singers were in many cases very different in wording, yet the spirit of what I have written is in keeping with their explanations. Interestingly enough, in some cases the singer was unable to give any interpretation of what he had sung. He was so much a part of the songs that he could not state his thoughts in any other words than those contained in the songs. So there is no doubt that if the explanations of some of the persons interviewed were set down here, the reader would be as far from an understanding of the songs as if no effort at all had been made to interpret them. In other words, my wish to put down the original sayings of the interpreters has been partly voided by the necessity of having to use my own words.

Chapter 5

Imagery and Nature of the Work Song

The work song has been the surveyor of the most famous and significant Negro legends. Here the great imaginative power of the black man is brought forth in all its untutored glory. Perhaps a truer kinship with real, classic racial creativeness is apparent in the work song than in the other products of Negro folk genius.

Throughout the ages, races that have produced great artistic geniuses have also produced great legends. Most likely these races have produced great legends because they had great artistic potency. The ideals that were not attained in practice were attained through the creation of characters and situations that served to satisfy to some extent the longing for greater power, knowledge, and moral virtue. When one considers the legends of Germany, Italy, France, Greece, Russia, Scandinavia, China, and Africa, and the rich artistic contributions of these countries in various art forms, the result is significant if not conclusive. For instance, Richard Wagner, who wrote the greatest operas in the German language, relied upon the richness of German legend for much of his inspiration, as indeed does Strauss.

The great significance of African legend has been made manifest by the comprehensive work of Carter G. Woodson and, to a comparatively lesser degree, Natalie Curtis-Burlin. It is not strange but only natural that the tradition should have been kept intact by the Negro slave in his new environment. The story-making abilities of the Negro having been made the theme of much white literature, it is necessary at this point to address ourselves to the subject as it affects our theme—Negro music. It so happens that there are instances when the desire for greater ability to do certain types of work brings a legend into being. These legends are always the result or source of work songs. These characters are always capable of doing the things the Negro longs to do, but longs to do in vain. The characters are exceedingly true to life in some respects. They are born normally, work under a white "cap'n," and, as wonderful as they are, they work themselves to death or meet tragic ends by their own strength of body or of will.

To know John Henry as he appears in the song bearing his name is to have a very shallow acquaintance with him. There is more than one legend about him, just as there is more than one song based on his exploits. Insofar as John Henry worked in different places doing different kinds of work, it is useful to understand that it was as a steel driver that he is generally best known and remembered by Negroes. Different states have taken the occasion to apply the local color of their respective provinces to the legend.

The legend of John Henry as told in Georgia is not taken from the lips of any one person.[1] As it appears below, it is in composite form, having been developed by joining together actual incidents gathered from various sources. No effort has been made to expand upon the collected material but only to link it together in its correct order.

John Henry in Georgia

John Henry was born in a place that no one seems to be sure about. According to the familiar words taken from the song, he was born somewhere around Macon, Georgia:

> He was born
> Down 'bout Macon,
> And he growed
> Lak de risin' sun.

This at least provides the vicinity and gives a dynamic suggestion about the life that such a Samson–Hercules–Don Juan mixture of a man would be expected to have. John Henry moved instantly from birth to having the ability to do the impossible, thus refusing the

---

1. This is not the only version found in Georgia; nor is this version found only in Georgia.

comforts of infancy in favor of the sterner ways of life. His first request was for his father's overalls and shoes. He held his father's hammer in the most severe contempt because of its lightness and shortness. His next, strongest urge was his natural desire to satisfy his hunger. To this end he ordered his astonished mother and humiliated father to provide him with a crisp side of bacon and a pan of biscuit. His thirst was satisfied by taking a cup of strong, black coffee. At the witnessing of these strange events, John Henry's father said his son was "gwine cause trouble fer wimmins and hell fer mens." It was John Henry who settled the matter by saying that he wanted to be a "steel drivin' man."

Having "growed lak de risin' sun," it must have happened that John Henry reached maturity on the day of his birth, which explains why no account of his childhood appears in this story. Furthermore, he left home on the day of his birth. As the train (which passed but a short distance from John Henry's home) blew for a nearby crossing, this young giant took his father's work clothes, gave his parents and others present "de high-ball sign," and with strides befitting his powers overtook and boarded the flying train. What would follow was a series of great exploits that startled the world. These exploits even startled John Henry at various times, as he admits in the words of the song:

> Ah got scar'd
> At Smoky Mountain,
> 'Cause mah hammer
> Wrecked de train.

The road was made for John Henry, and John Henry was made for the road. The first job he received was given to him somewhere between Macon and Savannah. The section gang was laying rails when John Henry walked up to the foreman and asked for work. Seeing that John Henry was rather young, the foreman asked if Henry had done railroad work before. To this question John Henry made his famous reply:

> Cap'n, Cap'n
> I ain't no lie,

Railroad hammah's
Bawn in mah han'.
I wears a rail fer my collar,
Spike fer my scarf pin,
Chain fer my tie.

So, the "cap'n" hired John Henry and set him to work. In less than ten minutes the "cap'n" and the section gang were overcome by the great brilliancy of John Henry's steel driving. They ran in all directions to call witnesses. Soon the entire right-of-way and the surrounding uplands were crowded with people who wished to see the hammering of John Henry. Five men were required to set up spikes for him and twenty men to keep up with the laying of rails. No matter how fast they worked, John Henry complained of the slow service he received. In fact, once when he was on the verge of destroying the work he had done, the "cap'n" saw to it that he was given the aid of an additional five men who volunteered from the onlookers standing by to see the miracle being wrought. The hammers were used by John Henry until they were all worn out, and the day's work so ended.

John Henry traveled almost incessantly. The great demand for his labor as well as the inborn traits of being a wanderer called him on and on, ever on to new labors, new surroundings, new women, and new problems, but never to a place capable of exploiting the many abilities he possessed. As he traveled, he never carried more than the very few things he considered absolutely necessary:

Jes gwine tak
His dice and hammah.
Dat's 'bout all
John Henry need.

When John Henry arrived at his new destination, the women worshipped him, the men feared and envied him, the children lived by him, and the section boss respected him. Day after day the section boss was forced to have larger and more durable hammers made for John Henry. His work was so tremendous that the "cap'n" frequently despaired over whether he would ever be able to cope with John Henry's ever-increasing demands. For example, when John Henry worked, his hammer became red-hot and burned away from the handle. If he missed the spike and smote the rail, he splintered it. If the "cap'n" could not keep a steady stream of water flowing in his direction in order to satisfy his thirst, then the work stopped. If the men could not keep the spikes set as John Henry demanded, then the "cap'n" had to procure a new crew at once. When John Henry made up his mind to drive steel, no interruptions were tolerated. So it was that this black giant strode over the face of the earth giving no quarter, asking none, despising the average man, and working the wonders of creation and the marvels of the age through the sheer power of his hands.

One day the "cap'n" came to a mountain standing directly in the path of the right-of-way, so that he was much distressed as to what he should do to overcome this seemingly insurmountable obstacle. The first idea was to lay the track around the mountain, but the shortage of time and rail prevented that. The second idea was to tunnel through the mountain. But this could not be done because it was well known that no help would come from John Henry, for he would work with nothing but his hammer. In the meantime, John Henry had taken advantage of his wonted prerogative and remained at his shack that day while the "cap'n" worried over what could be done. A thousand times the "cap'n" demanded that his men find a way out, for the road master had promised to have this new "cut" ready for service on that same day. In such circumstances the only hope was getting in touch with their champion and hero, John Henry. They ran to John Henry's shack and found him there snoring out his contentment under a fig tree, so they cast lots to see who would wake him up. When John Henry was finally shaken from his slumber, the unexpected happened. Contrary to all expectations, he did not become angry but merely looked drowsily out of the corners of his eyes in the direction of his gang, yawned cavernously, flexed the tremendous muscles in his arms and chest, pulled himself up to a sitting posture, and then said: "What de hell yawll want wid Henry?" He stood, a half-grinning, half-sulking, inviting personality.

After the "cap'n" explained to him what he was needed for, John Henry immediately set forth for the scene of the new conquest. Upon reaching the spot, John Henry ordered two men (as was necessary) to bring him his newest and biggest hammer, with which he swore to beat down the mountain. He girded himself a bit, spat upon his hands, turned his hammer over his shoulder and balanced it there, and strode up the profile of the mountain, singing:

> Take dis hammah
> In mah good right han',
> Beat down de mountain
> Lak a col' steel man.

As he reached the top of the mountain and began to work, the dust rose and drifted over the country surrounding the mountain so that it, together with the pounding of John Henry's hammer, caused the natives to imagine that an earthquake was in progress. The splinters of rock rained about, trees fell, and the fire from John Henry's hammer as it smote the rock flashed like lightning. The mountain came down in great chunks and dammed up the river. Finally there remained at the foot of the mountain but one big rock that obstructed the laying of rail. John Henry struck the rock twice with no result. Having faced the first thing in life that defied his great power, he was outraged. For his third blow he summoned all of the strength in his muscles. He double-jointed his knees and wrists and brought his great hammer down. Fire flashed and the rock rose like a cloud. Suddenly the gang saw John Henry reel, grip the handle of his hammer, and, with blood streaming from his head, fall down upon the trembling earth. Upon reaching his side, they realized what had happened. The hammer had rebounded with the blow that subdued the mountain and had struck John Henry in the forehead, killing him. He had been conquered by the only force on earth that could overcome him—his own strength.

John Henry's Funeral

John Henry fell dead while his hammer was still in his hand, and his eyes were still open. He did not look like a natural man in death, for he still was John Henry. The people who saw him cried and moaned, and the women who loved him had to be held back so that the boxcar could be brought up to carry him to the undertaker. When they lifted John Henry to put him in the car, they could not get him in the door with his hammer in his hand. Six men tried to remove the hammer but could not. But then one of John Henry's women walked up and called his name three times and fell down and cried, and when she fell down John Henry's big hammer fell down too. So they loaded John Henry into the boxcar and carried him to the undertaker.

When the undertaker saw John Henry's body, he said he was not going to touch it because he was afraid to work on "a unnatchel man." The section gang said he had better, so he laid out big John Henry on a commissary table and put a pick and a hammer by his side. He put a flagman's lantern to burn at his head and a coupling lock at his feet, and he made a casket from hewed-down cross-ties and dressed him in overalls. The section gang served as pallbearers, since the lovable John Henry did not belong to any church, and they buried him by the siding. The people stood in the driving rain and bitter cold to see and hear what is said to have happened:

> The first dirt they throwed on poor Henry
> It called John Henry's name.
> The next dirt they throwed on John Henry's feet
> Cried Lawd it's a pity and a shame.

> The next dirt they throwed on John Henry
> Sound like thunder ball
> And everybody that heard it say
> Sound lak mountain done fall.

> The next dirt they throwed on Henry
> Run like a rollin' stone
> But the next dirt they throwed on Henry
> Couldn't do nothin' but moan.

> The last dirt they throwed on John Henry
> Fell on the coffin top
> Made a sound like a hammer drivin' steel down
> Like the one made John Henry drop.

This legend is at least sixty to seventy years old, its story having been remembered throughout the lifetimes of many Negroes that old. No one has been found who has ever "seed" John Henry or who believes that such a character really lived, but here and there some doubt is expressed in both directions. It is very certain that the imaginations of many people have gone into the John Henry episodes. In fact, it is not uncommon for new exploits to be created "on the spot" for the entertainment of children as well as adults. For the working man, it is wholly apparent that John Henry existed as an ideal that could never be realized.

One summer day "Uncle Jim" (Jim Bowley) came to the front gate of our home in Jacksonville, Florida, and offered to "tidy" the yard for a modest sum. Having begun to work, he decided to make his chore more enjoyable by engaging in conversation. Being a man of very well preserved appearance, it came somewhat as a piece of the incredible when he gave his age in the indefinite but picturesque phrase "slavery-time critter." During the conversation I learned that he had been born in Louisiana, that he had worked as a roustabout on the Mississippi River, and that he was able to sing some of the roustabout songs. This was indeed the most gratifying of circumstances for a researcher, the more so since I was engaged in teaching in Louisiana and had already begun to do research on Negro music in that region. It was from Uncle Jim that I obtained the following legend in connection with the song "Hot Termolly Cholly." Here are Uncle Jim's words, as near as I can approach them, based on the several times I heard him tell the story, with slight variations.

Hot Termolly Cholly

Hot Termolly Cholly wuz bawn 'way up in de coldes' place in de worl'. Ennyhow, dats de way hit seem f'om what de song say an' how de boys whoop an' holler 'bout him back yonder on de river where we wuz steamboatin'—'specially doonce [during] de winter. De river is de coldes' place in de worl', dat is, sometime. Well, de boys settin' 'round, dey git ter 'nubbin' noggin' [taking small drinks of alcoholic spirits at very frequent intervals] an' singin', an' ter lyin'. Dey kin make up songs an' lies all night. Dat's how come dis song an lie 'bout Hot Termolly Cholly. We made dat up an' sung hit, an' all de boys an' gals learn hit f'om hearin' us sing hit.

Well, dis boy, Hot Termolly Cholly, never did care nothin' 'bout no col' wedder. De col'er hit come, de mo' he sho' off, but he couldn' stand no warm wedder for nothin'. Live mos'ly on snow an' ice, but he could eat pow'ful 'mount o'dese hot termollys—not dese here one yo' buy off'n de street, but a mo' special sample what he made hisse'f. De ool'les' mawnin' in de worl', dis ol' boy grab de line an' jump in de river jes lak nothin'. Never is had no clo'es sceptin britches an' shirt. No blanket, no fire, no coffee, no nothin' sceptin dat what I 'low him at firs'—plain britches an' shirt. Doonce de winter he spent mos' all his time out on de levee or messin' 'round on de deck. Nobody never could git him ter come nigh de boiler room er nothin' lak dat. All he want is col' an' mo' col'. When de wedder seems ter git de leas' bit lak she gwine break fer spring, he git res'less an' mean ez a rattle-snake. Den when de birds go norf dey allus (always) let him know 'fo' dey goes. Some way dey had ter tell him so dat he be sho don't be dere when de wedder break. He allus go norf a'ter dem.

Well, ter make dis long story short, de boys didn't lak de way Cholly do. When de wedder git too wet an' col' fer de odder boys ter work right, he go ter showin' off an' tell de cap'm 'bout how he doin' an' ter make dem do lak him. He knowed dey didn' had de temper fer ter stan' what he stan'. One day hit got ter drizzlin' an' blowin', an' hit wuz freezin' up an' down de ramp. De boys tol' de cap'm dey can't make hit no longer. Some wuz freezin', some wuz cryin', some wuz slippin' on de ice, fallin' in de col' river an' drownin'. All dis time ol' Cholly struttin' 'roun' lak a rooster, crowin' at de cap'm ter make dem bullys shine, an' de cap'm an' de mate wuz drivin' lak hell, cussin' an' knockin' roustys [roustabouts] 'cause dey couldn' keep up wid dat fool Cholly. So dat night when de boat lef' fer Newleens, dey dat wuz lef' waited 'til ol' Cholly wuz sleep out on de deck in de col'. Dey slip an' grab him an' hit him in his big mouf so he can't holler. Knowin' dat he can't stand no heat, dey takes him down ter de boiler room. Time he dark de do' he went ter sweatin' an' pantin' lak he been runnin' ten miles. Prutty soon he begin ter melt an' run jes lak a piece o' ice. He jes melt down ter nothin'. Ter be sho' he git plenty heat, dey tuk his water in a couple o' syrup kags an' poured him in the steam boiler. Dey thought dey wuz sho done wid him den.

De cap'm wuz crazy 'bout Cholly fer de way he stand enny kin' o' weddor an' 'buse, so de next mawnin' he ax de roustys 'bout where wuz Cholly. Dey course wouldn' say nothin'. Jes 'bout dat time de boat wissle blow an', man, soon ez dat steam o' Cholly's hit dat freezin' air, hit turn back ter Cholly. He sail 'round in de air fer a minute den drap down on de boat same ez ever. When de boys seen dat, dey wuz so scart dey all jump plum over boa'd, col' river er no col' river, an' course dey drown. When de cap'm seen dat he didn' had no crew lef' an' what a fix Cholly done got him in, he grab his gun an' shot at him ter kill, but Cholly start ter high-ballin' an' lef' so fas' he ain' been seen ner heard f'om since. De cap'm an' de mate got ter squabblin' 'bout which one er dem gwine ter take de blame fer all dis Hot Termolly Cholly mess. Dey gits ter fightin' an' falls over boa'd an' dey drowns. De boat, bein' widout nobody ter work her, run out on de bank an' bus' wide open. Dat end de whole bizness, sceptin' Cholly. He ain't been heard f'om, er heard 'bout neither.

The greatest truth of this story is that it teems with situations that make it authentically a part of the life of the roustabouts who lived on the Mississippi River in bygone days. During the five years I spent in Louisiana as a teacher and a student of Negro life and music, no trace of Hot Termolly Cholly could be found in story or song. As is the case with many songs found in the older collections of folk songs, this is due to loss through neglect on the part of those entrusted with the care of the songs. The songs that do have legends connected to them are not myriad, but when one does exist it invariably reveals itself "a gem of purest ray serene." It shines "lak forty thousand diamonds shining in de noonday sun." To ever redeem the lost is a wish whose fulfillment can be only hoped for. The work song, the source of these legends, has been neglected to such an extent that it is difficult to say how much, whether truth or fiction, has perished with it.

Taking a few reflective chews upon his worn wad of "chawin' 'bacco," Jim Bowley shot several violent, almost machine-gun blasts of amber from his mischievous mouth and continued with the legend of "Creepin Midnight."

Creepin Midnight

Say "Fess," you ever hear 'bout de time on dis here line when de boys went crazy on de account of little o' boy, 'bout fo' feet high, dat call hisse'f Creepin Midnight? You ain'? Well, ahm go' tell you. 'Cause ah wuz dere an' seed hit fer mah own se'f. Now here de way hit come ter be lak what ahm go' tell you.

Creepin had him a black cat bone. Now lemme axplain dat. You see, if he' git a bone f'om de lef' hind laig o' a black cat dat wuz de seventh in de' seventh litter of de seventh black cat he ever seen in de full o' de moon in de seventh month o' de year, an' if he see dis exactly at midnight he kin do mos' lak he please, an' dats de truth. How little o' Creepin wuz so lucky is mo' dan I can tell you. But I swear dat little bit o' boy wuz a mess wid dat bone.

He git in a crap game, win all de money. An' if de law come an' ketch ev'y nigger dere, Creepin grab dat bone, stick hit in his mouf, an' den he jes banish 'way to nothin. Sometime he go wid another boy's 'omam, an' dawg if he don't be dere an' hear ev'ything dey say an' dey don't know he dere. He wouldn' do nothing in de day an' he do his best 'tween midnight an' daybreak. Course, dats why dey calls him by dis here name.

Well, jes lak ev'ything else, he one day had bad luck. Here what he done. He went down to a 'oman's house ter good time an' he got drunk. While he drunk, dis 'oman's sho nuff man, Cue Ball, slip in Creepin's left hind pocket an' stole de bone 'way f'om him. I know you done hear 'bout how hit bad luck fer enny other pusson ter fool wid dem bones. Well, as ahm bound ter say, he got 'long all right 'til midnight. Den de mess started. He settin' on de side o' his bed takin' off his shoes when jes den a sharp piece o' wind blowed through de window an' blowed de lamp out. Man, befo' dat room got dark good, a big black cat rubbed up 'gainst his laig an' said, "Fetch mah bone home." His eyes wuz shinin' lak fire an' his hair wuz up lak pine needles, an' he wuz growlin' an' spittin' lak a steam engine. Man, dat cat wuz mad. He done come back out de ground ter see 'bout dat bone an' ol' Cue Ball knowed his time done come. Boy, dat bone start ter gittin' hot in his pocket. Fact is, hit turn ter a hot coal. Ev'y time ol' Cue Ball try ter git dat bone out ter cool hisse'f, dat big black cat slap his hand down f'om his pocket. Cue Ball jump up an' start runnin' an' dat cat right behind him. Ev'y time Cue Ball reach fer dat bone, dat cat slap him an' bite him. Dey run down by de railroad, an' by dat time Cue Ball wuz so scared an' hot he jump plum in de Big Pond an' de red hot bone sot de whole pond a bilin. Well sir, ev'y fish in dat pond wuz biled done an' float on top of de water. 'Bout dat time de section gang come, an' dem fish smell so good dey all start ter eatin' em an' wonderin' how come dey wuz dere.

'Bout an hour pass an' dem bullies begin ter feel de magic f'om dem fish, 'cause de power f'om dat bone got in em. Dey start ter workin' an' hollerin' an' dey wuz jumpin' over boxcars an' totin rails an' layin' em lak no mens had ever done in de worl' befo'. De cap'm got scart an' run off in de bushes an' den suddenly de bone made ev'y las' one o' dem niggers banish 'way. Dey could hear each other, but dey couldn't see nobody—dat is, one see de other. 'Bout dat time ol' number nine come 'long an' dey felt dey self so strong dey got ready ter throw de whole train off de track. De engeenuh couldn' see em so de train run into em an' carried all 'way. Dey ain' nothin' been seen f'om em since. Sho nuff, ol' Creepin wuz on dat same train, runnin' f'om de law. An' when dey foun' him, he wuz done drap out his seat dead; an' a black cat wuz settin' on his chest an' singin' lak dis:

> Creepin Midnight was here,
> Creepin Midnight done gone.
> He wuz done wrong by Cue Ball.
> Ahm gonna keep him till I git back mah bone.

'Course dey couldn' git back dat bone, so dey had ter let de cat stay dere. But when midnight come, Creepin wuz turn loose by de cat, an' dey stopped an' buried him by de track. So dey say when de train come 'long dere at midnight, dey hears a black cat holler an' dey hears a bunch o' railroad mens singin' dat same song what de cat wuz singin' settin' on Creepin Midnight.

His eyes closed but seeing beyond the distance, Jim Bowley lifted his aged head, smiled a lazy, lore-laden grin, cocked his hat with the swipe of his hand, hunched himself over his thighs with an elbow pivoted on each knee, and let go with "Big Joe."

Big Joe

Dis here tale is 'bout a mule, a mule dat wuz way back yonder befo' I wuz big enough ter be on public works an' hoboin' an' roustyin' on de river. I heered 'bout hit f'om a boy dat knowed de camp where all dis happen, an' where Big Joe wuz buried at. You see, dey didn' throw Big Joe out in de woods lak dey done de odder mules 'cause he was too mighty. Now dat wuz a mule f'om now on.

Well, one day some o' dese gypsies come by de camp out f'om Nowleens, an' dey had dis mule. He wuz 'bout a baby den. He sho wuz po' an' bad lookin', but dey said he wuz gwine be a sho nuff big un 'cause dey say he come f'om pow'ful stock. Ol' man McBride, de boss, bought him fer a little bit o' nothing' an' turn him loose ter graze, an' he sort o' growed up lak he please. Ter make dis short, Big Joe growed ter be de biggest an' de best an' de wortest critter dat ever wuz a mule. Dey couldn't do nothin' wid de rascal. He had ev'ybody scart ter come 'round him. He bust in de carrel an' he bust out de carrel. He buse an' kill de rest o' de mules an' jes natchally raise hell in gen'l. Fact is, ol' man McBride mos' got ready ter kill de big cuss a dozen time, but de big boss don't let him. He say Big Joe is worth too much ter de company. Same time he wont doin' nothin' but eatin' an' sleepin' an', ez I say befo', plain raisin' hell.

One day, a big ol' red boy come ter de camp an' got a job 'cause dey wuz pow'ful short o' hands. Dis ol' boy (dey call him Big Red) seen Big Joe an' say he go' make him work an' do lak he say. He say dere ain' no mule he ever see he can't rule, an' he go' show em dat same day. Big Joe seen Big Red an' bust out de lot an' went on 'bout his bizness. But dat showed dey wuz somethin' 'bout Red dat moved Big Joe ter act lak he never done befo'. He act lak de time done come fer him ter have trouble. Big Red lit behind Big Joe an' start ter whistlin' a strange tune an' talkin' a kind o' no-name talk, lak when you hear dese Chinamens an' such as dat talk. When Big Joe heered dat, he dawggone sho stop, turn 'round, an' come on up ter Big Red slow lak. When de boys seen dat, dey start whoopin' an' a-hollerin' an' run ter tell de white man.

Well, ev'ythin' wuz alright 'til Big Red say he go' hitch him ter work wid de wheeler gang. When Big Joe seen Big Red come wid de bridle, de critter jump at him an' tried ter paw him ter death. But Big

Red wuz so fast he jes couldn' git ter him. When de next time come, ol' Red had him a plan. He got him a long chain an' tie hit ter de bigges' an' talles' tree he kin fin' in de woods. When he got up dere good, he start to whistlin' an' talkin' lak he done at fust. An' sho nuff here come ol' Big Joe, 'cause he lak ol' Red when he do lak dat. Jes as dat mule come under de tree, Red throwed down a lasso an' hit caught Joe 'round de shoulders. Boy, dat big rascal lit out f'om dere an' tore down dat tree an' went flyin' through de camp wid dat tree hangin' ter him. He most nigh tore down all de shacks in de camp. He raise so much noise, done so much damage dat de folks thought day wuz havin' a earthquake. Funny thing 'bout hit was dat ol' Red didn' git nary a scratch.

'Bout dis time dat mule sho wuz mad wid Red, an' he wuz all sot ter kill him at de fust chance he had. But ol' Red black his face an' change his clothes an' walk an' went out dere an' call Joe ag'in, an' when de mule seen hit wont Red he come on up. Red, he had him a cigarette an' he blowed some de smoke up both de mule's noses. An' dat done dat mule good, 'cause he kind of clared his throat an' hung his head down on Big Red's shoulders. Ev'y time Red smoke, he give de mule some too. Ev'y time Red drink his likker, he pour some in de mule's mouth too. Dat mule sho love Red, but Red had ter keep hisse'f blackface 'cause de mule know him as he wuz an' he wuz go' kill him. So, de mule wuz ready ter do anythin' dat Red say so long he don't know hit Red.

One day, ev'ybody come out in de mawnin' an' see dis same Big Joe hitch up an' ready ter go. I mean ter tell you dat mule could go too. Talk 'bout workin'—dat mule wuz de same mongst mules ez dis fellow day calls John Henry wuz mongst mens. Dey had ter git him a scoup 'bout five times big ez de one dat fo' mules regular pull. He don't git tired in de heat, in de col', er nothin'. Boy, when one o' dem wheelers git stuck an' de mules river—dat is, give out—day jes let ol' Big Red know an' him an' Joe come an' walk away wid dat wheeler lak nothin'. When he git ter workin' sho nuff, he holler ev'y once an' a while. Sound lak thunder too. He could walk fast, so fast dat de rest o' de mules had ter trot to keep up wid him. Ol' Red could ride on de wheeler 'cause de load didn' bother Joe none.

You talk 'bout de day ol' John Henry got mad at de show an' slap down de elephin. Shukkins, dat ain' nothin'; wait 'til you hear 'bout dis. When de Bonnimen Baity [Barnum and Bailey] circus come ter town dey bet ol' McBride dey had a elephin dat could outdo Big Joe. So, dey git a boxcar an' hitch de elephin on one end an' Big Joe on de other, an' start em off on object ways. Big Joe drag dat elephin an' de boxcar off in de woods, on down through de swamp, an' jes drag so long he wore him out. Dey wont nothin' but de elephin two back feet. Dey was go' kill Big Joe 'bout dat, but de next mawnin de engine of de show train broke down, so dey had ter borrow Big Joe ter pull de train twenty-seven miles down de next road junction so dey could git de odder engine.

You ain' fergot 'bout de way ol' Big Joe hate Red? De funny think 'bout hit wuz dat all de time Red wuz doin' all dis he wuz foolin' de mule, 'cause he paint hisse'f up lak what I tol' you at fust. Ennyhow, de wedder hit git so hot one day, Red sweat all his paint off, yet an' still he didn't know he done dat. Now, when de twelve o'clock whissel blow ev'y day, dat mule turn 'round, look at Red an' holler. Dat mean ter git him ter place he gwine eat quick, 'fo' he git mad. He want dat cigarette smoke in his nose an' some likker too.

When he look 'round dat day he seen Big Red standin' dere, natchel, an' he knowed him. He bust loose f'om de harnesses an' lit out after Red. All through de woods, down through de quarter, dey had bizness. Now you know Red was flyin' when de mos' mighties' mule in de worl' can't ketch him. Ev'ybody wuz scart ter death an' dey wuz hidin' where dey could see, 'til de dust riz so high dey couldn'. When Red knowed ennythin' he wuz headin' fer de briar patch. He didn't want ter go dere, but dat mule wuz heatin' him so hot he couldn't make nary single turn ter de right er de lef'. He didn't have no shoes on 'cause in dem days dey didn't allow nobody in dat camp ter wear shoes but de mules an' de white boss man. When he hit dat briar patch, de mule caught an' tore him tar pieces.

When dey seen dat dey sho wuz through wid Big Joe. Dey sot him free an' lef' him ter do lak he want. But befo' long dat mule start fallin' off 'cause Big Red wuz hantin' him ter death. Ev'y night Big Red's hant would git him a whip made out dem briars an' ride Joe tell he drop. In de mawnin you could find him layin' out mos' dead. At fust Joe holler so loud all night dat de folks thought a lion roarin'.

But befo' long dey couldn't hear him no mo'; he too weak ter holler. Jes de same, ev'y night Red hant him an' ride him.

One day, de boys foun' Big Joe layin' in de briar patch, dead. De Big Boss come an' say dig a grave right dere an' bury him decent like, 'cause he wuz de greatest animal ever wuz. Dey done lak he say an' de next spring de briars an' de berries wuz de bigges' an' sweetes' in de worl', an' ev'ybody dat got ter eat em wuz a more pow'ful man after dat. Some folks say dat where John Henry got his strength. Say he wuz dere fust an' eat more berries den de rest. Dere wuz jes one crop o' dem berries, an' den de bush banish 'way an' ain' never growed no mo'. Sho nuff, dey say if you every goes dere, you kin see de shape o' Big Joe dere in the groun', 'cause dat place won't grow nothin' no mo'. De only place in de worl' where de shape o' de mule made in de groun'. Big Joe ain' never go' leave dis worl'. Yahs suh, now dat wuz a mule f'om now on.[2]

Some insight into the enormous mental handicap and physical pain suffered by the Negro laborer in some places in the far-flung South has been gained from the preceding material. The fact is, the work songs came out of these conditions. Hence, one cannot be unaware of the very vital reason for the lamentations frequently welling from the realm of the work song. More yet is necessary as a complete background for the real understanding of the spirit and fiber of the Negro work song. Though the situations pictured are on the receding tide, enough of them remain to render a knowledge of them invaluable to the reader's background.

When the Negro was emancipated after the Civil War, the problem he faced was one that made him a slave to a system rather than an individual. Being forced to live with an inferior status to those who had previously owned him, he again had to accept the treatment of a slave, insofar as his relationship to the labor was concerned. In order to make a bare living, Negroes were in cutthroat competition with one another. These conditions did not tend to improve the heart of the "driver," who was in many cases transferred to the status of foreman. For years the matter of "knowing how to work niggers" had

2. Songs from the above legends are found in the Appendix of this book.

been a rather special calling among certain classes of white men. So, the Negro laborer had been preferred for the labor field, which at one time or another has involved nearly every form of exploitation and injustice.

This situation at least put the Negro in a realm with other people who found themselves buffeted about on the ruthless swell of circumstances. That the songs do show a consistent resentment of the treatment accorded the Negro laborer is true. Yet people who are capable of taking cognizance of these very important and informative pieces of art have been content to ignore the sounding of truth at their very doorstep.

A study of the work songs reveals the life of the Negro as it existed and, to a lesser extent, as it exists today in some parts of the country. The road, river, mill, foundry, field, turpentine camp, and public works in general have been the places where the work songs have developed. They have also been the places where some of the most deplorable acts of social and economic violence have been inflicted upon the black man who worked in them.

At this moment there comes to mind the name of Henry Miller, a man who came to the Florida Baptist Academy in Jacksonville through the benevolence of N. W. Collier, the president. Henry Miller was a slender man (too slender for the work he had done) who looked more than forty but was in his mid-twenties. He had professed Christianity during his more recent life and had decided to further his progress by going to school, so he entered school in the fourth grade (a charitable fourth). The life he had lived seemed to haunt him day and night. He delighted to get the boys around him and tell of his life prior to being taken into school. His best stories came from the turpentine camps where he described men running through the woods like dogs of the chase, throwing their "box pullers" into the Florida pine all day long, and always on the run. The men took water anywhere they found it—creeks, gullies, ditches, puddles, anywhere. A "wood-rider" rode after the "gang," demanding more and more from the men. Although they were working "by the piece," a minimum limit was always set in defense of the company's interest. When it became a matter of further emphasizing his demands upon the gang, the wood-rider turned into a raging, swearing, kicking, horsewhipping, bullying inferno who went the limit in cruelty and intimidation.

Food was prepared by the men in primitive open-fire fashion. Each man had to cook his own meals as best he could, and that but once a day. The other meals were taken cold. Sanitation was unknown. Of course, the men who stayed in the camp were left to their own devices about all matters of personal welfare. Such a life must have taken a severe toll on Henry Miller. He remained at school long enough to show signs of improvement in every aspect of his personality, and then his heart gave way, causing his death.

The life connected with water transportation—whether it be river, lake, or ocean—has been noted for severity, cruelty, and the extreme penalty for those who worked in the capacity of menials. A strong chapter of this truth comes out of the period when the steamboat was the sole means of transportation in the Mississippi Valley. The roustabouts (Negroes who handled freight on the boats) were treated worse than beasts of burden. They were forced to carry tremendous loads on their shoulders in twos and sometimes singlehanded. A mate or foreman stood by, armed with a pistol and a long graduated hickory or oak club (called a "nigger teaser" by the white men). The Negroes philosophically referred to the gun and club combined as "de differ'nce." Armed to the teeth, these ruffians terrorized the "rousty" into abject slavery. They were driven at the will of the mate or overseer, beaten unmercifully for the slightest offense, and shot or knocked overboard for any attempt to show resentment. Strangely enough, they were well paid. The profits from their labors must have been enormous and the market for this kind of labor relatively small in order to create such a paradox. Considering the fact that the men who owned the boats had also owned the men who worked for them prior to the Civil War and emancipation, it is highly likely that the boatmen were never really emancipated.

Even today the longshoremen on the docks at Jacksonville, Savannah, New Orleans, and Charleston are among the hardest-working people in the nation. Whereas physical violence is seldom if ever resorted to, the verbal abuse often gets terrific. One of the most serious offenses is to retard a line of truckers loading a vessel. While in the employ of Captain W. M. Tupper, superintendent of the Clyde Steamship Company in Jacksonville, the writer was permitted to "walk abroad" the docks, a privilege not generally granted to everyone. On more than one occasion I have witnessed a foreman profanely imploring the men to run their trucks over some fellow who had been forced to stop through no fault of his own. If this did not suffice for immediate action, the foreman would dash after the offender, causing him to flee from the scene, for the moment at least. It must be said that this conduct did not represent the attitude of the Clyde Company, but more the attitude of the stevedoring agency through an individual.

The old road camps offer one of the most despicable of all pictures of Negro labor life. Here is a group of men working for a man who is scared to death of his job, scared because the "big boss" demands that he get the work done by a certain time, regardless; and scared because it is the best job he has ever had and he knows of nothing else he can do to earn that much money. His job is not merely to get the work done as fast as possible, but to make the supremacy of his position felt to the extent that there will be no questioning of the demands he makes in getting the work accomplished. His demands are never to be questioned or denied. He is the master, slave driver, jury, and judge. Little difference is made between the men and the mules they drive. The shacks or quarters where they live are even vermin-infested and presided over by a so-called "shack-rouster" (frequently a Negro who is obviously depraved), whose job is to drive the men out to work in the morning, regardless of their physical abilities or personal preferences:

> Buddy, raise up!
> Raise up!
> Raise up!
> An' git dis fo' day coffee.
> I ain't yo' ma!
> Dat ain't her bed!
> Call yo' ag'in,
> Gwine whip yo' head!

There are only a few alternatives here: go out, get out, get thrown out, or fight it out. In the end, of course, the "shack-rouster" always wins. Many men have been done to death in coups of this kind for no more significant reason than that they were persistent in their differences of opinion where the walking boss was concerned. Perhaps the men wanted to stop work at the appointed time; if so, there was never but one person who had the correct time:

Ain't but de one watch
In de worl' keep time;
Hit b'long to the cap'm,
Lawd, I wish twas mine.

Ain't but two eyes
Can see de sun;
Dey b'long to de cap'm,
But he won't come.

Ain't but one mouf
Can let me go;
Hit b'long to de cap'm,
His jaw is sore.

Men and mules on the "wheeler road" have been the recipients of some of the most pestilential brutality found in the annals of civilized labor. By way of explanation, it may be said that this period followed slavery, so the Negro knew nothing of justice or other forms of decent treatment. He accepted mistreatment as his lot. This era has practically passed, with the states and certain organizations looking out for the working conditions of laborers. Although the circumstances discussed here have been taken from the river and the road, others exist that are different in type but similar in effect.

Such is the stuff of which work songs are generally made. However, to say that those conditions, as given above, are the background in every case is to go a bit too far. However, it may be said in truth that the best and most interesting work songs were born of conditions similar to those given here. No wonder they often baffle the keenest wits in almost every line. They come from a life that is as heavy with its own philosophies as with the problems that breed them, and as strange to most people as the conditions in which they found their beginnings. They reveal a singular side of the Negro that has yet to come into a fuller realization and understanding. It may be that the Negro, as a personality, cannot be seen as a whole until this side of his nature is brought out in fuller lines.

The attitudes that have been formed concerning this newly tapped reservoir of racial expression have been very favorable on the whole, but there seems to be a tendency to "include everything in the net as worthy of the catch." There is reason for this in that the songs are new to many of those who are making a study of them. Then, too, contrary to the religious songs that by their very nature establish themselves as being of rather definite value, the work song must be, as must all seculars, called to suit the purpose of the author who undertakes to use them. His attitude toward the Negro will often help in this. The Negro himself has been on the wrong road in regard to his secular songs. This too was the result of his lacking the knowledge and interest to discriminate among them. Certain of the work songs were not made of the material that the more conservative element preferred; consequently, the entire field was eschewed. At this writing, it is safe to say that interest in the development of the work song of merit is going to continue apace. Composers and arrangers have not taken up the call yet, but public interest is destined to take care of this. The making of anthologies will also aid the composer in gaining the often elusive material he needs for this development.

My experience in Louisiana made me aware of the Negro songs that were developed from life on the Mississippi River. These were very old songs that had been born and all but forgotten prior to my days in this region. The songs and knowledge that I gained there led me to wish for an opportunity to investigate the singing of the long-shoremen. This desire was further stimulated by certain contacts I had made while I was engaged as a teacher in Mobile, Alabama. Realizing the unique type of Negro living in and near Savannah, Georgia, it became a real obsession on my part to go there for the purpose of song collection and study. This wish was realized in 1940 through a research grant I received.

I was fortunate in having two former schoolmates in Savannah who were of great help in my efforts—Dean W. E. Payne and Reverend Levi M. Terrill, pastor of the First Bryan Baptist Church. Reverend Terrill not only took me into his prayer meetings, where I heard some of the most interesting singing I ever witnessed, but also introduced me to Mannie Jackson. This man, Mannie Jackson, president of the Savannah Longshoremen's Local, was a thorough believer in Reverend Terrill, so much so that he had made Reverend Terrill an honorary member of his organization. When it was known that I was a friend of his, Mannie Jackson opened his office and his mind to me. He was a fine singer of the longshoremen's songs and used his influence to get other men to sing for me. We used to gather in his office on the very shores of the Savannah River and sing for hours. His "office" was adjacent to a large room where the longshoremen awaited the call for work. Thus, these men were always available, and they liked to sing their songs while waiting. The singing would start with dialogue about like this:

"Mannie, here 'Fess' an' 'Rev,' you know what dat mean. Dey want some sing."

"Yeh, Phillips. Git 'em a seat, an' take pain wid dey comfort; dey our frien'. 'Fess,' here come 'Snake' [Brown], he de man ain't go' sing. So, we ha' see 'bout dat."

"Naw! I ain' sing fo' nobody. I jis stay here an' watch em. Go head, fetch em. I ain' jine em 't all."

In a few seconds Mannie would have his song selected and "pitched." "Kid Jeff," Smith, "Big Gator," "Crit" Crittenden, Jim Green, "Rev" Terrill, and "Fess" James would be standing around an oil heater, facing the almost pure African features of Mannie Jackson, framed by a sooty window with a backdrop of the muddy Savannah River.

All I want is Union,[3]
Oh Lawd! hanh!
Union make me happy,
Oh Lawd! hanh!

3. This is the International Longshoremen's Association.

There, sitting rather sullenly in the corner with a cold glint in his small eyes and a sinister expression on his small, dark face, would be "Snake." Each time we finished a verse, he would clear his throat and shift his legs. By the time we reached the fourth verse, "Snake" would rise with a jump and let out: "Hol' em, hol' em. Stop! Y'ain't sing em right. Y'ain't ketch de true way. Sing em over. I jine em! Sho em straight." (His Gullah is beautiful.) When that happened everyone there knew the singing was going right. The day had just begun. The fire had just started to burn. When we had sung three or four songs, the men would usually "stop for breath." Here Mannie Jackson would begin to reminisce. His pet theme was how hard he had worked as a longshoreman and how much harder he was working "trying to make some self-respect fo' his people on de river." It was usually after such lectures that I would find the chance to get the songs in detail and to get the information that went with them.

The shanties (chanteys) they sang for me were very old and had passed out of use with the cotton jacks. The cotton jacks were no longer in use because the cotton was now compressed when it was baled and was thus in "ship-shape." Previously cotton had been packed rather loosely. In order to get as many bales as possible into the ship, the men pressed the bundles into the hold of the vessels with these jacks. These jacks worked on the same principle as the more common jacks used to raise cars and buildings. Such names as "dolly," "jag," "beam dogs," and many others that do not need discussion here were common topics with the men. It is better for our purpose to describe how the songs originated from the work.

Two or four men would get in a kind of square around the lever or bar of a jack. When the leader started singing, the men joined in and kept together through the rhythm of the music. As each man pushed the lever around, another man would snatch it and shove it to his left. This operation continued until the cotton was in place. At every turn the men would give out a snorting "han-nh." At times the men would mount the cotton in large numbers and tramp it down in cadence to a joyous chant. This was called "joy jumpin'":

> Oh jump fer joy,
> Oh jump fer joy,
> In dat mawnin,
> Jump fer joy.
> Jump to de middle,
> Jump to de side,
> Jump twell de cotton down,
> Don't git tired!

Sometimes, when the work was very hard, the men would sing in a facetious but earnest manner:

> Go in de town
> Hurry back,
> Do don't stay long,
> Need oil fo' de jack.

"Oil fo' de jack" was either whiskey or beer. This is typical Negro word-economy. The boss was never aware of what was going on. The indirect action of the "oil" on the jack did not always cause it to work more effectively, depending of course on the quantity and the brand used.

One song that seemed to be a favorite with all of the men was "Sweet Water Rollin'." This is not a true work song in the sense that it was created for the work done to it, or for any work at all. The religious version appears in *St. Helena Island Spirituals*. There is only one line of words to this version, but there are other versions. The version sung by Mannie Jackson, and finally by all of us who were present, was a lilting derivative:

> *Chorus*
> Sweet water roll,
> Sweet water rollin',
> Sweet water roll,
> Sweet water roll.

> *Verse*
> Oh, roll me to de shore.
> Boy, if I can't leave when you go,

Tell my best gal
Don't fool wid Joe,
Sweet water roll.[4]

Sonny "Snake" Brown was very fond of a song called "Come Off de Ilam" (Island). It goes:

Ho, hey, hey gal.
Ho, gal when yo' come off de ilam,
A great big gator,
Ho, gal when yo' come off de ilam,
Bring dat gator,
Ho, gal when you come off de ilam,
A ring-tail gator,
Ho, gal when you come off de ilam,
Sho nuff gator,
Ho, gal when yo' come off de ilam,
No two-leg gator!
Ho, gal when yo' come off de ilam.

At this point the laughter would end the song.

Not all of their songs were good or even genuine. Some were borrowed from the old British seamen who sang them in port. For instance, "Santa Ana" is the basis of "Sandy Andy." "Shaller Brown" (arranged by Percy Grainger and sung by John Charles Thomas) is sung as "Shiloh Brown." "Kid Jeff" Phillips once told me Shiloh was really on the river at one time but left to become the greatest railroad fireman in the South. One of the most interesting corruptions was that of "Blow the Man Down." This turned out to be "Knock the Man Down." The word "blow" is used in coastal Georgia at times for "strike." One will say "I'll blow you" instead of "I'll strike you." The transference makes for a very funny song for those who realize the connection. The tune is clearly borrowed.

The most powerful song sung for me was "Baby Ann." This was not very well known. Only one man knew it completely. When he

---

4. Music settings to some of these songs are in the Appendix of this book. This song is one of the most beautiful in the group.

saw me write it down, he refused to give me his name. As the music reached swell tide, the room changed from a mere location into a moving, riding ship at anchor. The air seemed to take on the reek of vessels long used to carry the multi-odored goods of the world. The feet of the men beat out a wild, syncopating rhythm that sounded like the wheels of a freight car moving empty in a distant night against loose-jointed rails. Each face caught the magic of nostalgia and swelled with the zeal born of creation. Even the sweat ran down and the jacks creaked. The men were loading cotton—"jackin' cotton twell de rivet seams cried and bust!"

> She don't draw but a foot o' water—
> My Baby Ann
> She belong to de cap'm's daughter—
> My Baby Ann.
> Load her when she come,
> Load her when she come,
> An' send her gwine on home!

There is a tenderness and charm about this which lingers and is real several days after you have heard it.

The principal loading at Savannah, Brunswick, Charleston, and Wilmington was for cotton and lumber. The shanties were about the same for both. Yet the greatest and best "shantying" was done around the cotton jacks when they "gave heel" to the "smilo" and made the cotton bales whisper and gasp beneath the force of black hands.

One cold, bleak morning I went down to the headquarters, as was my custom. A strange sight greeted me. The rooms were filled with strange-faced delegates. My friend Mannie was making a powerful Gullah-laden speech. "Snake" met me at the door unsmilingly:

> "Fess," de meetin' on. Ain't got no mo' time da sing. White man ain't pay us right. We got to meet de business.
> Snake, why are you carrying that stick?
> I go keep Mannie safe. I go beat hell out em if dey bot'er Mannie.

At that instant a commotion started in the assembly. "Snake" swung around in an eddy and made for the room. He raised a sawed-off pool cue and spat out an excited, violent warning. In a moment the man who had spoken out of turn was silent. "Snake" sat down on the edge of a desk. Through the glass door I am sure I saw the end of a pistol barrel beneath his coat. "Snake" was mean, dangerous, poetic, and lovable. All of the men who knew me were apparent strangers. They did not wish to be molested by a mere "music 'fessor" when there was important business ahead. I looked through the open window in the top half of the front door for a second and then left. I would not disturb them today. I had to leave the next morning.

Though we write to each other occasionally, we have never met again, or maybe we have. I am sure that on some cold, rainy, winter days those men hear and see "Rev" Terrill and "Fess" James there singing with them, even as I can from this distance. As "Snake" once said: "'Fess,' I believe you done jine em [us]; you done kept on sing wid we 'til you stay on me mind." That is mutual.

Finally, I wish to leave with the reader a brief statement regarding the form and style of the work song. There is only one real definite form found in the work songs, and that is in the "swings" or "hammer songs." Nearly all of these that are known to me have a "burden line" repeated three times and a one-line "sinker" (refrain). They are in four-quarter time, with a "channel" or "gut" on every third beat where the hammer falls or where the haul is made. Instead of a note being sung here, the men give out a kind of thoracic ejaculation, sounding like "hanch," "hunch," "janch," "huph," and "wan-n-n-n." The common but powerful name of this expression among some older Negroes was "muscle guttin," and no one was called a "good man" who could not perform it in a way considered correct. The use of cries in work songs causes some to consider the cries themselves work songs. However, a cry is not a song at all and thus deserves the separate treatment I have given it. Now, as for the songs of the river, road, and so forth, which are not "swings" or "hammer songs," no more interesting freedom of design could be wished for. The lack of form here in many cases results in freshness and interest that is not to be found easily elsewhere in the realm of art.

As for the aesthetic variants to be found, speaking generally, some are carefree:

I'm jes a workin' man,
A po' boy far f'om home.
Git likker wid part my money,
Wid 'rest give my gal some.
Ain't worried, ain't goan hang my heart, Lawd.

Some are beautiful:

She got forty thousand diamonds
An' I give her ev'y one.
When she walks out in de mawnin
She looks lak de risin' sun!

Some are pathetic:

Mamma, you ain't been told
How yo' son was hired as a man,
Den treated lak a dog in de cold.

Some are comical:

De pay train come,
De main line fell,
De cap'm got skeered
An' run lak hell.

Some are bitter:

Dam de cap'm!
Dam de comp'ny too!
I'm natchal bawn eas' man
Thoo an' thoo.
White folks don' cuss me!
Done buke me 'round!
I'll take dis here pick
An' tare yo' down!
Cap'm, cap'm, hear me,
Listen to what I say:
Cap'm, cap'm, hear me,
Dis here's my last day.

Several are magnificent:

> I'm a man,
> Tall lak a mountain,
> I'm a man,
> Steddy like a fountain,
> Folks all wonder
> What makes it thunder,
> When dey hear, Lawd,
> My hammer fall!
> It swin' lak thunder, Lawd, Lawd
> When mah hammer fall.

It would seem that these songs are just about like the individuals who made them. Indeed, these songs are the people.

Chapter 6

Characteristics

I. Definitions

When one thinks of Negro music, he usually has in mind the religious songs generally called spirituals. However, the spirituals constitute just a part of Negro religious expression and are used by the Negro to give meaning to his deepest and most sublime feelings toward God and His great universe. For this reason the spirituals are, as a rule, sung in a slower and broader line than are the jubilees, which are songs of great exultation and joy—joy that is the result of a belief in the power of God unto salvation. To make this point clear it is only necessary to consider two well-known songs. "Lord, I Want to Be a Christian" is a song of the penitent who stands, as it were, before the very throne of his maker and proclaims his unworthiness and at the same time asks for the power not only to be "more holy" and "more loving" but also to be like Jesus. The music to this song is, as one will find in most folk songs, ideally suited to convey the fullest meaning of the words. It is simple, broad, and highly religious.

Now, take the song "Down by de Riverside" as an example. It is the exultation of the victorious soul that has fought the good fight and kept the faith, and that, like the apostle Paul, is ready to lay down the armaments of this world and cross over Jordan where there will be peace and rest from the war against the evils of life. The tempo is vigorous and joyous with the basses thundering triumphantly against the happy chanting of the higher voices. Here we have the jubilee in true form, a direct contrast from the song previously discussed, which is one of the finest spirituals.

There are other songs that use biblical names and subjects in a humorous vein but are neither spirituals nor jubilees. An example of these is the familiar "Who Built the Ark?" There has never been any argument as to who built the ark, so this question and the humorous and witty naming of the various animals as they passed by on their journey into the ark are merely a facetious use of the elements of one of the greatest stories ever handed down to man. No one has realized this more fully than the Negro who wrote these songs. Thus a comic song is not a spiritual.

In a similar vein, "Sometimes I Feel Like a Motherless Chile"[1] is an example of a situation where the Negro is more concerned with his feelings than he is with religion, for he mentions things of religious import only in an incidental manner. This type has been wrongly called the "sorrow song," for such a name does not distinguish it from certain blues types. In fact, this type of song is difficult to name. The music is like the spiritual in fineness and dignity, but the words turn out to be highly personal lamentations. I have called them morality songs in order to give meaning to their obvious double nature.

There can be no justification for classifying Negro songs on the mere basis of words. In the case of folk songs, the music is the truest indication of what the words, when uttered, caused the singer to feel. If one takes the tune of a Negro folk song as the conveyance of the true spirit of the original maker at the time of the song's conception, he is likely to find a more moving testimony of the emotional qualities of the race than if he considers the words of the song alone. It is for this reason that one often hears the tunes without the words but rarely the words without the music.

It is strange that some people invariably try to force the general classification of "spirituals" onto all Negro religious music. Neither is all religious music sad, for no matter how sad a song is, it still points to a brighter day. It is here that we can see that words alone fail to convey the truest meaning of religious song. If this is true, then no Negro religious music is sad, for it all grows out of a belief that a better day is to be the reward of the Christian.

However, there must be a bit of suffering here on earth. So what of the songs that deal with the struggle here in the immediate sense?

---

1. The original version does not have the "true believer" refrain that is heard in some quartets nowadays.

I am a po' pilgrim of sorrow,
I'm tossed in dis wide worl' alone,
I heard of a city called Heaven,
I'm trying to make it mah home.

Ev'y time I feel de Spirit movin' in mah heart I will pray.

I been in de storm so long
Give me little time to pray.

What of the great songs of Christ's suffering—passion spirituals?
They are concerned entirely with the ideas of his grief and humility:

Dey crucified my Lord,
An' He never said a mumblin' word.

Calvary, Calvary, . . .
Make me sorry thinkin' 'bout Jesus.

These and many others cannot be arbitrarily called jubilees. They are spirituals. On the other hand, such songs as "Good News, de Chariot's Comin'," "Great Day, de Righteous Marchin'," "I Know I Got Dat Good Religion," and "I'm Goin' Down to de River o' Jordan" are unmistakably looking forward to and taking note of the happier things associated with the Christian religion. Thus, they are jubilees. Again, if one takes the music of each of these songs as a test, the music springs from the words in such a true light that there can be no doubt of the spirit that caused the original singer to give the song life.

No matter what various collectors and folklorists say about the labels assigned to songs by certain Negroes themselves, the responsibility for naming and classifying the songs finally rests with scholars. They must protect the songs by making their natures understood. Too many songs passing as spirituals are not worthy of being ranked with the real songs bearing this title.

II. Texts and Rhythm

The texts of Negro songs are in many cases the governing factors in the rhythms of the songs and are always the source of their messages. In most cases the length and form of the text govern the form of the song. In the first chapter the word-rhythms were discussed. Now it becomes necessary only to observe the actual text in an extensive manner. Before this is done, we may consider the various types of poetic form found in some Negro songs:

1. Repetition complete:

Send down power!
Power, Lord!
Send down power!
Power, Lord!
Send down power!
Power, Lord!
Send down power!
Power, Lord!

2. Repetition almost complete:

Somebody's here;
It must be Jesus.
Somebody's here;
It must be *de Lawd.*

3. Repetition of all but one line:

Guide my feet,
While I run dis race.
Guide my feet,
While I run dis race.
Guide my feet,
While I run dis race.
For I don't want to run dis race in vain.

4. Repetition of half of the lines with a constant refrain:

See fo' an' twenty elders
On dere knees.
See fo' an' twenty elders
On dere knees.

Refrain
An' we'll all rise together
An' face de risin' sun.
Oh Lord, have mercy
If you please.

5. Repetition of no lines:

Go down Moses;
Way down in Egypt Land.
Tell ol' Pharoah,
To let my people go!

6. Partly from literal scripture quotation:

Seek and ye shall find;
Knock and the door shall be opened.
Ask and it shall be given;
And de love come tricklin' down.

7. Line with partial repetition:

Gonna see my mother some o' dese mawnins,
Gonna see my mother some o' dese mawnins,
Gonna see my mother some o' dese mawnins,
Hope I'll jine de band.

8. Line with rhythmic interjections:

a. I'm gwine to Alabamy, oh!
b. Oh! rock me Julie, oh!
c. Read de sign o' de jedgment, aye!
d. Dis ol' hammer, hanh,
Kill John Henry, hanh.

9. Lines and humming alternately:

Sinner ain't yo' tired o' sinnin'?
Hm-m-m (long)
Sinner ain't yo' tired o' sinnin'?
Yo' better lay down de sins o' de worl',
Hm (short, used instead of conjunction)

Go' jine de band wid de angels.
Hm-m-m.

10. Line with constant refrain:

Bet yo' a dollar,
Rock back;
An' fifteen cents,
Rock back;
Dis lil' ol' cap'm,
Rock back;
Ain't got no sense,
Rock back.

11. Line with changing refrain:

Ho, hey gal
A great big gator,
Ho, gal when yo' come off de ilam (island)
Bring dat gator,
Ho, gal when yo' come off de ilam
A ring tail gator. . . .

12. Line with rhythmic syllables (nonsense):

Way down yonder by myself.
Dum-a-la-dum-a-lum.

13. Lines with only rhythmic syllables:

a. Da, da, da-da-do.
b. Doo, dah, doo-dah-doo.

14. Lines from hymns with original responses:

I wandered far away from God.
I wonder if de lighthouse will shine on me.
The path of sin too long I've trod.
I wonder if de lighthouse will shine on me.

When the Negro speaks through his songs, he is not aware of poetic feet and musical measure as formal aspects. He is guided by innate feeling. Not knowing the above, he is forced to fall back upon some fundamental rhythmic urge generated by one of the song factors. His first conception is the rhythm of the speech, for he feels the movement of the syllables of the words. Something of this principle was discussed in chapter 1. At this point, for clarity, we must reemphasize and enlarge upon the fundamentals of speech rhythm.

When someone speaks, his words form a natural rhythm that is not stilted in its poetic stresses. If a phrase is carefully listened to, the rhythm of the spoken words make a pattern that may easily be assigned to musical note-rhythm. For instance:

1. Good morn-ing,   how is ev'-ry one?

2.   I am a lov-er of Ne-gro mu-sic.

3. The Lord is my Shep-herd.

4.   I   think I am go-ing to school.

These rhythms may be generated as often as one speaks. The Negro realized this as a force rather than a principle. He therefore got much of his rhythm from this source:

1. Swing low,   sweet char-i-ot

2. Good news, char-i-ot's com-in'.

The strong rhythmic qualities in Negro songs are, alone, not enough for Negro feeling. Hence, foot-pats and hand-claps are added as intensifiers and fundamental regulators.

Differences in duration are a matter of notation. If larger note values are assigned to the above examples, then the time will be slower, but the note ratio must remain the same. If an examination of Negro songs is made, this principle is strongly in evidence. In varying degrees the same holds true in other folk music, especially in Europe. It is a very natural manifestation. As a result, the movement and dynamics of Negro songs depend largely upon the words. He who would sing Negro songs must realize this. A mastery of the Negro song text is three-fourths of the mastery of the song. Regardless of strong and weak beats, Negroes accent words in line with speech.

Since words are such an important part of song, their power and artistic value should be able to stand alone, as should the music. Several examples in different forms are given here for consideration. These examples need no words from me to give them merit. The list might well be from the pen of an inspired poet.

Religious Songs
Spirituals

Now We Take dis Feeble Body
Now we take dis feeble body,
An' we carry it to de grave;
An' we'll all leave it dere,
Hallelujah!

Now we take dis feeble body,
An' we cover it wid de sod;
But de soul will rest in God,
Hallelujah!

Now we take dis feeble body,
An' we dry our tear stain' eyes;
For in Christ we all shall rise,
Hallelujah!

Now we take dis feeble body,
An' we walk ourselves away;
An' we'll all go watch and pray,
Hallelujah!

When we take dis feeble body,
Don't you wring your hands an' cry;
Man was born to live an' die,
Hallelujah!

When we take dis feeble body,
Don't you wring your hands an' cry;
Mourner fix your faith on high,
Hallelujah!

Chorus
An' a-hallelujah!
An' a-hallelujah!
An' we'll all leave it dere,
Hallelujah!

Pure Religion[2]
You gonna need dat pure religion,
Hallelujah, hallelujah!
You gonna need dat pure religion,
Hallelujah, hallelujah!
You gonna need dat pure religion,
Pure religion takes you home to heaven;
Den you gonna need dat pure religion.

Death is ridin' all through dis lan',
Hallelujah, hallelujah!
Death is ridin' all through dis lan',
Hallelujah, hallelujah!
Death is ridin' all through dis lan',
Ain't gonna spare no gamblin' man;
Den you gonna need dat pure religion.

2. Sung by Mrs. Iona Floyd of Columbus, Mississippi.

Dar's a place in de Jordon you can't go 'round,
Hallelujah, hallelujah!
Dar's a place in de Jordon you can't go 'round,
Hallelujah, hallelujah!
Dar's a place in de Jordon you can't go 'round,
If you ain't got religion you gonna drown,
Den you gonna need dat pure religion.

When you crossin' de Jordon, don't have no fear,
Hallelujah, hallelujah!
When you crossin' de Jordon, don't have no fear,
Hallelujah, hallelujah!
When you crossin' de Jordon, don't have no fear,
Jesus gonna be my engineer,
Den you gonna need dat pure religion.

Doctor stand lookin' sad,
Hallelujah, hallelujah!
Doctor stand lookin' sad,
Hallelujah, hallelujah!
Doctor stand lookin' sad,
Said dis de hardest case I ever had,
Den you gonna need dat pure religion.

Mother 'roun' my bed a-cryin',
Hallelujah, hallelujah!
Mother 'roun' my bed a-cryin',
Hallelujah, hallelujah!
Mother 'roun' my bed a-cryin',
Lord have mercy, my child a-dyin',
Den you gonna need dat pure religion.

Ride death, don't ride so slow,
Hallelujah, hallelujah!
Ride death, don't ride so slow,
Hallelujah, hallelujah!
Ride death, don't ride so slow,
My heart's willin', I'm ready to go,
Den you gonna need dat pure religion.

De train is comin', done turned de curve,
Hallelujah, hallelujah!
De train is comin', done turned de curve,
Hallelujah, hallelujah!
De train is comin', done turned de curve,
I'm fixin' to leave dis sinful worl',
Den you gonna need dat pure religion.

Poor Blind Bartemeus
You read about it in the book of Mark,
Blind Bartemeus was his name.
He was blind and could not see,
He heard of the man of Galilee,
And said, I know he'll have mercy on me.
He healed the sick,
He raised the dead,
And brought the leper up from his bed.
He still' the wind, calm' the sea,
I know my Lord will have pity on me.
So when the Lord was passing by,
He stood on the road and began to cry.

Chorus
Poor blind Bartemeus stood on the road and cried,
Poor blind Bartemeus stood on the road and cried,
He was cryin', he was cryin',
Oh Lord, my Lord, please have mercy on me.

City Called Heaven
My brother and sister won't own me,
Because I'm walkin' in sin.
My father and mother will own me,
Because I'm tryin' to get in.

Chorus
When I was out on de mountain
Bright, but could not see,
I cried to my Almighty,
For to hand me victory.

I Want Jesus to Rock Me to Sleep

I want Jesus to rock me to sleep,
I want Jesus to rock me to sleep.
When I die, I'll have a home on high,
I want Jesus to rock me to sleep.

He rocked my mother to sleep,
He rocked my mother to sleep.
When she died, she had a home on high,
I want Jesus to rock me to sleep.[3]

Rock Me, Jesus, Rock Me

Rock me, Jesus, rock me in the weary lan',
In the weary lan', in the weary lan',
Rock me, Jesus, rock me in the weary lan',
He's a shelter in the time of storm.

He rocked my mother's mother in the weary lan',
In the weary lan', in the weary lan',
He rocked my mother's mother in the weary lan',
He' a shelter in the time of storm.[4]

Signs of Judgment[5]

You better get your ticket in your right hand.
The storm is ragin', oh Lord
The time is drawin' near.

My mother ain't dead, she is just sleepin' in Glory.
Goin' to wake up in the judgment, oh Lord
The time is drawin' near.

---

3. He rocked my "brother," "father," etc. Any relative's name can be substituted. Often the pastor's name is included.

4. He rocked my "father's father," "mother's sister," "lovin' mother," "father," etc.

5. This version is sung by Ella Madison of Dixiana, Alabama. She added many of these verses to this well-known song. She is a very gifted person and when last heard from had joined the Women's Auxiliary Corps (W.A.C.) and was serving with distinction.

Got my ticket in my right hand, gettin' ready to travel,
Goin' to ride in judgment, oh Lord
The time is drawin' near.

You can tell by the fig tree,
It ain't long 'fore it will be, oh Lord
The time is drawin' near.

It was 1917 when the storm was ragin',
It came through Bradford, oh Lord
The time is drawin' near.

See the people in this country,
Can't you hear them laughin', ha, ha, ah, ah, ah,
Oh! Lord, the time is drawin' near.

Remember 1936 storms began to rage,
They went sweepin' through Georgia,
Oh! Lord, the time is drawin' near.

Way down in Tuscaloosa, over in Northport,
God tore up the school court,
Oh! Lord, the time is drawin' near.

Chorus I
Read the signs of the judgment, aye
Read the signs of the judgment, aye
Read the signs of the judgment, aye
The time is drawin' near.

Chorus II
You see the signs of judgment (yes)
You see the signs of judgment (yes)
You see the signs of judgment (yes)
The time is drawin' near.

Must a Man Forgive His Neighbor
How many times must a man forgive his neighbor?
How many times, O, how many times?
How many times must a man forgive his neighbor?
Seventy times seven,

Says de good Lord, up in heaven;
You better mind, you better mind,
You better mind how you serve de Lord.[6]

Jubilees

I Know I'm a Soldier
I know I'm a soldier for my Lord,
I know I'm a soldier for my Lord;
He gave me a sword, He gave me a shield,
Said never git weary, stay in de fiel'.

I know I'm a servant for my Lord,
I know I'm a servant for my Lord;
If you don't know, I'll tell you how,
Settle your hand on de gospel plow.

He said be a witness for my Lord,
He said be a witness for my Lord;
Don't you never be asham',
Wherever you go, to own my name.

He said be a preacher for my Lord,
He said be a preacher for my Lord;
Tell my gospel, and tell it true,
You don't need to worry, I'll stan' by you.

He said be a teacher for my Lord,
He said be a teacher for my Lord;
Teach my people, and teach 'em right,
I'll guard you by day, and lead you by night.

He said be a watchman for my Lord,
He said be a watchman for my Lord;
Watch on de tower, and watch on de wall,
I'll be your capt'in, and I won't let you fall.

6. How many times must a man forgive his "brother," "sister," "elder," "en'my," "mother," etc.

Jubilee Song Sermons

The jubilee song sermon is a striking example of the Negro preacher's influence in the development of the religious music of the Negro. As compared with the more formal spirituals and jubilees, it outranks them poetically and often equals them musically. Because of its nature it has to be led by an exceptionally gifted person. Hence, it is not used in a general sort of way, but is more identified with certain personalities. Naturally, since the more formal spirituals and jubilees require less from the leader and therefore can be remembered and led more easily, they become more generally serviceable and better known.

My God Is a Rock

Oh look a-yonder at Mary and Joseph
An' de young child, King Jesus
On de journey to Jerusalem
For to pay their poll taxes.
On de way back dey miss de young child
An' dey went to Jerusalem
For to search for de young child, Jesus.

Where'd dey fin' him?
In de temple wid de lawyers an' de doctors
An' de elders
Ask'n questions one to another.

Den he turn to de doctor,
Said, "Doctor, state an' county doctor,
Can you heal some sin sick soul, suh?"
Oh no, oh no, dat's a question he couldn't answer.

Den he turn to de lawyer,
"Oh lawyer, state an' county lawyer, suh?
Can you plead some sinner's cause, suh?"
Oh no, oh no, dat's a question he couldn't answer.

Den he turn to de judge,
"Oh judge, oh judge, you de judge, suh?
State and county judge, suh,

Can you judge their righteous souls, suh?"
Oh no, oh no, dat's a question he couldn't answer.

Chorus
My God is a rock in a weary lan', weary lan', weary lan'.
My God is a rock in a weary lan',
Shelter in de time of storm.

God Will Straighten 'Em When He Comes
We have people in our country, in our churches, in our homes,
You can't straighten 'em,
I can't straighten 'em,
We don't know how to straighten 'em,
So let God straighten 'em!
He said He'd straighten 'em,
He knows how to straighten 'em,
An' He will straighten 'em
When He comes, when He comes.
God's gonna straighten 'em,
When He comes.

We have sinners in our country, in our churches, in our homes,
You can't straighten 'em,
I can't straighten 'em,
We don't know how to straighten 'em,
So let God straighten 'em!
He said He'd straighten 'em,
He knows how to straighten 'em,
An' He will straighten 'em,
When He comes, when He comes.
God's gonna straighten 'em,
When He comes.[7]

Chorus
Oh yes, He will straighten 'em when He comes,
Oh yes, He will straighten 'em when He comes,
God will straighten 'em when He comes.

7. We have "gamblers" and "liars" "in our country, in our churches, in our homes."

Moses in Egypt

Amram's wife was Jochebed,
They had a son, so de Good Book said,
Old Pharaoh held de Israelites,
And drove de children both day and night.
Pharaoh spoke and made it plain,
Every Hebrew boy child must be slain.
Jochebed saw de little boys drown,
She hid her child so he couldn't be found.
She laid de baby in a basket of clay,
Placed him in de water and begin to pray.
De Lord heard Jochebed when she cried,
Send Pharaoh's daughter to de river side.

She looked at Moses, began to smile,
For Moses was one lovely child.
De girl, she took young Moses home,
Showed him to Pharaoh on de throne.
Pharaoh said we'll let him stay,
To be a leader and point de way.
Moses stayed, grew tall and strong,
Walked in grace, sung Israel's song.
De young boy lived on de righteous plan,
And Moses 'come a mighty man.
Moses walked and talked you see,
And said all Israel must be free.
So on one day as he walked along,
He saw an Egyptian, big and strong,
Take a child of Israel, beat him down,
'Til de man cried out upon de ground.
Moses looked and raised his hand,
Killed de Egyptian—said, Git up, man!

God said, Moses tell Pharaoh,
His time is up! Let Israel go!
Pharoah heard what Moses said,
But Pharaoh's heart would not be led.

So God sent plagues in Egypt land,
On woman and child and beast and man.
Pharaoh began to moan and cry
Said, Moses take de chillun and fly.
But Moses had not gone so far long,
When Pharaoh said, I believe I'm wrong.
He set out after de Israelites,
Followed dem many days and nights.
De chillun cried, Where can food be found?
So God sent manna rainin' down.
A cloud by day and fire by night,
So Moses could lead de chillun right.
Moses crossed over on solid ground,
But Pharaoh tried and his host got drown'.

Chorus
Ride on Moses;
My Lord!
Ride on Moses;
My Lord!
Ride on Moses;
Thunder in de chariot—
Pharaoh's army got drowned in de sea.

I Never Mean to Die in Egypt Land[8]
Into de graveyard ah'm gonna walk,
With my Lord God ah'm gonna stand and talk,
Into the graveyard I been lead,
My soul's been fed with de heavenly bread.
I can't stay away, oh I can't stay away,
I will be fed
With de heavenly bread.

---

8. This song, sung for me by Mrs. Ross Allen of Daphne, Alabama, is a remarkable, mystical, powerful example of personal expression, although much of the text is borrowed from other Negro songs.

Talk about de river being wide and dark,
But de young child Jesus did die!
Walk to de marriage room,
Choose your seat and then set down,
Long white robe come try it on,
It fits so neat and so complete.
Never a seam to be seen,
Oh, you can't stay away (etc.)

God is on high although He looks low,
He knows what de people have to undergo,
He is lookin' right down into dere hearts,
He knows what they gonna do before they start,
You can fool man but you can't fool God;
What man misses, God surely will see.

Once in thunder, Jehovah spoke,
Top of Mt. Zion was fire and smoke.
Master come down de heavenly road,
Fire and thunder before Him rode.
He tol' He was coming by de rollin' of thunder;
Put all de people to 'sunder,
How can I sleep when the angels moan!
My Lord sittin' on a dazzling throne!

The darkes' night,
The gloomiest sight,
Between de walls,
Was de wonderful height,
De wind was high,
De path was dry,
Horsemen, chariot,
How they fly!
Don't dat look like judgment day!
When de stars will be falling!
God will be calling!

I want to have to stand,
Upon dat sea of glass —

De sea of glass,
All mingled with fire!
Then I'll join,
God's heavenly choir!
Talk 'bout de ditch where de scorpions creep,
You see de wild beast hovering 'round,
Three of these little bit of creeping things,
Got up in de ark and began to sing—
And poor Noah felt himself secore. (secure)
De Lord told him, He done close de door!!

I Never Intend to Die in Egypt Land
Come all de world and you shall know,
How you was save' from in dis sword.
I strove indeed but I could not tell,
How to shun de gates of Hell.
What to do I did not know,
I thought to Hell I would surely go;
I look' dis way and dat to fly,
I try salvation fo' to buy it;
I pray in de Eas' and I pray' in de Wes',
Seeking fo' dat eternal res'.

I am borned of God, indeed I am,
Sinner, deny me if you can.
While shepherds at dere flocks atten',
De Angel brought good news to men.
Over in Jerusalem, at de post,
See Simon filled wid de Holy Ghost.
Lord, let thy servant go;
Jesus Christ is born, I know.
De widow of Aneril came to see,
Who should bleed and die fo' me.

Through heat and cold Christ had to go,
To inst'tute His church below.
My father's fought de battle at las',
And all de days on earth are pas'.

My mother has broke de ice and gone,
And now she sings a heavenly song.
I hope to meet my mother dere,
Who used to kneel wid me in prayer.
Religion is like a bloomin' rose,
And none but dem dat feel it knows.

Way over yonder in de harvest fiel'
De Angel's workin' at de chariot wheel.
De chariot's down by de Jo'dan side,
In de chariot I expect to ride.
Some says I'll not make it so;
But I'll land my soul on Heaven, sho'.

You pray fo' me, and I pray fo' you;
Dat is de way de Christians do.
Run up Christians and get yo' crown,
And by your Savior's side sit down.
You can't get los' in de wilderness
Wid a lighted candle in yo' breast!

O, dere's a time when I must die
To stand befo' my God on high.
As I go down de stream of time
I will leave dis sinful world behin'.
Dere's no repentance in de grave,
Nor pardon offered fo' de dead!
Hell is ready to receive
De dying man who won't believe.
O, bless de Lord, I was born to die,
To stand befo' my God on high.

At las' I look to Calvary;
I saw my Jesus on de tree,
I felt de partin', I heard His voice,
My soul got happy and I rejoice'.
If ever I reach de mountain top,
I will praise my Lord and never stop.

Go down to de water when you dry
And den you'll get yo' full supply.

I'm gwine down to Jordan to pay my fare;
Jesus' lifeboat will meet me dere.
Jesus calls, "Come unto Me
Poor sinner, I will set you free."
He called His brethern on de sea,
Saying, "Leave yo' nets and follow Me."
On de cloud to Heaven He rode,
Now He dwells in de light wid God.
Bye and bye He will come fo' me,
When from sin I am wholly free.

De ol' ship's coming jus' like a whirl
To take God's chillun safe out o' dis worl'.
When I'm happy I'll shout and sing
And make de heavenly welcome ring.
De very time I thought I was los'
De dungeon shook and my chains fell off,
And Angel wid bright wings of gol'
Brought de glad tidings to my soul.

Here we walk de golden streets,
We tells to all de saints we meets,
De chariot runs to de mountain top,
My Lord bid de chariot stop.
My head was wet wid de midnight dew,
De morning star was a witness too!
I never will give up de shield
Until de Devil has made to yield.

Chorus
I cannot stay away,
I cannot stay away,
I cannot stay away,
I never intend to die in Egypt land.

The World Is So Low[9]

God's gonna build one angel in the East,
God's gonna build one angel in the South,
God's gonna build one angel in the North,
Ain't none of dem gonna rise,
Till the crownin' day!
Hmmm . . .

Once dere was no moon,
Once dere was no stars,
And once dere was no sun to shine,
But Heaven signed the 'cree,
That Adam's race must die.
One general ruin swept up low,
In the dust we lie.

Go angels around the wheel of time,
And bring here that welcome day!
Hmmm . . .

Job was sick and Job did moan,
But the flesh did come creepin'
Off of Job's bone!
Hmmm . . .[10]

Secular Songs
Spoken Selling Cries

The Peanut Vendor[11]

Yeee-hooo!
Come git dese fresh herbs.
Don't you wan' ter crush 'em?
Bettah quit stinchin yo' system!

9. Sung for me by the Reverend Dave V. Allen of Daphne, Alabama.

10. At this point, the Reverend Allen would switch to the words of the song sung by Mrs. Allen, his wife, "I Never Mean to Die in Egypt Land."

11. Heard annually from 1930 to 1933 at the Tuskegee–Alabama State football game at the Cramton Bowl in Montgomery, Alabama.

Dey's good fo' yo' constooshoon.
Come git 'em,
Ah knows you wan' to crush 'em!

Charcoal

Charcoal! Charcoal!
What's dat thing
Ah hyured you tol'
'Bout ah ain't got
De bes' charcoal?
Ah ain' got but a few lef',
B'lieve ah'll keep 'em fo' mahself.
Charcoal! Charcoal! Charcoal!

Shine Mistah

Shine Mistah?
Ah kin do a job-b-b on 'em.
Yo' kin see-e-e-e yo'se'f in 'em.
Look jes-s-s-s lak paten' leathah.

Shine-em-up?
You can't go wrong,
Doin' yo' feets a favah.
Ef dey don' 'preciate it,
Ah sho will.
Shine-em-up!

Independence[12]

I ain't got no sto'.
I ain't got no sign.
Jes de same I'm sellin',
And all I'm sellin' is mine!

My berries grows on de bushes.
My melons dey grow on de vines.

12. The first three lines of each stanza should be said rapidly in a sing-song manner, while each fourth line should end on a long tone.

Jes eat some dese here, you'll tell me,
Mister dey sho is fine!

My 'taters grows in de groun'.
My peaches grows on de tree.
I ain't workin' now fo' nobody,
I done sho hired out myself to me!!

I'm Yo' Ev'ything Man
Take jes a lil' bit o' yo' got
Fer jes a lil' bit o' my got.
What I got I has plenty,
Don't yo' want any?

Take a lil' bit o' my got
Fer a lil' bit o' yo' got.
Boy, dat will be hot!

Who got de money
Come an' buy!
Who ain't got de money
Sit on de curb an' cry.

Song Selling Cry

Ice Cream
I-i-i-ce cream!
Ice cream (said very quickly)
Made in de shade,
Sol' in de sun.
Ain't got a nickel,
You can't git none!
You ain't got no nickel?
You make me tickle.
Ice cream!

Love Song Ballad

Roberta Lee
De longes' day I ever did see
Was de day dat Roberta died;

I got de news ten miles from home
An' I walked back dat road an' I cried.

I been aroun' from town to town
From Texas to Santah Fee,
I done been dis worl' aroun'
But I can't find no Roberta Lee.

I dreamed las' night an' de night befo'
I was on my way back home,
But since I heard Roberta died
I got a mind to roam.

Roberta lived in Tennessee
Befo' she come to town,
Dere never was a girl like her
I been dis whole worl' roun'.
Dis worl' is high, dis worl' is low
Dis worl' is deep and wide;
But de longes' road I ever did see
Was de one I walked an' cried.

Chorus
I cried, oh pity an' a shame
It's jes a pity an' a shame—
An' if dis trouble don't stop worrin' me
I'll lay down an' die like 'Berta Lee,
Lawd, I'll lay down an' die like 'Berta Lee.

Work Songs

John Henry

John Henry walked upon de mountain,
Looked on the other side.
The mountain was so big and his hammer was so small,
He laid his hammer down, and he cried.

John Henry was a railroad man
And he said before he died,
"When I'm dead go and bury me beneath the cross-ties
So I can hear Number Nine pass by."

John Henry had a six pound hammer,
He carried it shoulder high.
He said before he'd let the steam drill beat him down,
He'd whip his hammer down 'til she cried.

John Henry had him a pretty gal
And her name was Julie Ann.
She said she loved John Henry with a natchel born love
'Cause he's a natchel born man.

His daddy took John Henry
And led him to the railroad line.
Said, "If you don't be a good railroad drivin' man,
You ain't no son of mine."

Then he took up little John Henry
And helt him in the pan o' his han'.
He said, "You are a little bit-a-baby, but yo' walk and yo' talk
Sho do seem lak a railroad man."

His daddy tol' John Henry
While he stood in the pan of his han',
"You got shoulders and your arms, and your ankles and your
     thighs,
Just lak de bes' steel drivers of any size."

John Henry spoke to de cap'm,
It was 'bout half-past four.
He said, "Cap'm, oh cap'm, I got to hurry lak hell
To be thru when ol' Number Nine blow."

John Henry said, "Cap'm, oh cap'm,
Let the boys line the track up right,
I'll nail it all down fo' de jack come rollin' by,
Or this six pound hammer weigh a pound."

Ah'm a Union Man
Some folks de big red diamond love,
Some choose de big black spade.
Ah loves de card dats in mah han',
De card dats union made.

A black man stays in union line
De boss man wonder why.
De union card won't change on you,
A union card can't lie.

A scab's highway mountain lion,
A standin' right an' lef'.
A union man stay union boun',
De scabs kin have what's lef'.

Chorus
Ah'm a union man,
Ah'm a union man.
Ev'rywhere ah go,
Let de good folks know,
Ah'm a natchel bawn union man.

Rollin On De Y. & M. V.

Here come de big wild-wagon[13]
Gwine to Buffalo.
Ef I git whar she's gwine,
Ain't never comin' back no mo'.

She got a great big fir'man,
A hundred inches tall.
She soun' lak de panter (panther) squall,
Run lak a cannon ball.

Chorus
Rollin on de Y. and M. V.
Rollin on de Y. and M. V.
Here come de big wild-wagon,
Rollin on de Y. and M. V.

De Pan (Palm) O' Mah Hand

Fortune teller come, Lordy,
Look in de pan o' mah hand,

---

13. A fast train of empty freight cars.

Say dere's one thing dere, Lordy,
She don't understand!
Look in de pan o' mah hand, Lordy,
Look in de pan o' mah hand.

Fortune teller say, Lordy,
Look in de pan o' mah hand,
Got a line thoo dere, Lordy,
Ain't lak no natchel man!
Look in de pan o' mah hand, Lordy,
Look in de pan o' mah hand.

Go an' tell de cap'm, Lordy,
Look in de pan o' mah hand.
Got de seaboard line, Lordy,
Runnin' thoo mah hand!
Look in de pan o' mah hand, Lordy,
Look in de pan o' mah hand.

Steel-Driver

Don't you never let me see you standin' aroun'
Like you hidin' 'hind me.
Tho' yo' driver down,
All de way from hyah to town;
Let de passin'-by people
See you drivin' iron down,
See you drivin' iron down.
Lawdy, Lawdy, Lawd!

Steel driver don't you never let yo' hammer fall light
When yo' workin' roun' me.
'Cause I'll tell de man,
'Bout yo' lowdown workin' ways,
Doonce (during) de balance o' yo days,
Lawdy, Lawdy, Lawd!

Hit (It) Sound Like Thunder

I'm a man tall like a mountain,
I'm a man steddy like a fountain,

Folks all wonder what makes it thunder
When dey hear, Lawd, my hammer fall.

Did yo' read it in de paper
'Bout de gov'nor an' his family,
Dey am 'cided to come to de new road
Jes to hear, Lawd, my hammer fall.

Boss got money—mo' den de government!
Come to town ridin' a chariot,
Drivin' forty big, fine race horses
Jes to hear, Lawd, my hammer fall.

Chorus
An' hit sound like thunder,
Lawd, hit sound like thunder
When my hammer fall.

Work Song in Ballad Form

Hyah Come de Cap'm
Hyah come de cap'm
Stan' right steddy
Walkin' lak Samson,
Stan' right steddy
He totin' his talker
Stan' right steddy.

Lookin' fer Jimbo
Don' say nothin'
Go 'head Jimbo
Don' say nothin'
Cap'm cain't fin' you
Don' say nothin'.

De houn' dawgs come
Oh! hab mercy
Start to runnin'
Dey cain't fin' you
Oh! hab mercy

Good ol' Jimbo
Lawd, Lawd.

Boy you mus' be flyin'
Lawd, Lawd.
Some good day
Lawd, Lawd,
Ef ah git de drop,
Lawd, Lawd,
Ah'm goin' on
Lawd, Lawd,
Dat same good way
Lawd, Lawd
Dat Jimbo gone
Lawd, Lawd.
Good ol' Jimbo
Lawd, Lawd,
He done gone,
Lawd, Lawd.
He done gone.

Social Work Song

Got Her Loaded, Now!

Got her loaded now,
F'om back ter bow,
An' I know it, boy, boy.
Let her roll, boy!
Let her roll, boy,
Down de river, boy, boy.
Jes soon ez ah git off dis boat,
Gonna grab mahse'f a box-back coat.
Let her roll, boy!
Let her roll, boy,
Down de river, hey, hey!

Well, a rampart sheet
Is long an' sweet,

An' I knows it, boy, boy.
Let her roll, boy!
Let her roll, boy,
Down de river, boy, boy.
Spen' a dollah here, a dollah dere,
Make som' mo' mos' everywhere.
Let her roll, boy!
Let her roll, boy,
Down de river, hey, hey!

Let de capt'in yell,
An' I raise o' hell,
Ah knows him, boy, boy.
Let her roll, boy!
Let her roll, boy,
Down de river, boy, boy.
Ah'm built up jes lak Stagolee,
Ef yo' don' b'l'eve it look an' see.
Let her roll, boy!
Let her roll, boy,
Down de river, hey, hey!

Work and Dance Song

Rock Back

Bet yo' a dollah,
Rock back;
An' fifteen cents,
Rock back;
Dis lil' ol' cap'm,
Rock back;
Ain' got no sense,
Rock back.
Ef he ax you sump'n,
Rock back;
How to lay dis track,
Rock back;
Don' say nothin',

Rock back;
Jes rock on back,
Rock back.
Bet yo' a dollah,
Rock back;
An' a quartah mo',
Rock back;
De bear (heat) gwine git go,
Rock back;
Fo' de whissle blo',
Rock back.

Big boss a-come,
Rock back;
Wid de money bag,
Rock back;
De cap'm didn' git none,
Rock back;
An' I sho' was glad,
Rock back.

De pay train come,
Rock back;
De noo track fell,
Rock back;
De cap'm got skeered,
Rock back;
An' run lak hell,
Rock back.

Chorus
Rock back,
A-way back, buddy,
Rock back,
A-way back, buddy,
Rock back,
A-way back, buddy;
Lay de col' steel down.

Dance Songs

Shoo-Long Sally Brown

When Sally went away,
De boys said she'd come back no mo',
But when I passed her house today,
She was standin' in her do'.

I love my Sally Brown,
De clothes she wears is fine,
De boys don't lak to tell de truth,
But dey know dat she's all mine.

Chorus
Shoo-long Sally Brown,
Da da da de-o.
Shoo-long Sally Brown,
Da da da de-o.
I'm a left wing hopper,
And a right wing loper.
Shoo-long Sally Brown,
Shoo-long Sally Brown,
I'm de best buck dancer in town.

Oh Jump for Joy

Jump up high,
Jump down low,
Jump tell you can't jump no mo'.
Jump to de middle,
Jump to de side,
Jump on de narrow,
Jump on de wide.
Jump on me, I'll
Jump on you! We be
Jumpin' like de kangaroo.
Jump to de left,
Jump to de right,
Jump all day and
Jump all night.

Jump on de corners,
Jump on de round, I'm de
Jumpin'est man ever
Jumped in town,
Jump on de cotton,
Jump on de bale,
Jump on de cap'm den
Jump in jail.

Chorus
Oh jump for joy,
Oh jump for joy,
Jump in dat mornin',
Oh jump for joy.

Cap'm Riley's Wagon
Cap'm Riley, O Cap'm Riley,
Ah dunno yo' be so mean,
Yo' step all on mah baby corn,
Reachin' fo' de sewin' machine.

Cap'm Riley, O Cap'm Riley,
Yo' meanes' man I knows,
Jes git yo' big roots of'm dat dress—
Dems mah wife's Sunday clothes.

Cap'm Riley, O Cap'm Riley,
Yo' got me trouble so.
Yo' clear dis house from wall ter wall,
Eben down dust de flo'.

Cap'm Riley, O Cap'm Riley,
Yo' stayin' mighty long.
But yo' sho' can't stay all night,
De beds is done all gone.

Chorus
Cap'm Riley's wagon been yar (here)
An' tuk all de fu'niture,
An' car'ed um 'way.

Cap'm Riley's wagon been yar,
An' car'ed um, car'ed um way.

Blues

No Money Blues[14]

I ain' got no money, baby, no friend to take me in. (2x)
And when I meet you on the street, my trouble start all over
again.

Last night I was wandering 'round, blue sky coverin' my head.
(2x)
Thinkin' bout my sweet baby, and wishin' I was dead.

Remember the night we parted, my love was ridin' high. (2x)
When you said you didn't want me no more, baby, I prayed God
I could die.

Now listen here, sweet baby, I'll love you just the same. (2x)
I love the way you kiss me, and I love to hear you call my
name.

You're just a sweet lovin' daddy, don' mean no harm at all. (2x)
'Cause you know I'll always love you, and be ready to catch
you when you fall.

Now tell me, baby, won't you try me one more time.
Now tell me, baby, won't you try me one more time.
I swear I won't break your heart,
And forever you'll be mine.

Arkansas Blues

Some folks singin' blues
'Bout de Spanish an' 'Merican War;
De blues I'm singin', come from Arkansas.

Ten years in jail 'bout made me lose my min';
De work didn't worry me,
Jes my woman I left behin'.

14. Written by Ella Madison.

Ef I had a musket, carry it shoulder high,
Wouldn' kill nobody;
Jes fight so I could die.

Don't ask me why de cause I'm lookin' sad,
Jes can't make it—
One mo' day lak dem I had.

War Songs

A Woman Is Born for Trouble
A woman used to be somethin',
If she married a workin' man.
She had clothes, a car, and a radio,
An' plenty good money in her hand.
But since de draft board's callin',
A woman's got a worrin' mind.
She work all day for her money,
And can't sleep at night for cryin'.

Chorus
A woman is sho born fer trouble,
Fer trouble as sho as you born.
Since draft boards start to callin',
De good mens will all soon be gone.

Rationing
Dey done ration ev'ybody—
From de cradle to de grave.
Roosevelt says de war is on,
Ev'ybody got to save.
Sometime you can't get no sugar,
Sometime you can't get no meat,
Sometime you can't get no shoes,
To go on your aching feet.

Dey done start to ration ev'ybody—
Ev'ything from water to wine,
Roosevelt says de war is on,

Ev'ybody got to stay in line.
It don't make no diff'rence—
I ain't gonna moan an' cry,
I'm po'—I ain't never had nothin',
Now I'm glad de rich folks can't buy.

Reduction Papers (Induction Papers)

I got my reduction papers,
Dey say I got to go.
I got my reduction papers,
Where I'm goin' I don't know.
I got my reduction papers,
I read 'em line for line,
I heard someone say, "Chollie",
And my gal done start to cryin',
I say look here my darlin', let me dry yo' eyes,
If Hitler knowed I was drafted, he'd hang his head and cry!

Chorus
I may be go to England,
I may be go to Jaypan,
No matter where dey send me,
Uncle Sam gonna have a hell of a man,
Uncle Sam gonna have a hell of a man.

Satire Songs

De White Horse an' de Black Horse

De white horse an' de black horse
Workin' side by side;
De sun got hot, de black horse run,
But de white horse downed an' cried.

De white horse left de black horse
Laid down in de shade,
De black horse eatin' wormy corn,
But de white horse eatin' sweet hay.

De white and de black horse
Went to de big race track;
De black horse run, de white got lame,
But he got all de money jes de same.

De Black Jack and de Tall White Pine

De black jack said to de tall white pine,
Don't keep that sun off me.
De white pine said to de black jack,
Don't run your mouth at me.

De black jack said to de tall white pine,
How come you grow so tall?
De tall pine said to de black jack,
I eat better then you, dat's all.

De black jack said to de tall white pine,
Just 'cause you high in de breeze,
You need'nt talk so biggity (bigoted),
Trees ain't nothin' but trees.

It is inescapable that such texts as the preceding would drive the singer in a path that has been rhythmically and emotionally hewn out. Therefore, the nature of the song structure is determined by the words given out by the leader as a "call" motive. If his call is short, the chorus comes in quicker, by necessity. Since he is the leader, the next move is his. This results in a quick entry by the leader, thus forming the song pattern:

Leader:	Good news (leader pauses)
Chorus:	Good news
Leader with chorus:	Chariot's comin'
Leader:	Good news (leader pauses)
Chorus:	Good news
Leader with chorus:	Chariot's comin'
	An' I don't want her to leave me behin'.

If the chosen call is long, then the chorus is kept out longer and takes its pattern from the call. The result is a broader song style, not necessarily slower:

Leader:	Swing low, sweet chariot
Chorus enters:	Comin' for to carry me home.

Since these two are the main divisions, it is but natural that mixtures should appear:

Leader:	My soul is a witness
Chorus:	Fo' my Lord (couplet repeated 4x)
Leader ("preaching"):	

> We read in de Bible and we understand,
> Samson was de strongest man.
> Samson went out at one time,
> Killed about a thousand of de Philistines.
> Delilah fool' Samson, dis we know,
> De Holy Bible tells us so.
> She shave' his head jes clean as yo' hand,
> An' Samson's strength come as any other man.

The speed and character of these songs springs from the spirit behind them. The words express this more clearly than music could, but neither as beautifully nor as powerfully as when combined with music. This seems to be the point of balance between the two powers.

From the point of view of musical analysis, my friend John Work gives a scholarly treatment of this subject in *Folk Song of the American Negro*. He divided the religious songs into the call and response chant; the slow, sustained, long-phrase melody; and the syncopated, segmented melody. The difference between his approach and mine seems to derive from our opposing conceptions rather than purposes.

III. Modes

Among the many good things that Henry Krehbiel did for Negro music was to compile a table showing the actual modes. It has become standard, and it is submitted here to clarify the nature of Negro song modes:

Ordinary major	331
Ordinary minor	62

Mixed and vague	23
Pentatonic	111
Major with flatted seventh	20
Major without seventh	78
Major without fourth	45
Minor with raised sixth	8
Minor without sixth	34
Minor with raised seventh (leading-tone)	19

The major mode is the boldest and most natural to the ears of most people. To my mind it is not stronger than the minor mode, if the spirit behind the minor mode is powerful. In fact, the opposite may be true in certain cases, yet it seems that people have used the minor modes to express gloom in a rather specialized way. The preference of the Negro to use the major mode is one reason I object to calling Negro music "slave songs." It is music out of slavery, but it does not express the spirit of that institution any more than does music created more recently. Similarly, songs of more recent vintage are too often labeled "slave hymns," "slave chants," and so forth. But the nature of each song should be taken as the basis for understanding the song.

With regard to the seculars, the reader should do some analyzing on his own. Blues especially offer patterns that are striking. The flat third and seventh, also often heard in primitive religious songs, plus raised seconds and sixths in major, give to these songs a charm and interest quite different from most folk songs found in America. The great mixture of scales used seems ample to put the Negro musical feeling in line with, and even beyond, what is generally known to be musically basic.

IV. Traditional Rendition Prerequisites

(Addressed to the prospective user)

Negro songs require a folk-like rendition, more so than any other prerequisite. A failure in this is a failure indeed. There is no one method that may or should be given as standard. However, there are some general principles that may be given as factors necessary for an authentic rendition. The list given below comes as a result of many years of observation at the source.

Fifteen Factors

1. Use simple harmony for traditional renditions.

2. Use steady rhythm, even in slow tempos.

3. Feel the hand-clap and foot-pat, but do not use them unless driven to do so by inner urge or for special preconceived efforts. Never use them for show.

4. Use dialect consistently and very sincerely. Avoid "operatic" voice projection.

5. Take care to observe the relationship between the spoken word and the notation, especially where rhythm is concerned.

6. Get dynamics by emphasizing the words that Negro folk do in their singing. Be careful of the verbs and prepositions, as they usually hold the key to the movement. The adjective usually has a little crescendo. Proper and common nouns should be sung with sharp emphasis but not exaggerated.

7. The conductor must not do more than is necessary. Too much control on his part makes for stiffness and coldness, no matter how otherwise perfect the singing may be. (It may easily be too perfect.)

8. Instrumental accompaniments are all bad—comparatively.

9. Listen to real folk singers as much as possible. Note their virtues instead of their vices. Go beneath the surface and listen to the melody and words.

10. Do not try to imitate their singing; imitate their spirit and their principles, rhythm, tone color, and spontaneity. (This is good to apply in general.)

11. Do not try to find effects in the use of strange and loud harmonies. End on the key note at "low-tide" rather than on the "raging-billow."

12. Combine all of the above factors with your own personality. There is the test. If the latter is sincere, able, and honest, the result is invariably good. A failure may represent a lack of one or more factors. Never have I seen all absent. The music is too natural to permit its complete destruction.

13. Select song leaders more on the basis of their spirit and musical talent than on sheer vocal power. Allow them to sing the lead as much as possible in their own way, with a suggestion given here and there.

14. Avoid manufactured dynamics, sudden stops, sudden changes of tempo, complex cross-firing of parts, radical changes in tone volume (*ff* to *p*, *mf* to *pp*). Follow the feeling produced by the first phrase of the song. This may be relied upon as being the birthmark.

15. "De" is pronounced like di, duh, or dah in its general use when having the pronounciation based upon "d" rather than upon "th."

Where do Negro songs originate? This question is becoming harder to deal with as the years go by. It is a question that might well be left alone if it were asked merely to satisfy a querious urge. It becomes another matter when it is asked by the interested collector or scholar who wishes to attach the proper historical and sociological understanding to a song or group of songs. It also becomes very important in the matter of directing research, so that one's research will have as little lost motion—time and expense—as possible. First of all, it should be understood that some localities produce large numbers of songs, while others produce moderate numbers, and still others scarcely produce at all in comparison with the more productive areas. These conditions are mainly the result of social forces operating in various ways in a very inconstant series of situations. Where Negroes are brought together in a situation that requires them to rely mainly on each other for interest and recreation, the production of songs of a secular as well as a religious type is likely to be greater than in situations where they work individually and live very different types of lives. This is largely due to the fact that group action aids the imagination in subject matter and at the same time serves as a kind of interactionary force in the developmental stages of a song pattern or subject.

For instance, Charles P. Ware, during the three years following the Civil War, was able to obtain from Coffins Point, St. Helena Island, South Carolina, the first 57 (out of 136) songs appearing in *Slave Songs of the United States.* Fully 79 of the songs came from the Sea Islands grouped off the coast of South Carolina. Very recently Nicholas George Julius Ballanta collected more than a hundred religious songs at the Penn School on St. Helena Island. It is of interest to note here that in a radius of ten miles or so, two volumes of spirituals have been compiled. If we add to these the various songs taken from this region by John and Alan Lomax and Lydia Parrish, then we get some idea of the tremendous creative forces active in this so-called "Gullah" country.

Consider the geographical situation on St. Helena Island, and the grounds for my previous assertion regarding the necessity for creativity will be apparent. In this instance we have a group of islands off the coast of South Carolina that are inhabited largely by Negroes who were brought over to America from the Barbados coast. Having been isolated on these islands for generations, they have become closely acquainted with one another. They have produced a language that in a striking manner sets them apart from other Negroes, and they have taken on a strong provincialism. This latter fact is noted by their having set up a separate district in Savannah known as Yamacraw, where those who have migrated from the Sea Islands live together in accordance with their customs.

An event occurred during the Civil War which also worked hand in glove with the promotion of group feeling among these Island Negroes. During the year 1862, the forces of the Federal Navy captured the coast embracing these islands, forcing the owners of the island plantations to flee to the mainland. Suddenly the deserted slaves found themselves in charge of the territory and responsible for maintaining themselves in this new situation. At this point the favorable circumstances for the creation of folk song must have reached a new height. With added responsibilities and privileges came new inspiration and new ideas for song-making. The effect of this welding together of group interest made it easier for the folk poet and composer to gain insight into the life problems, joys, sorrows, and ambitions of the people around him. Whereas a man previously had been bound to one plantation, he now was free to visit many. Whereas he previously worshipped with restrictions, he now could worship at will.

A comparison of the contents of *Slave Songs of the United States* and *St. Helena Island Spirituals* shows the interesting fact that they overlap only in four instances: "Roll, Jordan, Roll" (an indigenous version), "Wrestle on Jacob," "I Can't Stay Behind," and "Hunting for a City." But even here we have different versions, so much so that the two books may be said to have scarcely any duplication. One other interesting fact is apparent. *St. Helena Island Spirituals* is now as highly localized in color as the older and sometimes more primitive *Slave Songs of the United States*. The answer to this difference is found summarily in the dates of the two publications. *Slave Songs of the United States* was published in 1867 and was, of course, made possible by the singing of slaves and ex-slaves. The songs contained in this work are strongly suggestive of unity in origin, especially in their treatment of religious experiences. The people who composed this group of songs had been deprived of practically all outside contact and virtually all opportunities for educational experiences. There were practically no forces operative to make any conceptual difference among them. Hence, when one looks at *Slave Songs of the United States*, it is very likely that he will recognize, without any suggestion, that the first portion of the book (those songs from the island) is a singularly unusual and unknown group.

In looking at *St. Helena Island Spirituals* a similar feeling may result, but to a lesser degree because of the familiar spots here and there in this highly significant anthology. Here one finds, for instance, "I Am Boun' fo' de Promised Lan'" (hymn), "De Blood Done Sign My Name," "Yo' Must Hab dat True Religion," "I'm Goin' Down to de Ribber o' Jordan," "Give Me Jesus," and "All My Sins Done Taken Away," as well as a few others used with acknowledgments to other sources. These are songs generally known all over the country, at least by those who profess a fair knowledge of Negro religious music. In fact, one of these songs, "All My Sins Done Taken Away," was the first Negro folk song I can remember having learned as a child of about six in Pensacola, Florida. It was learned from another small Negro boy who brought the cows to pasture next to our home every morning. Since he always came singing this jubilee at the top of his voice, we learned it by absorption. The presence of these last-mentioned songs in *St. Helena Island Spirituals* is evidence of the action of outside musical influences of no uncertain nature. However, I wish to emphasize the fact that most of the songs contained in this book are indeed the products of the island whose name they bear. An investigation of the contents will bear this out in a striking way. Also some slight authentic alterations here and there are to be encountered by those who are familiar with the religious songs of the Sea Islands, thereby heightening the book's individuality in a musical and poetic sense.

St. Helena Island Spirituals, published in 1925, came out fifty-eight years later than *Slave Songs of the United States*. As a product of much later times, it bears the stamp of social intercourse. The graduates of the Penn School have gone on to the Hampton Institute, where they have learned the songs of the outlanders, and in some cases the outlanders have come in to teach and have brought new songs with them. Besides this, the entire population of the islands has been opened up to the course of social interchange. The people are of necessity far less static in their habitation than in the past. Each year will no doubt see greater changes in the course of denaturation among the Sea Islands inhabitants—in a folk sense, at least. I am not overlooking the fact that even in slavery there was social intercourse among slaves on plantations of various distances from one another, but the kind of social intercourse that has been constantly developing since the coming of emancipation hardly compares with slavery times.

To return to the point by way of other illustrations, it can be said with ample support that the same principles discussed above can be applied to other sections of the country and to both religious and secular songs. The Alabama Black Belt, the mountains and shore regions of Virginia, and the Mississippi River and Valley sections are cases in point. As proof of this thesis and to show some of the forces that are now at work in the creative field of Negro music, I wish to devote the following paragraphs to an area I recently visited. Studying seculars is a matter of considering public works, industrial centers such as foundries and coal-mining areas, and the various prisons and prison camps. A discussion of secular songs has already been undertaken.

Of the many places I have visited in search of Negro music, the Alabama coal-mining district I recently visited was by all means one of the most interesting and fruitful. There I was brought face to face with creative forces working together in a perfect pattern of production. These people are exceedingly group-conscious for three main reasons: (1) they are bound together by the common necessity of being members of the coal miners' union; (2) they are for the most part living in the same area in close formation; and (3) they have been, in the case of the T. C. I. Company, encouraged in the matter of singing some of their own songs, especially those that are related to the mine and to the life of the mining camp. There is more interest in singing in this section of Alabama than in any other similar area I have visited.

One Sunday afternoon in August 1943, I sat down in the home of Allen Lockett and heard ten male quartets that were kind enough to spend several hours of their time singing for my edification. When I asked where these many quartets came from, the answer was merely, "'Mongst de boys 'round here. You ain't seen nothin' yet. You ought to hear dem boys over in de Edgewater camp. Sometime all us get together and has a contest." Then I asked the question, "How many songs can you sing?" The answer came slowly: "Well, 'Fess,' d'ain't no tellin'. We ain't never give out nowhere. Sometime the songs outlast us. Don't worry 'bout us giving out. We can sing 'til yo' ears git hot." Songs, songs, songs, and more songs—it seemed that the end would never come, nor did I wish it to come. Each song was a stranger to my ears. Later, my investigation showed that there were no persons in Birmingham whom I could find who knew any of the songs I collected that day at the camps.

After I heard these quartets, it was brought out that each quartet knew the songs that had been sung by the others but had avoided repetition. This caused me to think that perhaps all of them could sing together. Without any preparation at all, the forty men banked themselves into the suffocatingly hot front room at Lockett's home and sang four more songs in a most thrilling manner. At this point, not only were my "ears hot," but all of those present were at the point of suffocation.

The reader will wonder why such a small place was used for the purpose of having these men sing. The previous Thursday, Lockett told me to come over and he would "have a few of the boys sing a song or two." When I arrived at his home, there were two quartets. Within an hour or more there were seven, and certainly within an hour and a half the quota had been reached. While this song galaxy was proceeding, Lockett was kind enough to offer to "step 'roun' de corner and git a few mo' boys," but this offer was turned down for a lack of room. Plus, there was ample chance to hear them on another occasion.

When it became apparent that all of this music was produced from what one might call a single neighborhood, it seemed incredible. My nephew, Charles Anderson, who accompanied me for the occasion, had not fully realized the situation. After we went out into the yard, "the boys" contented themselves with laughing and passing witty remarks about our upset mental and physical states of being. After this experience the most natural procedure was to follow up with personal interviews directed toward those who seemed to have the responsibility for leadership in the groups. One of the men interviewed was Cleveland Perry, born in Marengo County forty-eight years ago:

> Ain't never sung befo' 1920. Hit jes started ter worry my min' ter sing. Never is finished de third reader. Sung so many union songs 'bout de mines, de big mine boss don't want me 'round de reservation. I makes up a song 'bout ennything I see goin' on 'bout here. When hit come down ter songs, dey kin milk me but dey won't dry me. Is yo' got any chaw terbaccer or dip er snuff? I uses sitch ez dat when I git ter steddyin' 'bout songs. I gen'ly lays in bed at night an' fixes up ma songs an' verse 'em out an' sing 'em de next mawnin'. What you gwine do wid dese songs? How do I know you ain't up ter some devilment? Yes, I done sung fo' 'bout twenty thousan' people off an' on and dey loves ter hear me yet. Don't let yo' hongry run yo' off: my Ol' Lady bilin' some greens, I b'lieve.

Perry, who is an untutored genius of melody and of insight into his environment, sat on his very scant front porch for three torrid afternoons and sang songs he had composed or adapted to words he thought more fitting or words he wished to have presented to the local union or some special audience. Here, before my very eyes, was a man who had created songs from his experiences and the life around him in a manner that was indisputably authentic and real. No full value can be placed upon the work he has done, since other song makers in the vicinity claimed to be the authors of some of the songs he sang. Upon further investigation it developed that there were factions supporting the authenticity of each individual claiming authorship. This confusion was very dismaying at times, but it did have value in supporting the fact that the songs were created among the particular people who inhabited this locality.

In my study there were only a few cases where the authorship of a song was not contested by two or three "trainers" and by so many factions, usually comprising those who sang with the particular trainers. But Cleveland Perry, known as "Singin' Perry," convinced me that, compared to the other trainers, he possessed the greatest amount of originality in the quantity and quality of his creations. One of his greatest delights is to take a spiritual and put original words to it, thereby making what he calls a "work sperrichil" or "union sperrichil." Whereas this policy is not to be advocated, it is a strong index to the man's creative abilities. It also shows what actually happens to the songs of the Negro as they pass through the hands of highly gifted people who are honest in their efforts at self-expression, sometimes at the expense of another man's idea, which they happen to possess. That this process is creative in the final analysis, none can deny. Compare the following verses:

Original Version
O, hear me Jesus, hear me,
Hear me ef yo' please.
Ef yo' don't hear me standin'
I'll fall down on mah knees.

Perry's Version
Dere's people, dey don't like me
'Cause I'm a union man
Go'n' stay in line wid de union
Ef I die wid my card in my han'.

This is a very popular jubilee among the mining-camp Negroes entitled "O, Didn't It Rain." These specimens are part of the verses in both forms. The chorus is sung in the original form.

When asked why he had not changed the wording of the chorus,

Perry explained at once that the chorus was adequate for his purpose, so he had not changed it. He showed beyond a reasonable doubt that he had a definite and highly developed plan in his treatment of the song. Here is his own explanation:

Yo' see hits dis way. Dere's some people in de worl' dat won't jine nothin' dats for de good o' dem an' nobody else. Well, dere's some folks dat wants ter work in the mines but dey won't jine de union so dey kin he'p deyse'f. I had ter change dem verses so as I could git dem scabs good and tol'. Well, when hit come ter de chorus I didn't had ter change nary word 'cause hit struck em jes right. Here de way de chorus go:

O' didn't hit rain, children,
Didn't hit rain fer my Lawd?
O' didn't hit rain, Lawd,
O' didn't hit rain?

Yo' see, dat say plain dat de day comin' when dese scabs gwine be out in de worl' wid no pertection, jes standin' dere wid trouble comin' down on him. Go'n' be jes lak when Norah tol' de folks 'bout de ark.

Here are the other verses:

Dere's people o' ev'y nation
Fightin' de union plan.
Let me tell yo' what yo' better do,
Hurry an' jine de union ban'.

De supintender don't like me,
De bank boss hate me too,
De section fo'man can' he'p hissef
'Cause I'm gwine wid de union through.

It is a pity that so interesting a character cannot be dealt with at greater length. However, in a work of this sort it is necessary to pass on to other situations. More of Cleveland Perry will appear in a later section.

James Craig, the youngest trainer in Fairfield, is only twenty-five years old. He speaks very creditable English and takes pride in saying that in school he has been no further than the fourth grade: "I was born in Philadelphia. My mother was very pious. Never sang a spiritual until I came down south seven years ago. These boys taught me at first. Now I teaches them. What you going to do with these songs? Did you hear 'bout me before you came out here? I don't bar nobody when it comes to training a bunch of fellows how to sing our stuff. Yes sir, 'Fess,' I composed a heap of songs, but I kind of loss track of 'em after a while. When we get tired of one we just let it go."

There was nothing quite so fascinating to me as to sit and watch this young man train his group of male singers with full authority and unbelievable resourcefulness. He was immediately able to sing any part that did not progress as he wished it to. Most of the songs claimed by him are also claimed by others, but the beautiful and powerful jubilee, "John Wrote My Mother a Letter," is generally credited to his genius. He sang two versions for us, one of which (the one he asked to be used here) is included in the Appendix of this book.

Albert Hunter was famous among the miners for one song. He had built his reputation upon his composing ability as much as upon his singing. The training he gave his singers was rather taken for granted by all except himself and a few close friends who echoed his frequent bursts of self-praise:

Yes, Lawd, I was born way back yonder in '94. I ain't no good now. Been worked ter death. Shukkins, man, I was railroadin' in Macon, Mississippi, when I was twelve years old. Yes, Lawd, I comed over here in '15. Caught plenty hell in de army. I'm on compensation now. Was in de hawspital in Nawleens. Dat's when I done some sho nuff singin'. Us boys dere in de hawspital jes sung all de time ter keep from thinkin' 'bout home so much. Plenty time I be layin' in bed dere at de hawspital an' I feel somethin' hot an' wet run down 'side my ears, an' I know I done gone ter cryin'. Raise up den an' sing "Home, Jim." Nurses, doctors, nobody couldn' stop me twell de feelin' git off my ches'. In my good days I was trouble in dem mines over dere. Don't do nothin' now but sing an' mess roun' here an' dere de bes' I kin.

Got a bunch er boys over dere in Wylam kin sho nuff go. I'm de trainer. Sir? Ah, I ain't been mo'n fourth grade. I don't know nothin' 'bout no school ef dats what yo' gettin' at. What you gon'n do wid dese songs? Well, what yo' say sounds alright ter me but yo' better go on over dere an' see my ol' lady too. Yes, Lawd, I don't do nothin' widout she know 'bout it.

We did not get the opportunity to hear Albert Hunter train his group, but many of the members of his group sang for us at other places. The songs that Hunter sang were largely those we had heard elsewhere, yet there was one song he composed that is of singular merit. It is a work ballad he named "Mining Boys Song." Aside from having beautiful music, it has the type of verse that is instructive and picturesque at the same time. We consider "Mining Boys Song" one of our most prized trophies. We say "trophies" advisedly, for many of our songs are obtained after the most trying struggles. This was especially the case in getting this song. "Home, Jim" proved to be an old album song of the "prodigal son" type. It had no Negro atmosphere about it at all. Its appeal to the Negroes throughout this section is amazing. It must be that it depicts the lives of many of the men who work the mines. Hunter claims to have brought it back from Nawleens from a "little ol' Geechee boy." It is not too much to say that this man is a genius in the true sense of the word. His mastery of his abilities is one of the amazing things encountered during this particular venture. My acquaintance with "Mining Boys Song" is sufficient to warrant the space accorded him here.

Mack Free sat on the front porch of his small miner's quarters one August afternoon and looked on very curiously as two friends, who were guiding me around the camp, directed me up to his little home. He said, "Well, ef yo' lookin' fer singin' I b'lieve you come ter de right place. Fact is, we 'bout ter have a practice ennyhow. Dis is our regular meetin' night. Where mought yo' be from? Dat's de same thing I seed a man doin' befo'. Go git dat basser, tell him ter hurry, we got comp'ny ternight." After having all of us unite in saying "The Lord's Prayer," Free led his singers through ten spirituals and jubilees, the likes of which we had not heard before. At certain places a man who was an uncanny harmonica player joined the singers with his instrument. His was a most powerful performance. The sincerity of the whole thing was of such a nature as to hold one enthralled if he but had the capacity to realize what was transpiring in front of him. Again it was insufferably hot in the small room. When asked if the recital could not be held on the porch, I was told that the voices would "scatter 'bout" out of doors. So we again surrendered the comforts of life to the god of melody.

Here was a group of singers with an exceedingly well-balanced set of voices singing verse that had been largely created by them. The melody was often augmented to take care of added lines. Here and there Free would look proudly in our direction and say, "All of dis here one is ours." The singular nature of these songs seemed to prove his point. They had not been known to me before. There were five songs, and in some of them, such as in the magnificent song "De Han' Writin' on de Wall," the united singers reached great heights of creative accomplishment. It seemed to me that here the perfect blending of purpose, poetry, and music had been realized by these unsuspecting bards. Although the whole of "De Han' Writin' on de Wall" appears further on in this book, it is impossible for me to keep one of the stanzas from the reader any longer:

> Now, God got angry on His throne,
> Angels in heb'm begin to moan,
> Dey droop dere wings to hide dere face,
> An' Lord have mercy on de human race.
> Now, go down angels an' consume de flood,
> Blow out de sun an' turn de moon ter blood,
> Den go back angels an' a-bolt de do',
> Time done been, won't be no mo'.

This is art to the manor born, and there is no doubt on my part but that it was created by these singers. "De Han' Writin' on de Wall" has several versions, but in none of them have I heard anything that was comparable to this stanza. That it was worked out according to group ideas is a significant cause of the great amount of folk atmosphere pervading it.

The following day one of the group challenged me: "Is yo' got a union card?" I said, "No, I don't belong to a union as such, because I do not happen to do the kind of work that would require me to have a card." The man continued his questioning: "I didn't say nothin' 'bout no work. Is yo' got a card? Ev'y man have some principle ter stan' on. Ef he ain't got none he ought ter git one er git where nobody can't fin' him." It was in connection with this conversation that the evils of playing checkers were pointed out to us. These singers were the most religious of all the religious groups it has been my pleasure to work with, and the matter of singing their songs was a serious undertaking. The songs were developed largely for the purpose of communal good, no thought being given by the creators to the shallow purpose of personal glory—hence the difficulty of being able to find the persons who had been the original vessels of the songs indigenous to this section. This has been the custom here for a long period, and it is apparent that it is the same principle that has governed the making of Negro songs over the years.

My purpose for going into this community was to gather work songs. That so few were gained is largely due to the fact that the miners work underground on a comparatively individual basis, which prevents the gang spirit so essential in the production of work songs. Additionally, the fact that the miners work constantly under the threat of death, which could be caused by a slight error in judgment, causes them to be rather religious. This was the impression I got when questioning the Negroes who work the T. C. I. Mines. I am not suggesting that the miners used the foregoing songs as work songs, for just the opposite was the case: Singing among the Negro miners is a chief means of diversion.

Singing these songs also has its financial rewards, for the miners would sing for some compensation at various small churches in nearby Birmingham, Bossemer, Ensley, Fairfield, and so forth. The singing in a training session is very different from what transpires in a rural or primitive Negro church. The former is prepared music designed to be sung for money in concerts. The churches that would not tolerate many forms of entertainment sponsored by other institutions would eagerly support a concert or contest by those who "sing de gospel." How well the Negro fathoms his circumstances and ravishes the chances of his existence through his artistic genius!

Perhaps the description of a typical training session, as practiced in the Alabama mining districts during my visits, would be a fitting close to this chapter. This experience is one of the most enlightening lessons one may be privileged to receive. But the proof of the statement may be best realized by the training as here set down. In the trainings I visited, the leader or trainer always sat in with the singers, who numbered anywhere from four to a dozen. The sexes were never mixed. When the wives of the miners wished to organize into a singing group, the trainer from one of the male groups was called in to get them started, but afterwards one of the women would serve as trainer. In the case of the women, things move a little more decorously. The trainer and the women under her care are less inclined to joke. They work hard and they sing with the same technique as the men, since their example is found in the male trainer.

As the session is about to begin, the trainer in many cases will conduct a prayer, in spite of the fact that the smell of alcohol might be present. This does not mean that all the singers drink liquor or that the persons smelling of liquor always drink at times of rehearsal or performance. Some of these men never drink or smoke, while some smoke, drink, and chew. The important point is that these practices have no bearing on the religious beliefs that accompany their "singin de gospel."

After the preliminaries, the trainer has the singers rise, stand in a line, and sing some familiar song, frequently a theme song. Then, moving to the end of the line, facing in the same direction as the singers but standing a bit to the fore, he brings down his hand with a rather violent chopping motion. This action brings absolute silence. Then, with an air of considerate but firm authority, the trainer says what he wants done. His statements usually run about as follows: "Well, boys, yawl done come together ag'in to do some singin'. Now, yawl knows dat I'm yo' trainer an' yawl 'pendin' on me to lead yo' right. Now, ez I said befo', I can't do dis by myse'f. Yawl got to do bes' you kin all de time. What was de matter wid yawl over yonder to Wylam d'other night? Better stop doin' lak dat. Folks gwine git tired yawl foolin' roun' wid dey money. Now, we got a new song here tonight. I versed it out muse'f. I 'spect yawl done heered it. H-m-m-m, but yo' ain't heered it lak dis."

At this point the trainer sings and explains what he has in mind.

Like a flash the men catch on and the song starts moving. Since most of the harmony assumes a basic pattern, little difficulty is experienced by the group. However, when it comes to extras—the novel effects set in by the trainer—special care has to be taken to keep the rhythm moving in the right manner. Some of the songs are worked over in style and text. Others are imitated from the singing of other groups. Still others are well known. Not at any time have I seen a trainer show the least bit of impatience or brashness in leading a group to the mark he has set. A good trainer takes pride in his work and wishes to "outdo dem other boys," so these trainings are clearing-stations for the religious singing of our time.

Invariably a trainer manages to get the results intended, and in a short time, too! When reproof does come, it usually takes the form of comedy: "Hawkins, what's de matter wid you? Is you a grown singer or is you a baby? Keep on doin' dat, I'm gwine sen' yo' over dere to Smithfield wid dem lil ol' boys dat calls deyse'f singers, an' ain't—Wha! Wha! Wha! Whooee!" (all laugh). Or the reproof may sound like this: "You knows I'm's a singer, Free! Yawl jes done shet de do' on me. Yawl jes natchel singin' so tight I can't force my way in. Howsomever, since you talk lak you is, I'm gwine bust my way in! Now ef yawl can't stan' me when I throws my bass at you, it ain't gwine be my fault. Yawl knows I been grown ten years" (a grown singer is one who is able to sing in the accepted manner with almost any group on short notice). "Come on Mack, git her sot. Le's go!"

Immediately the singing is begun again, and all goes well until the trainer gives a sharp stamp of the foot, emits a shrill whistle, or gives the aforementioned chop of the hand. "Dats mo' like it," he says. "Now come on let's go fo'm here." With these words of approval the singers relax into a joyous, almost shouting type of singing—patting the feet, working the shoulders, swaying the body at will, flexing the knees, beaming in ecstasy. The trainer then moves into another song, always allowing the men to sing as freely as possible and thereby to create for themselves. It should be well understood that a good trainer is able to and often does take individual parts and sing them to the singers for the sake of example. At no time is there any directing in the real sense, for a movement of the eye, a flick of the finger, a very subtle change of dynamics or rhythm is all that is needed to change the procedure at any given moment without it even being noticed by the listener.

The final segment of the training session is a songfest of rare power. Frequently, when the weather is good, an audience collects in the door and window of the little quarters while other singers in the neighborhood enter and join in the festivities. Sometimes, when the spirit of the singing rises to a feverish heat, a man will leap up, or let out a yell, or both. I have often heard men say, while a powerful song was being rendered, "Yawl better stop dat now, I can't stand it," or, "Sing it, sing it! Sing it!!" or "When I hears dis song I can't be 'pended on!" A training does not end formally but rather just "runs out." Often the trainer does not realize when the end comes. When "tall tales" and "big talk" take place, the wise listener will realize that the training is done, but he will not leave until the "bull session" has also "run out."

After a discussion such as the above, the question of the historical period, in regard to the origin of various Negro songs, is bound to rise in the mind of the reader. No agreement can seem to be dependably reached here, nor is one altogether desirable, except in special cases. Once in a while the texts of the songs help a great deal. However, the most generally helpful means of determining the historical period are as follows: (1) consulting various collections of different periods; (2) consulting very old people who know the songs in question; (3) acquiring songs from contemporary persons who acquired them from verified sources, such as collections of older or younger persons; and (4) acquiring songs from present-day song makers of known ability, followed up by verifying their originality through research, testimony, and examination. For those who place all Negro songs in certain periods based on purely philosophical considerations, these four principles may appear inadequate. However, they are our safest guides when this type of study is undertaken.

I

The great number of books that have been written about the Negro and his songs is constantly increasing, as the addition of this volume suggests. The attitude of most of the authors has been to create interest in a fascinating subject. Many of the books deal with the Negro through the words of the songs he creates, in a sense permitting the Negro to tell his own story. This is good from a purely sociological point of view, but it obviously represents only half of the creative side of the Negro. Then there is the writer who seems more inclined to view the songs through his own eyes and write a more personal reaction to his observations, but such an account runs the risk of being fictional. Finally, there is the type of book that deals with the song of the Negro as a whole by presenting to the reader its melody, poetry, and interpretation. This latter would seem to be the most desirable from a general point of view.

The most difficult element of song to handle, insofar as the general public is concerned, is the music. My feeling is that, although the average person is not sufficiently versed in solfège to gain any benefit from having the notes printed with the words, the presence of the notes in no way hinders the reader who has a preference for the words alone. At the same time, the notes furnish an indispensable source to the person who is wholeheartedly interested in the offerings of Negro music.

Insofar as the Negro remains a factor not generally understood by the white man, there should be no further emphasis in the direction of generalized reference to the practices that accompany this music, particularly since these practices are as foreign to many Negroes as they are to the white man. Too often the impression is given that all

Negroes are given to dancing, jumping over benches, sweating rivers of perspiration, rolling their eyes until they start from the sockets, jerking their heads perilously, and creating a scene of general emotional carnage while they engage in singing their religious songs. In fact, some writers have carried these manifestations as the main burden of their message. Certainly, there are many instances where some of these manifestations are present, but there are also many instances where they are not. There is also the misconception that whenever the "shouting" type of Negro sings a spiritual or jubilee that the shout remains the ever-present accompaniment.

There has always been a type of Negro who was not given to the shout. "Shout," as used here, is not to be confused with the shout indulged in by an individual who is aroused to vocal and physical demonstrations by the trend of a sermon, song, or prayer. The shout, as it is meant here, is a deliberate procedure on the part of the entire church membership which is carried out in due form and practice. During and in preparation for this ceremony, the benches are pushed back to the walls and the members of the congregation form a ring as they sing and dance with a shuffling gait (undoubtedly imported from Africa in the conceptual state). The shout occurs in two general ways. It may serve as the medium for an entire evening or morning of worship, or it may serve as an aftermath to the regular worship service. I have observed this practice not only in rural churches but in many urban churches as well. At the present time I have recognized more of a denominational character in the shout than a general racial trait. The point I am making is that there is no justification for making the shout the basis for generalizations about all Negroes, just like there is no justification for taking the frenzied worship found among some whites in the Holiness churches as the basis for generalizations about the white man. Even the poorest student of logic can see the fault in such arguments.

Perhaps what is more interesting is the fact that even among Negroes who practice the shout there are times when religious folk songs are sung and no shouting is done. It all depends on the situation, and it is the situation that usually chooses the music. The shout has its own music, despite the fact that there are times when some borrowing goes on between the various musical types. The same holds true for the baptism, the funeral, the revival, and other occasions—the shout being itself an occasion. So, the less one considers the fact that Negroes in America represent many different tribes and customs, the more he is likely to make generalizations about a circumstance that may be true enough in his city or state but untrue elsewhere. For instance, there is a great difference between the musical renditions found among the Negroes in coastal Georgia and those in central upland Georgia. The same is true of Florida, Virginia, and Alabama, and within given cities there are differences between the various denominations. Some denominations use more spirituals, while others use a mixture of musical types. So, the church service is not to be dealt with in generalizations, at least as far as singing and shouting go.

Here I will quote from *Slave Songs of the United States*: "The shouting step varied with the tune. One could hardly dance with the same spirit to 'Turn, Sinner' or 'My Body Rock 'Long F'ever' as to 'Rock O' Jubilee' or 'O Jerusalem, Early in de Morning.' So far as I can learn, the shouting is confined to the Baptists; and it is, no doubt, to the overwhelming preponderance of this denomination on the Sea Islands that we owe the peculiar richness and originality of the music there." This statement, coming from the scene of one of the great strongholds of Negro custom and folklore, supports the theory advanced earlier, that there is substantial variation in the practice of shouting itself as well as in its denominational manifestations, all of which prevent the possibility of making generalizations about the shout. I should say that during the years immediately following the close of the Civil War, the Sea Islands did not support this conclusion. Perhaps the years have caused a gradual change to take place.

As a result of more than twelve years of research, I am strongly of the opinion that the shout, with its accompanying eccentricities, is found mostly in the Sanctified and Holiness churches and the other more recent religious faiths among Negroes. Indeed, some of these new faiths have included the tambourine and bass drum as a means to guarantee more audible rhythm in their services. This idea was likely gained through seeing these instruments used by the Salvation Army in their outdoor services, but the urge to accept and practice this custom is African. Instruments of rhythm are a fundamental part of Negro folk ceremony because the Negro is a very rhythmic being. So it is natural for these instruments to appeal to the Negro, but it is not natural to find them in his church.

One often reads that most urban Negroes no longer sing spirituals in their churches. This is another unfortunate misconception. The truth of the matter is that in many cases urban Negroes just happened to have sung no spirituals at the time of that particular writer's visit. Sometimes a group of white people go to a Negro church and ask that a great part of the service be sidetracked so that they may be entertained by the congregation. When the minister does not agree to this procedure, the opinion is developed that the Negroes at that church are not the type who sing spirituals or that they are ashamed of them. The spiritual does not make up the entire body of a church music program anymore, as it did twenty-five or thirty years ago in many sections of the country. The Negro church has become more and more literate and ambitious, and the ministers are becoming more capable in the matter of church organization and general management. In many Negro churches the services are well organized and a regular program of music and worship is followed. This is the result of a greater emphasis on the organic phase of worship than on mere emotional guidance.

If one goes to many of our Negro churches today, he will be aware of a formality that is not different in many respects from that generally found in metropolitan churches. To be sure, after the sermon there is occasionally a spiritual that is led by an older member of the church who obeys the impulse rather than the ritual. At such times the entire church will join in and sing most inspiringly. Otherwise, the service will be completed and no spiritual will be sung. It should also be mentioned that often the minister leads his congregation in the singing of a favorite spiritual. This seems to suggest that despite the fact that there are many times when spirituals are not sung at all in Negro churches, the feeling for the spiritual is often still present. Indeed, there are times when a spiritual simply must be sung as a direct and powerful summarization of the entire service. Consequently, one cannot safely think that whenever he goes to a Negro church he will be rewarded by the bountiful singing of spirituals and jubilees. The best time to hear spirituals or jubilees in a Negro church is on prayer-meeting nights, when the religious expressions are more spontaneous and personal. So, one may go to a regular church service and hear not a single spiritual and leave feeling that those people do not sing any spirituals at their church, whereas if he were to go back on Wednesday or Thursday night, he might be rewarded by hearing many spirituals sung in the most authentic style.

It is not strange that the Negro, in spite of his good nature, is capable of resenting the invasion of his house of worship by outsiders who seek entertainment. The Negro's power of understanding along this line is exceedingly keen. He has a well-known high esteem for his church and his religion,[1] and he generally is not willing to assume the role of performer for the satisfaction of some song collector, novelist, playwright, or curious listener. The mere presence of such persons, especially if they be of a different hue, will very often modify the immediate course of events. No, the white man cannot always judge the Negro by what he is able to get out of him, even in so free a field as his songs. Many factors must be considered and understood.

Very recently I was engaged in some very important research in the Yamacraw division of Savannah. Alfred Roberts, who is a very young and capable chorister at the Bryan Baptist Church (generally considered to be the oldest Negro church in America), took me into several rich spots during my investigation. Although we were Negroes, we found it best not to let our mission be known. In fact, we finally got our best results by not going into the church at all. It so happened that it was the month of July, so that the windows and doors of the church were wide open. Our method was to stay outside and record the songs through the windows. Roberts would take down the words, while I would take down the music. This was always done on prayer-meeting night, and the results support my aforementioned thesis with regard to the singing of spirituals. Of course, this situation was not a general one, since there were many other cases when

---

1. The fact that certain Negro preachers and their congregations have made phonograph records and appear over the radio does not contradict our point. Here the participants were essentially worshippers and were performers only incidentally.

the opposite was true. The point here is to show that generalizations about the Negro and his attitude toward his songs are not acceptable if made on the basis of a few writers' observations.

II

Perhaps after the foregoing thesis the reader is in a position to ask what the attitude of the more enlightened Negro—the Negro in colleges and professional walks of life—is to the Negro's religious folk music. I have been asked this question repeatedly by white people after lectures on Negro music. The question itself is evidence of an opinion that the more intelligent Negro in America has a distinct dislike for Negro folk music of the spiritual and jubilee variety. It is my opinion that this is due in large measure to the fact that the spirituals came out of slavery and thus cause the Negro intelligentsia embarrassment. This opinion has gained impetus in recent years because of the attitudes expressed by some college students and in some articles in Negro newspapers.

Such an attitude is not found in the exceedingly vast majority of intellectually developed Negroes. Indeed, the true Negro intellectual does not share in the aforementioned warped notion at all. It is the province of the pseudo-intellectuals among Negroes and the other races to become champions of false gods. If one wishes to know the true attitude of the Negro intellectual to Negro folk art, he may find the answer in the work and lives of such Negroes as Booker T. Washington, W. E. B. Du Bois, John Hope, Robert Russa Moton, James Weldon Johnson, Alain Locke, Carter G. Woodson, Benjamin Brawley, Frederick Douglass, William Stanley Braithwaite, Langston Hughes, Mary McLeod Bethune, Charlotte Hawkins Brown, and many others. These intellectuals have consistently maintained the virtue of the black man's rich artistic heritage, and many of them have, by their own deeds in the field of literature, taken the occasion to glorify the folk music of the Negro. Others of them have, by their positions of leadership in the field of Negro education, made tremendous contributions to the preservation and perpetuation of the religious music of their ancestors.

It is a significant fact that all of the scholars of Negro music have shown a preference for the thematic material found in these same folk songs. A detailed account of this is reserved for another place in this work, yet it may suffice to say at present that, for faith in the musical idioms of his own race, the Negro has not been surpassed by any other race. It is a strange fact that the Negro composer has never found it necessary to go out of his race to find material for any of his major works. It may be that the Negro musician's major works are major because he has chosen to set them in the Negro idiom rather than in a foreign one. This point would not be objectionable to him, insofar as it is in line with the ascendancy of Negro music as a folk medium. However, with regard to those people who hold that the Negro cannot create out of his own idiom like Georges Bizet, Antonín Dvořák, and Nikolay Rimsky-Korsakov were able to do with their native folk idioms, we can take some of the fine work of Samuel Coleridge-Taylor, Harry T. Burleigh, and R. Nathaniel Dett— composers in the cosmopolitan manner—as evidence to the contrary. The fact is, the Negro composer uses his own folk music out of the necessity of love rather than the necessity of "thou must."

Surely, too, the many Negro artists performing in North America and Europe must solidly appreciate and value the very fiber of Negro music. They have each consistently placed a group of spirituals at the end of their programs, thereby evincing their pride in this music. As I have already mentioned indirectly, many superior Negro singing organizations are today giving programs of Negro music for an entire evening. The vogue of the Negro music festival, now so prominent throughout the country, is possibly one of the most wholesome signs, in that it represents a larger percentage of people than the Negro intellectuals alone. The thousand-voice chorus singing spirituals, jubilees, lullabies, work songs, and other seculars is not uncommon from New York to California.

The Negro college student often has been misunderstood in relation to his folk music. This misunderstanding has been caused by a certain unrest on the part of the students at some colleges where questions were raised as to why spirituals were being sung on special occasions while being omitted from the regular calendar. In other words, the students felt that they were being asked to sing spirituals merely because a visitor had come to the campus and wished to hear them, and that they would not be encouraged to sing spirituals again until another similar occasion presented itself. It is very possible that a situation like this may be present on one campus and that these students are justified in their disregard for being asked to sing spirituals, but I am prepared to say, by right of my lifetime as a student of Negro music and as a teacher in Negro colleges, that Negro students enjoy singing their own songs. They enjoy singing them for anyone who genuinely appreciates the Negro's native songs. They enjoy singing them as a part of the regular school exercises and on concert programs. They do not enjoy feeling that the spirituals are unwelcome on campus until some visitor comes and asks for them to be unleashed, as it were.

To speak with further authority upon the subject, I cite the situation as it exists at Morehouse College, Spelman College, and Atlanta University, where I have been both student and teacher. The spiritual has always been an integral part of the life of these institutions, occupying a place in the regular chapel and Sunday exercises. Frequently the entire service is devoted to the singing of spirituals, so the place of the spiritual is thoroughly taken for granted. One might even say that a tradition of veneration has grown up around the spiritual. I am sure that this same situation can be found at most Negro colleges.

There is undoubtedly the type of Negro who, without any good cause, has no sympathy with the singing of spirituals in any form or for any purpose. But no justification can be found for these asinine attitudes that some students maintain. The situation is undesirable but far from serious, since it has very meager and unsound support. In regard to this element, it may be useful to resort to an old African fable related to me by a fellow African student during my early school days. It goes as follows: Three men left their tribe to look for a place to make a new home. They came to a very beautiful shady grove and decided that they would set up residence there. Suddenly one exclaimed that while the place was very desirable from every point of view, they had been forced to walk too far to find it. So the three, agreeing upon the point, decided to walk whence they had come. On the return journey they were all overcome with fatigue and sat down to rest. At this point one of them asked if it would not be wise to go back to the place they had just left, since it was a few miles nearer than their old home. They agreed that it was and so returned to the beautiful location they had found. Upon arriving, one of them declared that they could not stay there because this time they had been forced to walk doubly far to find it. They thus spent their lives contradicting themselves, remaining nowhere, gaining nothing.

It does not discredit Negro students to sing spirituals in a beautiful manner, even if there are occasions when the effort brings undesirable results. Moreover, there is adequate proof that the vast majority of people who visit Negro colleges and ask to hear the students sing spirituals are of the opinion that this is one of the most sublime artistic experiences to be had on the American continent. They are visibly moved by the music, and the results are often decidedly in favor of the cause of Negro education. Ever since the Fisk Singers began the vogue of singing spirituals, the world has agreed that any race that can produce such art has a right to the benefits of educational development. One might even say that the singing of spirituals by Negro students has received more wholesome appreciation than any other group effort among students, regardless of race. No one can deny that the broader education of the Negro is and has been a philanthropic education and that the spirituals have been ambassadors not only of art but of racial cooperation. These facts are known to the collegiate Negro.

While a student at Morehouse College, I performed with the college quartet, which was called upon to sing at various types of white meetings. The response to these appearances was usually of the finest type, while the undesirable incidents were so few that they cannot be considered significant. Indeed, these few incidents suffer miserably by contrast as we look back over the years. In fact, the students who make up the different singing organizations on the various college campuses are zealous about the proper place of the Negro folk song in art, as are their brothers who constitute the student body politic.

The clan that has negative feelings toward the spirituals does not begin and end with the Negro student. Here and there one finds a minority among much older Negroes of a different economic and developmental status who openly show contempt for spirituals in any form. To be sure, these supercilious souls are prompted by an inferiority complex that throws down the truth for a fleeting morsel of satisfaction. In seeking to find the reason that certain persons do not like to sing or hear spirituals, I have noted a pattern of thought or opinion based on factors I will try to discuss in the following paragraphs. I am not claiming to give the reader a comprehensive list of all the causes for this pattern of thought, but I do feel confident that what follows is a fair appraisal of the situation.

The first reason given by most who express disregard for spirituals is that the spirituals represent the Negro's inferior social status. These people think that because the songs were born among the Negro when he was held in slavery, any attempt to preserve them or use them is a tribute to the memory of slavery. This logic is indeed strange. Why should one feel that the flower is the same as the soil? There is nothing in the songs that refers to the status of slavery as being longed for. In fact, it is noteworthy how very seldom one is reminded of slavery in the spirituals. So, generally there is no way of knowing that the Negro spirituals originated in slavery. The spirituals would have developed if there had been no slavery, provided the Negro had been here in sufficient numbers. I am aware that the line of demarcation is slim here, but I am saying that slavery created a social condition that caused Negroes to embrace a new religion and to hold to it with a peculiar zealousness. This zealousness begot songs based on the faith and teachings found in the new religious leaning. With regard to the spirituals, these did not represent the rise of a "slave song." To the contrary, the spirituals link the Negro with the highest and noblest spiritual expression known to man. It has been agreed upon, too, that the religious songs of the Negro are among the finest expressions that have grown out of the Christian faith. Moreover, it is evident that the spirituals hold a place unique among artistic expressions of the world.

The second reason I think certain persons do not like to sing or hear spirituals is that the spirituals perpetuate Negro dialect. Of course, dialect is merely a new shade of art in the realm of speech and is powerful in its own right. In many respects it is more beautiful than the speech from which it springs. No one is suggesting that Negroes continue to use dialect simply because the spirituals require it as a prerequisite to real and powerful rendition. Of course the standard is the English that is found in books and on paper, but no one needs to be ashamed of Negro dialect. One needs only to understand it and see the power of Negro word and tone blended into utmost beauty. Those who are afraid of dialect are evidently not sure of themselves in their use of the English language. The use of dialect in art forms—such as songs, books, plays, and operas—will not perpetuate it as the language spoken among Negroes in America. Rather, it will preserve a unique and powerful heritage.

The third category of individuals who do not like to sing or hear the spirituals are those who do not have a real reason. They "just don't like them," and indeed their reasons may vary from day to day. It seems that behind their emotions lie deeply entrenched feelings of inferiority that cause them to flee from any scene where there are manifestations of Negro culture. There is no argument or remedy that I can provide here, since I am no psychologist.

In spite of my foregoing theories, there are a few well-grounded reasons why students in various schools and colleges may express some dissatisfaction with the spirituals. First of all, there are too many schools that do not teach students about the true dignity of the spirituals but merely request the students to sing them. So, the nature of the songs, especially the texts, is not always understood by students. The song characteristics are not studied from the traditional folk point of view, so as to bring out the charming rhythmic movement so characteristic of Negro singing. Often the songs are given a strange coat to please only the taste of the director, so that all of the traits that make the songs vital and artistic are squeezed out. The song then becomes anemic and wan, lacking in the fiber that gave it birth and sustained its life.

Negro college students do not really know many Negro songs. Of course, this is also true of urban Negroes in general (to be studied elsewhere in this volume). If one travels through the South, one cannot hear many new or rare spirituals or Negro songs in general. What are the same, old standard ones? "Swing Low Sweet Chariot," "Lord, I Want to Be a Christian," "Ev'rytime I Feel de Spirit," "Couldn't Hear Nobody Pray," "Steal Away," and "Jacob's Ladder" (which is not a Negro song in the version used, although there is a Negro version).

Other standard spirituals are "Down by de Riverside" and "Down to de River o' Jordan." Heard a little less frequently than these are "Go Down Moses," "Roll, Jordan, Roll," "When de Stars Begin to Fall," and (at Christmas time) "Go Tell It on the Mountain" and "Dere's a Star in de East." These songs are sung so much that they become rather taken for granted by the young students, and they are grown tired of in the sense that they no longer offer learning experiences to them. Added to this is what I said earlier about the students often not knowing the true meanings of the songs.

Song leaders are frequently the only persons in a congregation who have a reliable knowledge of the spirituals as a whole. This is proven by the fact that it is almost impossible to get a spiritual going if certain people are not present to lead in the singing of the verses or stanzas, since the congregation is only able to sing the refrain or "burden." The fault here rests with the directors for having failed to teach the entirety of a spiritual to all of the students. In an emergency, there are students who possess good voices but who are unable to take the initiative in a folk song rendition, mainly because they are either ignorant of the texts or too timid or both. It was only in recent years that I began teaching all of the spirituals to the students in my care. Prior to that time, the only thing that saved me from an embarrassing situation was the fact that I am able to lead spirituals myself. Since then I have learned that a more serious approach to Negro music on the part of Negro teachers would be to remedy the general misunderstanding about the spirituals on the part of students (and people in general), particularly since these students will often go on to become teachers. In addition, there should be an effort by more schools to consider the folk cultures of various peoples and to discuss Negro culture for the sake of enlightenment.

Another source of disturbance for all Negroes is the type of performance that one encounters on certain occasions where Negroes are called upon, by their own choice or by others, to imitate the real folk-level Negroes in singing and dress. In some cases, educated Negroes don the red handkerchief and affect the shout, cotton-picking, and so forth, in an effort to gain what does not seem desirable in this situation. I am not speaking of what occurs in folk plays and the like, where the situation can be understood as character portrayal. I am speaking of that ridiculous behavior that adds nothing to the matter of singing and much to the matter of perpetuating stereotypes. The Jews, while in Babylon, refused to sing their religious songs for the sake of mirth-making. This principle is not understood by everyone. Those who do not comprehend it must be led by those who do.

Chapter 9
The Influence of
"Shape-Note" Singing

One of the greatest hindrances to the growth of Negro music both in a creative sense and as an expressional medium has been the advent of the "shape-note" hymn book in the rural church and the life of rural Negroes. This is a case of great misfortune in a twofold sense, insofar as it affects the spirituals that are already a part of the Negro's musical repertoire.[1] First, it causes the Negro to confuse his traditional songs with the shape-note songs. Second, it places in his hands an inferior substitute for his folk songs. These forces tend to cause a deterioration in the very singing itself, insofar as they rob the singer of his wonted melodic development. Shape-note songs are designed to suit the market requirement, so that the few songs that are worthwhile in some of the shape-note books are not able to offset the disadvantages of the majority of the songs.

The question has been asked many times why the Negro can be so easily persuaded to lay aside his own music and take up that of the shape-notes. The answer has something to do with the Negro's great hunger for familiarity with the printed page. He has noticed that the book has been the medium through which his children are taught at school and that the exigencies of his existence—from the Sunday school card to the puzzling tenancy accounts—are contained in written matter. This is the source of his inability to believe that anything he has created is better than that found in a book. Perhaps there was a time when the Negro would have been less eager to take up the present trend, but the age of educational process is upon him. Additionally, too often he seems to be misled by the suggestions of those who

---

1. The fact that certain Negro preachers and their congregations have made phonograph records and appear over the radio does not contradict our point. Here the participants were essentially worshippers and were performers only incidentally.

are unqualifiedly trying to raise him above his own foundations. Thus, some effort must be made to encourage the rural Negro to take pride in his own musical abilities.

Throughout most of the Deep South there are well-organized singing conventions. Among the Negroes these conventions are controlled by certain "professors" who form a type of musical oligarchy. These professors are for the most part very able in the matter of handling shape-note singing, whether it be in the very rudimentary stages or in the conducting of a chorus or convention composed of veterans. The whole process is done without a piano or organ. The professor sets the pitch, the rhythm, and the parts. Then, at a gesture, the syllables are sung, the "do, re, fa" of the common scale being used but usually being pronounced as "dah, ree, fah," and so forth. After this has been done to the satisfaction of the leader, the words are sung. This will be followed by another song that is treated in the same manner, only perhaps by a different leader.

Different districts or associations are frequently engaged in contests. No cause is more sufficient to start a contest than the casual boast of one leader in the presence of another or the avowed superiority of a rival organization. When these organizations are engaged in heated combat, the audience, which comprises the judges, is frequently left in a state of disagreement, which is sure to call for another battle at a designated time. It is necessary to see one of these contests in order to appreciate the great zeal put into them by all concerned. It is likely that most of the appeal is found in the rival leaders as they race about in front of their charges, gesticulating and giving audible encouragement.

If this type of music left these people developed culturally, then there might be some justification of it on that score. But even when one has learned all there is to know about shape-notes, he is still ignorant about the practices of singing legitimate music. Nine-tenths of the music and verse he has sung cannot do for him in fundamental good what some of his own magnificent songs can.[2] There would be

2. The fact that the better grade of music is not included in the shape-note books relegates the singer to inferior practices. If legitimate notes were taught, then the horizon would be enlarged a hundredfold.

less objection to the practice of shape-note singing were it not squeezing all of the creative interest out of these particular Negroes— Negroes who by right of association and of birth are best prepared to carry on the fine traditions founded by their forebears. There would also be less objection if the shape-notes formed only a part of the musical culture of these people. However, when one sits for an entire day and hears a group of naturally talented Negroes singing naught but the cheapest white hymns, he is forced to ask, in all fairness to the cause, "Quo vadis?" The fact is, I know of no case where a similar interest is taken in the singing of Negro music by Negroes in the rural districts, and my research has carried me into a great many rural districts of the South. As I have mentioned, there are a great many Negroes in these sections who are holding forth in the traditional manner of singing Negro music, to the extent that they are still creating spirituals, but this is not comparable in effect to the strength and influence of the shape-note singing conventions.

One day Professor Benjamin F. Bullock, one of my colleagues, carried me out to Red Oak, Georgia, to hear some Negro spirituals. When we arrived, we found that most of the people who sang in the church had gone to shape-note singing. This situation can be multiplied many times in various places in the rural South. The great fascination that shape-note singing holds for the talented Negro in these sections is a potent threat to the very existence of the spiritual among the people. It must be noted that the rural manner of singing the religious songs of the Negro is the real authentic source of information to which we must turn for authoritative examples. If the rural Negro entirely forsakes the spiritual (for any reason whatsoever), it would take only a generation for creativity in the area of Negro music to become sterile. If this were the case, then surely the following generation would be forced to function in the dimly charted sea without a compass. Even in this age of our proximity to folk sources, we are frequently in error, as I have shown. Without the stabilizing influence of the rural districts, the whole field associated with the spirituals is bound to suffer. It must be apparent that the aforementioned system of neglect and dilution caused by the growing zeal for shape-note singing is bound to take its toll at the gate of sound Negro heritage.

Not long ago I saw a book of spirituals and jubilees arranged for mixed voices in four parts, which was issued in two forms by a leading Negro publishing house. One form used the shape-note and the other used the standard note. One gathers from this situation that the shape-note edition was created with the rural Negro in mind, since urban Negroes do not use the shape-notes. Now, here is a strange case indeed, a case where "the patient has prescribed for the physician." The natural manner of the Negro should be permitted fuller development in the matter rather than be throttled by the injection of the arranged versions. Indeed, there can be very little, if any, justification for applying shape-notes to the spirituals in view of the fact that urban Negroes do not use them and rural Negroes should not use them.

While I was the director of music at Leland College in Baker, Louisiana, I had every opportunity to compare the students who had sung shape-notes with those who had not. The shape-note singers were superior in regard to the relationship of tones in the scale. Yet because of long practice in the wrong pronunciation of the scale syllables, together with various theoretical inaccuracies, the shape-note singers were forced to unlearn some things, in terms of their musical development, along legitimate lines. This proved to be a requirement that these students were all too often unwilling to meet. So, while both the students who had sung shape-notes and the ones who had not were about equally helpless when given a page of standard notes, in most cases the non–shape-note singers were more teachable and useful in the practice of singing music that required a knowledge of printed notes.

The final factor favoring the non–shape-note singer was the matter of the shape-note singer's unchallenged preference for standardized notation. On this point I have sometimes been asked whether or not the teaching of even legitimate notes in the rural schools will tend to weaken the development of the spiritual in the authentic manner. I am forced to say that it appears that such instruction would weaken the natural development of the spiritual. However, the existence of the rural school without the music would produce the same effect. Educational progress is indispensable, but it also exacts a toll. An exceedingly hard bargain should be driven in the unavoidable exchange: the greatest possible good must be asked in return for the obstruction of progress in any line.

The decline in the use of the old religious folk songs of the white man in America is largely due to the fact that these songs were taken up by the shape-note masters and placed in books bearing the general name *Shape-Note Hymn Book*. These books were the source of financial benefit to certain people and were thus looked upon as their property. Therefore, the general population did not feel that they really owned the songs. They looked upon the songs as belonging to a small group of experts who merely permitted the singing of the songs.

The use of shape-notes created a vogue which gave the South a special type of singing. But the shape-note singer was really a different kind of singer, one who was unorthodox from the standard point of view. So, as time brought the knowledge of standard notation into the possession of less developed people, shape-note songbooks were pushed aside. Standard notation, requiring greater scholarship and general intelligence on the part of its users, caused shape-note adherents to be considered musically antiquated and backward. Thus, the songs that were carried in shape-notes and set in the manner peculiar to their composers became socially as well as musically undesirable. In other words, when the vogue suffered, the songs did likewise.

The use of these shape-note songbooks also took away the freshness of the shape-note songs and delayed scholars' interest in them. If these songs had remained in the custody of the people, they would have picked up great folk color and would have been refined by the general use of the people, who alone could make the songs theirs by placing their creative stamp upon them. On the other hand, the Negro songs have been in a different situation. The collectors have taken these songs to heart as authentic representations of the folk. I harbor no disfavor with shape-notes as such, but when the cause of art is affected adversely by the means of conveyance or communication, then the purpose and duty of the scholar should be to point out the situation impartially.

In the example below, the scale is divided into trichords rather than into tetrachords. The first three notes make the first trichord, and the second three make the second. The fourth shape is placed in parentheses in order to make its suggestion clearer. Being the leading tone, the seventh degree was used less than the other tones. Hence, the people named this system "fa so la singin'."

Four Shapes

fa   sol   la   fa   sol   la   (mi)

The system below, with seven shape-notes, is more developed and is therefore more difficult. It is an attempt to compromise with the seven-note standard system. It is therefore named "do re mi singin'" by the people.

Seven Shapes

do   re   mi   fa   sol   la   si

The examples are taken from the *Harp of Columbia* by W. H. and M. L. Swan, who worked in the latter half of the nineteenth century.

The benefits of the shape-note, insofar as they affect the development of the rural Negro, surely cannot enter claim here. The standard music note, on the other hand, contains the glorious universal language of Johann Sebastian Bach, Ludwig van Beethoven, Richard Wagner, Frederic Chopin, Samuel Coleridge-Taylor, and R. Nathaniel Dett. Even there we would not want to welcome a total exchange. Throughout the years it may not be possible to manage two desirable but conflicting forces so that both may survive in the form of original design.[3] Only the ringmaster of time can assign a place to each

3. In a desire to develop the opera, Italy lost her interest in producing great song classics. Germany, in an effort to improve the opera musically (Wagner), lost interest in the production of great vocal technique.

of the factors. Let it be said, however, that if birthrights must go, then let them not go "for a mess of pottage." The Negro has bought his songs at a vicious, exorbitant, bludgeoning price. He is paying on the account yet. Only God knows how long he will remain the debtor.

Chapter 10

Has the Negro Borrowed His Songs?

The great volume of articles and books now being written on the subject of Negro music demonstrates the awareness that its inherent worth has generally awakened. It is doubtful if this folkloric interest finds a parallel in any other country or age known to man. Whereas most of the contributions have been inclined toward genuine appreciation and better understanding, the expected dissenting few have also made their way into print. The great preponderance of constructive work on the side of Negro music prevents the need for a general rebuttal to the claims of some writers who would change the public's mind in regard to the situation. However, there is one claim about the source of the spiritual that has gained a following far out of proportion to its apparent worth—the notion that the Negro borrowed his songs from the white man. In speaking to this subject, let me say that if Africa was incapable of creating the spiritual and the jubilee, so was America until the Negro came upon the scene. Two seemingly divergent continents found a medium in the black man, in whom they became an articulate power in the creation of art. It seems that this fact about Negro folk music is the most fundamental of the many facts I have discussed.

It can be said with authority, backed by a good deal of vigorous evidence, that the Negro often finds his music claimed by the white man with a sense of proud possession. When it is understood that the two races have lived side by side for so many years, it seems very reasonable that the white man has been stimulated into using Negro themes and motifs in his hymn-writing, especially when his avowed fondness for all forms of Negro music is considered. But it is less resourceful and less practical on the part of whites to resort to the use of slightly different words and, in some cases, to take over a spiritual entirely for use in a hymnbook while making no reference to its origin and then lending further obscurity to the songs by using English instead of the dialect.

We know definitely of two such cases in *The Revival No. 1* hymnal, a book very popular in the South during the 1890s. Here we find two well-known Negro songs, "Gimme Dat Ole-Time Religion" and "Pilgrim Song." In the case of "Pilgrim Song" ("Poor Wayfaring Stranger" in *The Revival No. 1*), we find that the person who set it down was not on the best terms with the music. One finds the tune set in a major key but trying to force its way to a minor key at every step. The time is four-four when three-four would be better. Any person who takes the time to compare these songs with the versions found in *Religious Folk-Songs of the Negro*, edited by R. Nathaniel Dett, will be rewarded. There are many titles in *The Revival No. 1* that suggest Negro verse, such as "Roll on the Gospel Chariot," "I'm a Pilgrim," "Some Mother's Child," "Oh, Mourner in Zion," and "Walking in the Light." The last-mentioned is found in *Religious Folk-Songs of the Negro* in a version very much like the one in *The Revival No. 1*, there being no similarity between the verses but a strong similarity between the refrains.

Of special interest to all students of folk songs is the rather recent attention a few scholars have given the so-called "white spiritual." Here is another instance of Negro spirituals being misconstrued as white, in this instance in the minds of collectors, because the spirituals were sung for them by white people. It must be borne in mind that many white people sing spirituals that were taught them by older members of their families, who had learned them from the singing done by their slaves or from old Negro servants who sang in their houses while working.

The mode of the white man's singing often lends the spiritual a resemblance to the jubilee. I doubt the advantage as well as the propriety of referring to the religious folk songs of the white man as "spirituals," insofar as the word is now synonymous with Negro music. Also, the fact that the word is an adjective and is used in this case as a noun supports the contention that it is a part of the Negro's early language. Of course, the word "spiritual" is English and was therefore learned from the white man. However, when the white man sings, he sings about the Spirit; whereas the Negro sings through his own spirit to and from the Spirit: "Ev'rytime I feel de spirit movin' in my heart I will pray," "Lord, I want to be a Christian in my heart," etc. Further, "spiritual" is a word inextricably bound up with the most unfortunate period in the history of the American Negro and was primarily molded by the coordinates of unrelenting sweat, abortive hope, and the driver's bullwhip. If indeed there be any justification in using the term "white spirituals," it seems to be a proposition entirely overlooked by the mass of white people, who at present are expending their efforts in a determined manner to sing the spirituals of the black man.

The success of some white singing organizations in rendering spirituals is remarkable, if judged from an unarbitrary viewpoint. This fact seems to vindicate Harry T. Burleigh's age-old contention that anyone who is sympathetic in his effort to understand and does not try to impersonate is capable of singing a spiritual effectively, if not in the same manner as a Negro would. Finally, it may be said in relation to this point that the Negro's conception of the word "spiritual" is in all appearances different from that of the white man. We have found instances of agreement only in the several cases where Negro spirituals are credited to the white man. Some of these instances have already been referred to, but I cannot refrain from mentioning a very striking case where a "white spiritual" and a Negro spiritual have a very striking similarity. Even in this case, as in regard to "Poor Wayfarin' Stranger," the white version is in the major and the Negro version in the minor.[1]

An examination of these two versions showed me a striking similarity in word and music, in spite of the difference in mode. This spiritual, in its Negro version, was sung for us by Ross and Stone of the Georgia Industrial College in Thunderbolt. A comparison of both versions would be of interest to the reader. It is, of course, impossible to prove that they are of the same origin or to prove which one came first. However, if the saying that "the late branch is inferior to the old" is adopted, then the Negro version must claim priority, for its

1. "The Other Shore" appears under the section containing white spirituals in *American Ballads and Folk Songs*, by John A. Lomax and Alan Lomax.

superiority speaks for itself, especially from a musical point of view. Certainly it is an instance where the Negro does not seem to have taken his leave of genuine, creative power.

There is another Negro version of this song called "Wonder Where Is Good Ol' Daniel" in R. Nathaniel Dett's collection *Religious Folk-Songs of the Negro*. This version is best related to the white version by its relationship to the preceding Negro one. The similarity between the two versions of the same name is even more striking. However, if the three are compared at once, the general pattern of all of them is arresting in its suggestiveness. There is certainly not an effort here to show that the white man has molded his religious folk songs from those of the Negro. This would be a very ungrounded surmise. However, it is the purpose here to show that while much has been said about the fact that the Negro has sometimes used the white man's motifs in his songs, it is also apparent that the white man has used the Negro's.

Here we have sought the truth, but not for the general application of a few instances, no matter how striking. The potter is greater than his clay, and it is to him that we must finally give homage rather than to the material that is molded in his hands. But for the Negro, there is little doubt that the songs now so eagerly claimed by white scholars would never have been generally known, even if one were to truly discover that in general Negro music did come from the white man's songs. It should be noted that only recently has George Pullen Jackson come forth with the volume *White Spirituals in the Southern Uplands*, a collection that comes more than a half century later than the first volume of Negro spirituals. This may lead one to believe that the Negro collection gave Jackson his cue. This would suggest that the folk activity of the Negro took root in a manner not discovered by others, and that he at least got his creative incentive in operation before the white man realized what was going on at his doorstep. This would further lead one to believe that the case against Negro music is in a large degree hypothetical. It certainly has to look backward through an uncertain past. The fact that the Negro has in certain cases done the natural thing of adapting an idea from his neighbor race is to be readily admitted. In fact, I am in favor of this being generally accepted by Negroes, but it simply is not true to say that all Negro music is nothing more than warmed-over white or European folk and church music.

If the Negro had produced only religious music, then the case would not be too strong against him, considering the evidence presented heretofore. For there are numerous examples of religious songs that in design and character are different from any of the religious songs of the white man. As an example, let us take one of the sermon-type jubilees. This style of singing, as the name implies, grew out of the preaching of the uneducated Negro. When he preaches, his voice intones his statements in a manner very much like that of the singer. In fact, at times he actually does sing phrases over and over, like weird cadenzas.

On the other hand, the minister may use a very few notes in the relating of a story taken from the Bible and ask the congregation to join in chanting a refrain at regular intervals. Out of this type of preaching grew a new mode of religious song, which I have named the song-sermon because it has all of the characteristics of Negro folk sermons. An example of the Negro song-sermon in shorter form is the well-known "Who'll Be a Witness?" which tells the stories of Daniel and Samson. However, one that is in longer form may serve our purpose better. There are enough of these alone to create an entire collection. The text follows:

De Han' Writin' on de Wall

Now God got angry on His throne,
Angels in heb'm begin to moan,
Dey droop dey wings to hide dey face,
An' Lord have mercy on de human race.
Now, go down angels an' consume de flood,
Blow out de sun an' turn de moon ter blood,
Den go back angels an' a-bolt de do',
Time done been, won' be no mo'.

You read in de Bible an' you understan',
King Belshazzar was a wicked man.
God walked down in Babylon one night,
You never did see such a wonderful sight.
De han' writin' was on de wall,

Go git Daniel, he can read it all.
Ol' Daniel come an' read de sign,
King Belshazzar den lost his min'.

Well Daniel come an' dere behol',
He read de writin' like a natu'al scroll,
Daniel read upon de wall,
King Belshazzar was about to fall.
Dere de writin' upon de clay,
Was de sign of de reck'nin' day.
King Belshazzar tremble' an' wail',
But he couldn't balance on my God's scale.

Chorus
Oh, what is dat yonder
On de wall?
Ah can't understan' it—
De han' writin'.
Oh, go an' git Daniel,
He can read it—
De han' writin' on de wall.

Other examples of this song type may be found in various anthologies of Negro music. (For the uninitiated, a few titles may be found in the Appendix of this book.) These are among the most powerful and convincing of any folk songs to be found in the world. As I have said, they represent a type unlike those sung anywhere else in this country.

Now, as to the Negro religious songs of a more conventional form, let us take "Swing Low Sweet Chariot," "Lord, I Want to Be a Christian," "Go Down Moses," "Steal Away to Jesus," and "Couldn't Hear Nobody Pray" and compare these to the mass of religious folk songs of the white man. What we find is that they, too, have an individuality that is worthy of being called original. Of course, in speaking of this whole matter, I am taking into consideration the fact that the pattern of folk music in this country, like many others, has a tendency toward the repetition of a given line and a refrain (also of one line). Also, I am aware that in many cases there is strict evidence of borrowing, but I insist that this borrowing works both ways. I also insist that the abundant majority of Negro music is not borrowed from any source. The Negro's music sprang from an actual need, and was born in most cases out of actual situations.

For an example, let us consider the early Negro concept of "getting religion." In order to be converted, one had to "go down in de lonesome valley" and find a praying ground, a place of solitude where he could go and fight out his salvation to the best of his ability. At his church he could and did have others praying for him, but this was merely a kind of spiritual encouragement for him to find salvation on his own:

> Brothers, if yo' want to find religion
> Go down in de lonesome valley.

This valley, of course, was a state of mind and was called "valley" in order to represent meekness and the subjugation of the spirit. In another example we have a literal statement from the scriptures referring to the above subject and emphasizing the method by which Negroes "got religion":

> Seek an' you shall find.
> Knock an' de door shall be open—

The devil was always presenting himself in different forms and seeking to prevent the seeker from remaining in the valley and visiting his praying ground:

> As I went down in de valley to pray, oh yes!
> I met ol' Satan on de way, oh yes!
> What do you think ol' Satan say, oh yes!
> You too young to die, so you too young to pray, oh yes!

The struggle with the devil was so severe that the seeker only came out from his praying ground supported by the Lord. This is one of the characteristic statements that give Negro songs the sign of genius and at the same time lend an unmistakable authenticity to their origin:

Ef you want to see Jesus
Go in de wilderness
Leanin' on de Lord.
I give de devil a battle
When I come out de wilderness,
Leanin' on de Lord.

The language and style of all of these statements must be acknowledged as belonging to the Negro by all who profess to know anything about his manner of expression. The circumstances that produced the inspiration also belong to the Negro folk heritage.[2]

Wherever primitive people live side by side with people of higher culture, it is true that the people of higher culture become fascinated with and adopt certain aspects of the primitive art. Music is one of the phases of art most desired; another is unique language expression. Where the Negro has gone in South America and Cuba, the influence of the Negro's music has been felt and adopted. His natural rhythmic endowments as well as his melodic gifts have produced a new music in each of these places. This is proof of the fact that Negroes have the power to create a music when confronted with a new order of life in a new environment, and that the singing of the southern white man in the United States was not the sole inspiration of the Negro in making new music. Of course, the situations are not entirely similar, but the principle is the same. It is not reasonable to assume that the Negroes brought to the United States had less native endowment than those carried to the Latin countries. Neither is it apparent that the feeling of Negro music has influenced the national music less in North America than in South America.

It is remarkable that it never occurred to the white southerner that the Negro had no music of his own—that the Negro was merely singing white music for these many years—until recent years, when such statements have been made repeatedly. The fact remains that in the South the music of the Negro is generally considered his, and the white college choirs and other white singing organizations have

2. These stanzas are not here to prove anything of a musical nature. They merely show that the Negro is capable of putting his actual life experiences into art forms which incidentally were set to music.

been eagerly singing Negro music and trying to render it as they have heard Negroes perform it. This indicates that the Negro folk feeling, which is at the core of all Negro music, is sought by white singers as much as is the music itself.

In order to be specific in this chapter, it is necessary to refer to George Pullen Jackson's chapter in *White Spirituals in the Southern Uplands,* entitled "Tunes of the White Man's Spirituals Preserved in the Negro's Religious Songs." In this chapter, Jackson, along with many others of his race (notably Richard Wallenschek, Guy B. Johnson, Newman White, and C. Sprague Smith), takes the position that Negro folk music in America is nothing more than variegated songs sung by the rural southern white people in camp meetings and conventions. In the first place, it should be understood by the reader that Jackson and Johnson use an unusually small number of songs in "proving" their point. As everyone knows who has been associated with Negro folk music, there are hundreds of Negro songs not in books — in fact, most of the Negro songs remain in the possession of the folk. Jackson uses about nineteen actual songs and cites twelve of those studied by Johnson. It goes without saying that this is not a reliable percentage and that anyone who makes such a general statement as the one made by Jackson would have to show a much larger percentage. In fact, the only fair way to support such a statement would be to make the large majority of Negro music available to the public and then show its relationship to white music in a direct line. Further, the songs used by Jackson are merely one small portion of one segment of Negro music. Surely one would not say that the music of the Negro can be summed up in so sketchy a manner as that shown in the chapter referred to above. Also, it is clear that the songs that Jackson uses are compared with Negro songs in other books, which means that the number and the field are further restricted.

When it comes to Negro folk music, much more is heard by ear than is seen when the notes have been set. The settings in many cases are and can be only approximations. Since white songs were sung to and from syllables, a setting of notes can be much more authentic for them than for Negro songs, which are always sung spontaneously. Additionally, the graphic aspects are not too reliable in Negro music, because there are so many versions of the songs. No such single analysis is sufficient to make a statement that Negro music is merely the worked-over music of the white man. It would have been better if these gentlemen had gone into the field and made a study of the variations in Negro music and then made comparisons with their holdings. If this had been done, it would have been seen that Negroes are never content with one version of a folk song, but that they constantly change the words and melodies of many of their own. Practically all of those that remain in constant use are so treated.

The five-tone scale is another evidence submitted by Jackson in his thesis. Here again it must be pointed out that the proof is not specific enough. The five-tone scale is not the sole property of any one person in the sense of origin. It was known and used by the Chinese centuries before China had free intercourse with the outside world. It was used by primitive peoples all over the world in the past and is used by many different races today. If some of the music of the East has more complex scale systems, it is no point against the principle here—that a common scale feeling is based on the natural three stages of vocal music development, namely, the shout stage, the pitch stage, and finally the song stage. All of the stages were, of course, founded upon the natural ability of the human instrument to find its way into full musical usefulness. If the five-tone scale "sounded good to the ears of the Negro," it naturally had the right to do so.

In regard to the songs sung in the early rural South by the settlers, it is true that they did not have songs that bore only the marks of their musical feeling. It is a fact, therefore, that the principle of song—using the voice with music and words—was worked out by the cooperation of many peoples. The fruits of this activity found a meeting ground in ancient Rome where, during the time of Nero, song became homogenized and later, under the influence of the early Christians, became the working force of the church. Later, through the work of persons of different nationalities in the Catholic Church, the art of group singing became a finished product, reaching its highest stage of development in the sixteenth century in the hands of Giovanni Pierluigi da Palestrina, Tomas Luis de Vittoria, and

William Byrd. The singers referred to by George Pullen Jackson were and are direct beneficiaries of these forces, which means they have done in principle what the Negro has done: They have used the musical development of peoples other than themselves to express what they felt. The pattern of the religious songs used by rural white people in the South show this fact all too clearly for it to be misunderstood. However, I take the position that this power on the part of a people is evidence of alert creative genius and not one of weakness, since the principle applied in general is the basis for the entire progress of the world. Nor do I agree that because of some similarities in artistic products that the conclusion should be drawn that the producer of the second product drew all of his inspiration and power from the producer of the former.

Immediately following Jackson's above-mentioned chapter is another entitled "White Man's and Negro's Spirituals Texts Compared." Here Jackson takes twenty-eight pages of texts from white songs and Negro songs and arranges them side by side in order to show that the Negro texts are duplications, modifications, or remnants of the white texts. Again, the material is not of sufficient quantity. However, something may be said in regard to the quality of the comparisons. It seems that in many places the comparisons bear out what is hereby admitted, that the Negro did and does take some of the white man's music and words both with and without modifications. However, it does not prove that he has created nothing of his own. In fact, many of the comparisons seem to be strained; for instance:

1. *White*
   And will she have other comrades on board
   Negro
   She's loaded down with angels

2. *White*
   She's waiting now for a heavenward gale
   Negro
   O de ship is at de landin'

3. *White*
   Come along and go with me
   Negro
   Come along if you want to get to hebben[3]

4. *White*
   The cords wrapped around his sweet hands
   Negro
   O they bound him with a purple cord

These are mere suggestions of the many similar situations found in the above-named chapter. They shed an interesting light on much of Jackson's procedure.

Of course, the words do not prove anything about the music, since the two are entirely separate considerations. If the Negro had taken all of his texts from the white man's hymns, it would not mean that the music was necessarily the same. The use of the same words has been a practice of composers and peoples for ages. When one speaks of folk music, one is thinking primarily about the tune and only secondarily about the words. I realize the importance of the words, for without words we cannot sing. However, words cannot prove anything about the music, and music cannot prove anything about the words. The two are separate arts, each in its own right. Again, I must mention the fact that the Negro resets his own texts. This is an important factor with the Negro, because his folk music has been more active through the years than that of the white man. It is not necessarily a racial peculiarity. It is my opinion that folk music is at its worst when found in books. Yet no other way has been found to preserve it for general purposes—performance and discussion, in particular. Therefore, one must be careful, when consulting books, not to be influenced too much by the mere appearance of things.

The development of Negro music in the United States resolves itself into the following:

3. Surely the Negro's religion caused him to desire to get to heaven, if it had any meaning at all to his primitive mind.

1. Negroes adopted many songs outright.

2. White people borrowed many songs from the Negro. Stephen Foster was not by himself. He was completely honest regarding his inspirations. He was a great songwriter who did not have to rely on Negro themes. He merely loved them. Many other white composers on the folk level who used Negro songs are not so famous.

3. Many songs are in a state of doubt because of the two influences being shown in them on an almost equal basis—Negro and white.

4. A great wealth of Negro songs are independent of white origins. A great store of these are to be found in the seculars as well as in the religious realm.

5. Having great gifts as folk composers, Negroes reworked many white songs and thus saved them from oblivion. Their treatment extends to the words, tones, and rhythm. This principle of composition was followed by every great composer who ever lived. They all took inspiration from sources outside of themselves and refined the original until it shone in eternal luster.

Chapter 11
The Wheel in a Wheel

Religious folk music of the American Negro is proving to be a constantly widening enigma for those who, by right of birth and association with its fundamental idioms, should not find themselves so puzzled. Recently we have had a rather copious, determined effort on the part of some men in America, Europe, and even Africa to reduce Negro music in general to its simplest terms, and perhaps they have done the best that their knowledge has permitted. On the one hand, we are happy that our music has attracted such scholarly attention. But on the other hand, we are forced to feel unhappy about the fact that some of the damage done to our sublime songs is in a sense irreparable.

Certainly every man has the right to react in a very personal way to his life experiences, but it has to be admitted that these reactions often overstep the bounds of good judgment, leading to most unfortunate practices and then, inevitably, to unhappy ends. Much of the white man's work in Negro music has been legitimate and serviceable. But when it comes to the point where our white songwriters take unto themselves the right to compose jazz songs and refer to them as new spirituals, a sad day has come for them. It is a sadder day for American artistic values. Such profane, avowedly commercial attempts are always certain to place the perpetrators in the position of not being in harmony with art. When it is true that so many remarkable songs of the Negro are as yet unknown to the general public, it is obvious where the emphasis of these enthusiasts should be, if they are to persist in their work in Negro spirituals.

There are three main sources from which these so-called "new spirituals" come. One is the surge of interest (recently seen in the moving-picture industry) to find commercial media for things Negro.

The commercial industry is first and most flagrant in its lack of understanding of Negro music. To fit the industry's commercial needs, such titles as "Going to Heaven on a Mule," "Bend Down Sisters," "Sing You Sinners," and so forth have been used as themes for jazz songs. In some cases they have been sung by comedians and referred to as "new spirituals." However, when one considers the commercial setting in which these songs appear, it is difficult to determine which is the greater evil—calling the above songs "spirituals" or using the real spirituals in such unseemly settings, distorting their Negro heritage.

The second source from which so-called "new spirituals" come is the composed opera. Here the situation seems paradoxical enough. The Negro spiritual is not sufficient to bring reality to the score, so the author writes his own "spirituals" so as to add luster to the Negro theme. He objects to having them referred to as anything but Negro, because his vaunted original purpose would be undermined. However, in his eagerness for acclaim as a maker of "Negro spirituals," he proclaims boldly that he has originated some "Negro spirituals"—a question that can be best determined by a test. There are several sources in the country qualified to be of vital assistance in this matter. Up to this writing I know of no single instance of favorable comment coming from any of them.

There also remains the situation where the jazz orchestra has invaded the realm of the spiritual for so-called novel dance effects. In fairness, it should be stated that if the white man created the vogue, he did not do so without help from the Negro himself. The deplorable sterility of some dance orchestra arrangers is notorious. Their leeching rapaciousness is too well known to warrant treatment here. It should be pointed out, however, that they are indeed becoming almost intolerably indifferent to musical values as well as to religious prerogatives. Here, for once, it seems that the public has not been in agreement with the system that would cause it to dance to religious music that has been wrung from the very souls of black men by generations of sorrow. Perhaps it would be best not to mention names, in view of the fact that there has been no effort on our part to prepare a catalogue of all those who have been guilty of the aforesaid malpractices. Nonetheless, this condition is well known.

We are particularly aware of the deplorable dance treatment of the universally loved "Swing Low Sweet Chariot" and the jazz version of "Deep River." Practically all of the leading Negro dance orchestras have used the latter spiritual with a different word setting.

There is a third source from which so-called "new spirituals" come. In some respects it is even less desirable than the two preceding sources. It is the present standard for programs encountered in some of the concert halls, those heretofore "holies of holies" for the music patron. Whether the times have caused some concert singers to cater to the masses in an effort to fill the box office cash register, or whether the general taste has been warped by so much musical confusion poured out over the radio, the fact remains that the so-called "program novelties" are very much on the increase in the cases of several well-established singers. Press notices preceding various concerts point out with emphasis that the singer is by public demand going to sing several novelties of various temperaments. I reserve the following discourse for an appraisal of one of these novelties that has a Negro background and has been referred to recently as a spiritual by some commentators in their program notes.

My first hearing of the composition of which I speak was at a concert in a large southern city given by a then-eminent singer, Clement Wood. The program note called the piece a "new Negro spiritual" composed by Jacques Wolfe.[1] The rendition of the song was received with great acclaim, and the singer was forced to resort to every courteous resource in his nature to avoid having to repeat it. This state of affairs is striking when it is understood that this happened in a city of the South, which is accustomed to genuine spirituals being sung in the traditional manner. Upon leaving the concert, my interest led me to procure a copy of "De Glory Road" and make a careful examination of its makeup.

Clement Wood has written at least three Negro poems that have been set to music by Jacques Wolfe. No reference is made on the cover of this particular song which would suggest to the layman that a spiritual was the goal of the collaborators. We are therefore forced

1. We cannot say that Wolfe or Wood had in mind that the composition should be called a spiritual. We are dealing with effects.

to accept the notice given in our concert program—that it is a "new spiritual." Wood's poem reveals that he has engaged in careful study to acquire a proficiency in writing Negro dialect. His method of spelling and his sentence structure seem characteristic enough, except in one or two places where the past participle would have been better than the simple past tense of the verb and where the use of an apostrophe would have been better than the use of a spelling invention. For instance, "back or sin," should be "back o' sin," just as "de Lord sang" should be "de Lord sung."

When Wood's message is unraveled from the poem, it is disappointing in every way to those who have any true conception of the religious makeup of the Negro. In his spirituals and jubilees the Negro always conceives of God speaking as He spoke to Moses and to Paul and to Elijah. No record is found where God is represented as being ridiculous. His horses are always milk white and never scarecrows. His voice is sometimes terrible and sometimes soft and comforting, but never does it suggest to the Negro the hooting of an owl, as one would glean from Wood having God call "whoo-ee!" to the sleeping Negro. The climax of the episode comes when Wood has even God call one of his disciples "niggah" and when the Devil proclaims, "I am gwine ter kotch a Niggah fur ter roast in Hell." The mere suggestion of roasting "niggahs" seems to lessen rather than strengthen the hope that the approach is sympathetic. No one uses "nigger" more than the Negro himself. He does so rather facetiously. I have found the word used in many seculars, but I have never heard the term used in any Negro religious songs.

From a musical point of view, Wolfe has done practically the same thing as Wood. The piano accompaniment uses rolls, syncopates, and various jazz movements without regard for any of the style of the spirituals. The composition abounds in sudden dynamic extremes and variegated rhythms, seemingly in an effort to arouse a feeling of austerity. However, at best it does little more than travel along in a vain attempt to bring reality to an unreal situation. Perhaps there are those who feel that the music is good. However, when it is understood that the religious folk music of the Negro is the background out of which "De Glory Road" was drawn, the best that can be said is that the song is a very unkind and ungrateful caricature of a most important form of American music. I am wondering where a parallel situation can be found in the religious music of any other country.

In the foregoing matter, only casual reference has been made to the Negro's part in creating a serious misunderstanding of Negro music. The Negro has been called upon in so many different circumstances to sing his songs that he has sometimes become confused as to whether he should sing as he does when there is absolutely no hint of beckoning approval from the gallery or whether he should sing for the circumstances. This statement is not meant to berate our Negro students for the many instances when they have sung spirituals on the concert stage. On the other hand, we are in a position to say that the Negro college alone is the most convenient purveyor of their performance. Since Fisk University so ably pioneered the performance of Negro religious music, the Negro colleges of the South have, with a few exceptions, maintained the dignity and sincerity so inherently a part of the songs. Indeed, Fisk, Hampton, Tuskegee, and Atlanta have without exception been bulwarks of tradition in keeping the religious music of the Negro before the Negro youth and the general public.

Any person fortunate enough to hear the students in these colleges sing spirituals during their regular chapel services is familiar with the great inexplicable power the singing always brings to the listener. There is undoubtedly a difference between this singing and that heard at a rural Negro church or a camp meeting, but the striking effect is similar in both instances. The peculiar vocal timbre and mass harmonic effect of voluntary parts, together with the authentic relationship to the mood as well as the mode, have cast an inspiration not like that found elsewhere over those who have come under its spell. Likewise, a person hearing Roland Hayes sing spirituals for the first time is suddenly aware of a swelling tide of all those finer emotions involved in the pursuit of life surging through every fiber of his being. The effect here is quite extraordinary, though Hayes lacks the advantages of a harmonic pattern formed by many voices and many sympathetic, understanding spirits. It seems that this comparison of effect would tend to support the principle that it is necessary to feel as well as to understand the spirituals in order to sing them as they should be sung.

Unfortunately, some Negro singing organizations have evidently taken the singing of spirituals and jubilees as a matter of personal privilege. Seemingly in an effort to give a realistic presentation of the spirituals, they have attempted to depict the actions of Negroes under the spell of religious excitement. Of course, this suggests the ridiculous insofar as it is done for the audience's benefit. Additionally, the piano has always been out of place when used to accompany the singing of spirituals. Not only do many of our groups use the piano in their concertizing, but they do so in a very questionable manner. The accompaniment is too often played in a manner that suggests the fox trot or ragtime. The only reason I can think of to explain this kind of accompaniment is that it meets the commercial interests of the performers.

While visiting a Negro college some years ago, I had my one and only experience of hearing a college student body sing spirituals to piano accompaniment, although I had heard a few high school groups do so. In this particular instance, a white visitor on the rostrum asked that the piano be omitted. My chagrin was complete. In my opinion, the singing of the Hall Johnson choir is a fitting challenge to the various professional organizations specializing in spirituals and jubilees. Johnson's choir shared equally with Richard B. Harrison in making *The Green Pastures* the artistic success that it was. Although the songs sung by this choir were all arranged, and although the progressions were in many places striking in their individuality, the manner as a whole was always compelling and true to life. How else could it have produced such thrilling effects throughout the play, especially the tramping scene where "Lord, Ah Don' Feel No Ways Tired" is sung? Here again it is a matter of sympathetic understanding being unremittingly wedded to sincere purpose, which conveys to the listener an unfailing sense of vital realism.

During the last fifteen years a type of Negro quartet has appeared in the theater, the concert field, and often over the radio which is not suited by temperament or experience for the task it has undertaken. Too often it is obvious that the popularity of the jazz quartet's singing has decoyed the attention of these otherwise potentially useful organizations. Instead of the ever-beautiful humming accompaniment so characteristic as a background for the leader and his verse, a jazz motif is emitted often in an altogether unintelligible species of growls, and the song is deliberately ended on the tonic seventh. This situation is not a deliberate attempt on the part of the untrained Negro singer to cheapen his songs, but is rather a lack of the power to differentiate between values brought to him by radio, phonograph, and direct contact. Naturally, he chooses those that seem most acceptable to the public, wishing thereby to gain public favor for his own effort. Despite my foregoing criticisms, there are yet many Negroes who hold to the sanctity of the spiritual. The fact that they will often sing them for profit in no way differentiates them from the minister who looks for a reward for his services.

It should be understood from the foregoing discussion that the jazz quartet style has been brought under attack. Obviously the point stressed here is that, insofar as it is largely the frank imitation of a Negro jazz band, the style should by all means be relegated to its proper place. If there can be any virtue in the voice being employed as a trumpet or saxophone, I leave it for other hands to prove. To be fair, it must be said that the Blue Jay Singers, a Birmingham quartet that antedated the present period by several years, used a jazz style very much like that being used today. This instance would seem to indicate the possibility that this practice had been going on unnoticed for quite some time, until the great exploitation period after the First World War caused it to be publicly disclosed by the phonograph.[2]

During my teaching period at the State Teachers' College at Montgomery, Alabama, the "L. & N." and the "Maggie Street" quartets frequently appeared on the radio, singing spirituals and jubilees in a manner very similar to that of the Blue Jay Singers. It is very likely

2. Very often a collector may venture forth in an effort to find the traditional Negro singing so much talked of these days. When he has made several records in various places, from "barber-shops to baggage-wagon," his research will not always be the kind of representation it is intended to be. The process of selection based upon first-hand knowledge of the subject must aid the collector. He would do well to remember that Negro music is sung inspirationally. The social status of the Negro who sings it is not the sole guarantee of its authentic worth. In *American Ballads and Folk Songs,* William McDonald, a Mississippi State Farm convict, added to his rendition of "This Train" a coda representing a train whistle. While "This Train" is a very cheap jubilee, it is never sung that way except in an effort to "show off."

that these two quartets were inspired by the Blue Jay Singers and that their being elevated to the status of radio performers caused other more authentic groups to follow in their wake. The solution to this condition rests entirely with the Negro. The great mass of Negroes must be made conscious of the vastly inferior qualities found in their false conceptions of stylistic advantage. More training is needed in the schools, especially the rural schools, with regard to the true nature of Negro music. The time has come when the great mass of Negroes can no longer be left to their own methods insofar as public performance is concerned. It is a challenge to the Negro, who by right of primary contact with the source, as well as by right of training, is qualified to look forward and backward and visualize a focal point of balance. This is necessary if Negro music, especially religious music, is to be used as a performance medium. Otherwise, no unity of purpose can ever be attained.

The spirituals and jubilees would then be happier left undisturbed in the use for which they were created—to be the sole possession of the people who make and use them from real necessity. To understand this last phase, more detail is needed. Hence, chapter 12 should be considered a projection of the ideas suggested herein.

Chapter *12*
The Folk Festival

Fort Valley State College has the most unique enterprise of a folk nature held by any of the Negro colleges to come under my notice—the Fort Valley State College Folk Festival. The origin and history of the festival is best told by the man who conceived of it, Horace Mann Bond:[1]

> The Fort Valley State College Folk Festival began as an annex to a conventional college–high school music festival. The idea of a Folk Festival came to several persons at Fort Valley, including the President, Horace Mann Bond, after a visit one day to a rural church. The singing of the people was wonderful. There is no better word for it; yes, it was exactly and perfectly wonderful. So, then, at a Festival intended to teach young Negro high school students an appreciation of music, why not have a session or two devoted to the Folk and to their perfectly wonderful music?
>
> A sound idea; in practice, it did not work. The Folk need a Festival of their own; the people do not like to be on exhibition; they have come to the Fort Valley State College Festival because it was their own, and among themselves they felt at home. After 1940, therefore, we have held the Folk Festival separately. Beginning in 1941, we scheduled the Folk Festival at the same time that the annual Ham and Egg Show is held. This ancient event, now in its 29th year, is purely a folk event; the Father of the Ham Show, County Agent O. S. O'Neal, is a man of the folk, and for a quarter of a century the annual Show has brought the folk

1. W. W. E. Blanchet, dean of the college; L. R. Bywaters, business manager; C. V. Troup, now president of the college; and Troup Daniels, bus driver and talent scout, have been invaluable in their efficiency and cooperation.

to the College for a day all their own. The Folk Festival added a last touch needed to round out the Ham Show, the natural element of the people's music to the people's holiday.

So, the festival at Fort Valley was the outcome of two significant events. These were, first, the development of the Ham and Egg Show under the guidance of County Agent O. S. O'Neal and, second, the coming of Horace Mann Bond to the college as its president.

Any description of the festival would be a half-truth if the Ham Show were neglected, for this spectacle furnishes the atmosphere for the secular phase of the festival, which occurs on Friday night. The festival is held in the auditorium of the academic building. It is a room ideally suited to the purpose of housing this event. It is a rather plain room with a blind side where a hallway passes along the west wall. The stage faces south and is rather modestly draped with curtains of maroon velour, which do not have the newness that would cause them to seem artificial. Directly facing the stage is a low balcony equipped with rural-church-type benches. The outside wall, on the east, opens by windows and doors onto a perfectly rural scene— shanties, gardens, farms in the distance, a lone dirt road only twenty feet away, and magnificent trees. The ceiling vaults up two stories, giving the well-worn oak floors the proper counterbalance to produce a very resonant tone quality. Singing sounds delicious here.

O. S. O'Neal drapes the stage, and in fact the entire northern end of this very unique room, with hams of all sizes, shapes, and degrees of cured odors. There are whole cured pigs and whole sides of cured meat hanging over head. Thousands of eggs garnishing the proscenium spread out toward the audience and descend gradually to the floor. They find their way over a ramp suffering with more hams, more bacon, more eggs—more and more and more. There is always enough room on the stage for the participants who have come "to be in de festival."

After a day during which all who wished have had barbecue, soda water, and much good fellowship, the people move to the auditorium, and soon "de firs' night" is under way. The participants are presented according to number. Each person or leader draws a slip from a hat, which determines his place on the program. These performers are "geetah pickers," "hawp blowers," "banjer pickers," "pieanna playahs," "washboard beaters," and a variety of lesser lights. Some use childish inventions involving bricks, wire, Coca-Cola bottles, "quills," saws, and bones.

An experience never to be forgotten is seeing and hearing Bus Ezell come onto the stage, "geetah" in hand and "hawp" on a rack about his neck, and take his introduction with all the dignity of Caesar Augustus. I had not yet spoken to him personally, but I could see that he was a remarkable man. He is a genius who, but for this festival, would be unknown to most people. In fact, as he sits in his chair, one might mistake him for one of the more personable rural preachers or "big" country farmers. He is a man of rather stocky build, with a bronze complexion. His age is uncertain, but he is well preserved. Except for a slight limp, the result of an accident sustained during his "loggin' days," he is physically active to a very satisfactory degree.

As he gives his performance, Ezell sings and plays his harmonica alternately. His voice is one of the most powerful vocal organs I have ever encountered. He shakes the large room with his music, as both feet beat out a folk rhythm and his guitar twangs a very metallic accompaniment. Suddenly, Ezell begins a monologue, which grows out of the text of his song, only to swing back into the singing in perfect time and harmony. Before he has gone very far, the excitement of the capacity audience (more than a thousand) has reached such proportions that even the great voice of Ezell cannot be heard to advantage. It is almost pandemonium. His pet rendition reaches its climax in:

> Hitler tried to fool de Negroes
> By sayin' dey ought not to fight.
> Dey has no home or country,
> No flag or equal rights.
> But de Negro knewed de bes',
> Dey deeds did prove de res'.
> Dere's strange things a-happenin'
> In de lan'.

Once when I spoke to Ezell about his having won the first prize so often, he said: "'Fess,' you knows me! I plays de songs lak dey ought to be. Dem' other boys jes tries." By comparison, he is right. In fact, on more than one occasion the other contestants threatened never to return if Ezell continued to compete. He makes it difficult for them because of his great creative ability and his native histrionics. For instance, he sings:

> Airplanes cross de ocean
> Ninety-nine miles in de air.
> All our soldiers boun' to lan' over dere.

> Goodby mamma and papa
> Don't you moan an' cry.
> All us soldiers knows we's born to die!

Other talented and clever performers who have shown their wares at the festival are Gus Gibson (singer and guitarist), Sanders and Duffy (guitarist), Duffy and Snead (guitarist), and Buster Brown (harmonica player). All of these men show originality and a unique sense of performance quite out of the ordinary. With the exception of Gibson (now deceased), they constitute the real fiber of the festival's night of secular music. The people love the festival. They really own it. The festival moves by, through, and for them.

As has been noted, the main instrument of this occasion is the guitar. Negroes have long loved this instrument. It is melodious, cheap, and easy to play their music on. It is carried easily, and it blends well with their feelings. The tuning of the instrument is a thing of interest, in a folk sense. The tuner uses both accepted and personal tuning systems. We find the instruments tuned in "Spanid" (Spanish), in "stancher" (standard), and in various other personal ways. Sometimes a man will tune his guitar in a personal way and name the tuning after himself—for instance, the "Johnson Special." While I will not take the time to try to explain these systems from a technical standpoint, it may be said that the tunings used represent a variety of harmonic possibilities. In playing, however, the performers use few chord changes, but rather depend on dynamics, figurations, and rhythms to do the main job of accompanying the words. Seldom does anyone play the guitar as a solo instrument.

The grandest and most worthwhile part of the festival comes on

Sunday afternoon, following the Saturday-night barn dance. This occasion, which brings the festival to a dynamic close, is what may be called "the light"—the light that shines through the artists like multifaceted prisms. During the four years I served as director of this festival, the singing and the occasion always left its mark on my spirit. Whenever I hear Negro music anywhere, there is a spontaneous reliving of that music within me.

The singers are invited to come to the festival by postcard, handbill, letter, word of mouth, and, on a few occasions, radio. The people who come are instrumental in bringing others. One of the thrills of the whole venture is the vigil that begins at the college on the night before the rally. This waiting and watching to see who is going to arrive is like any other game of chance—the die is cast, so you must wait. Despite the fact that we receive assurances from some of the singers that they will participate, some of them do not show up. Some arrive who were not expected, and some arrive who are always present. Others come and leave, only to return later, sometimes too late.

The main arrival of the people on the campus formally starts at about noon on Sunday and continues to gain force until the affair begins. The modes of transportation constitute an entire folk experience of their own. All kinds of cars, trucks, and buses of every vintage are lined up, representing the progress, the patience, the bravery, and the daredevilry of the human race. Strolling about the college yard listening to the fine-spirited conversation, the beautiful laughter, the greeting—all create a human symphony that seems to catch up the full sweep in the folkloric score. For instance, Sam Jackson says to me: "Hello 'Fess,' how's you gettin' 'long. I sho-o-o is glad to see you. You ain't give me up, is you? When Sam Jackson say he go' do somethin', he mean he go' do it. Is I got some new songs? Hm-m-m, ev'time you sees me I got some. I loves 'em."

Singin' Sam Jackson is one of the most gifted folk singers in the South. His singing is not as loud as Ezell's. Neither is it of a particularly pleasing tone quality, but it is fascinating in a stylistic way. It has the spark of a genuine genius behind it. The voice resembles the man—dark, rather small, energetic, friendly, and authoritative. Jackson is also marvelous as a leader of people. Jackson's means of livelihood is that of "spiritual doctor." He claims to have "set down" (not to have learned to walk) for more than twice the period children usually do. He claims that during this period he was in the process of getting his superior powers. At any rate, when last heard from, Singin' Sam was established in Atlanta. From there he found time to commute to Fort Valley once or twice a month to "look a'ter bizness" there. On one occasion, Jackson showed Horace Bond, John Work, and me some candles of rather familiar appearance, which he said would do remarkable things for anyone who would "burn 'em at odd hours."

Just alighting from a truck is an aged brown man with a barrel chest, a mischievous face, a pair of squat legs, and a personality so fetching that the mere presence of Bill Edwards on the stage or on the floor sends a tingling sense of approval scudding through the audience.

"Professor" Bell, from Baxley, Georgia, is one of the most sophisticated leaders. However, he is definitely on the folk level. His arrival is generally effected by a large orange-colored bus and white driver. He indeed looks the part of his title. Although he worked at a Baxley "sody water factory," from appearances Bell could have been a small-town dentist, lawyer, or doctor. He would say to me: "Hello 'fessor. Now anything you don't understand, I'm willing to help. Ef you don't min' I got some new ways o' singin' this year. But I guess yo' better tell me what yo' think dese folks will like—same as las' year? All my boys ain't here. De war got some." When it comes to sheer organic singing, Bell's group is the best group ever to come to Fort Valley. He comes infrequently, but percentage-wise he has won more "firsts" than anyone else. He is not the singing character that some of the others are. He is a teacher.

At the main door of the auditorium, everyone is greeted by Maggie Clark, a master singer from New York, Georgia; Beady Gay, composer-singer from Byron, Georgia; and Consiwella Soloman, a summer student of Fort Valley State College and a teacher in Montezuma, Georgia, who also is a very good trainer of singers a bit above the folk level. One also meets many others who come to hear the performance. They too are a part of the festival. Just inside the main door of the auditorium is a table that is arranged for registration. Each leader registers the name of his organization and his two or three selections. He is straightaway given his place number and checked to see if his songs are really Negro folk songs and not just hymns. While this is taking place, other groups are singing in the various classrooms, in the hallways, and on the stairs in a last "warmin'."

At three o'clock the auditorium is more than full with the various singing organizations, which are seated across the front of the room in close order. The audience is seated in the rear and in the balcony. The master of ceremonies rises from his chair, at the extreme right of the stage, and speaks a word of welcome before introducing Horace Bond, who gives a brief summary of the "Festival Idea" and expresses his desire that each participant will have a joyous visit to the campus and festival. The master of ceremonies returns to center stage and explains the rules and the conditions governing the competition, as set forth on the handbills. These items are as follows:

Cash Awards

Best Choir	$20
Second Best Choir	$15
Third Best Choir	$10
Best Glee Club or Quartet	$15
Second Best Glee Club or Quartet	$10
Third Best Glee Club or Quartet	$ 5

Rules of the Singing Rally

1. All choirs and quartets must sing only Negro spirituals or jubilees.
2. All choirs, glee clubs, or quartets are asked to be on the grounds by 2:00 P.M., Sunday, July 26, 1942, to register.
3. All music must be sung without piano or any music sheets or books.
4. All organizations which have not been on these programs before must "try out" before being admitted.
5. The judges and not the audience will make the decision for the awards.

With this done, the master of ceremonies announces the opening prayer, usually led by either Deacon Walker of Oak Grove or Deacon Smith of Byron. One of these men brings the meeting into focus with a devoutly uttered supplication. The voice rises, falls, and breaks away into unbelievably beautiful cadences. The figures of speech are the kind that have made the Negro unique as a master of praying and preaching. One finds in these men praying in the college auditorium the same earnestness one would find if they were praying while kneeling on the bare, unfinished floors of their humble churches. The audience catches the spirit of the moment and begins to "answer." The thread of inspiration spins itself into a maze of moving power that is felt more than heard. The great moment is present. But, content with this service, Deacon Smith leads a song, an art of which he is a master. As his tremulous voice begins to sing the first phrase, a thousand others catch up the melody. A foot-patting rhythm begins to move the tempo along and the sound swells into a flood of sheer power and vocal beauty, a power not realized often during an entire lifetime. Charged by this spell, several other leaders will "raise" their own songs, moving to the front and giving an exhibition of rare song-leading mastery. The birth of the "rally" has been achieved by the folk impulse. So moving is the moment that the master of ceremonies must be careful not to become too engaged in the group action.

Eventually the number calling forth the first group of singers is announced, and the leader begins his "marchin'" song or theme song. Slowly, with an almost flowing motion, these singers take their places on the stage. The titles are announced and the singers begin. There is no singing like that of a group of Negro folk singers inspired by the presence of an audience composed largely of the people to whom they are accustomed, and supported by those who may be looked upon as better trained (but less efficient in the things that make up real living).

Sam Jackson stands on the end of his choir line for an instant. Then, making a sort of genuflection, he runs to the fore, turns himself half around, and "sets off" his choir. As the music grows in power, Jackson raises his hand or hands above his head as though giving a sermon at its highest point. When he comes to the verse, there is a peculiar catch in his glottis and a vital, fiery glow in his eyes, and his long, keen face moves in a series of powerful spirit-reflecting nuances. Wheeling like a frightened child, he will dance upstage with the shuffling gait that was borrowed from his ancestors of the dim past. Spinning dervish-like, Jackson again takes personal note of his fascinated singers, leading them more by the power of what he has just accomplished than by further action. The excitement of the audience is such as to make mere formality impossible. Even Jackson must surrender to his own charging spirit.

William ("Professor") Bell mounts the podium, clad in a white silk jacket, white pants, and holding a baton. He beats a rather personal cadence and causes his sixteen male singers or his twenty mixed singers to sing as though he were not present. His flair for costume has his mixed singers attired in high school graduation gowns, although most of them are above thirty years of age. The matter of shoe color is left to the pleasure of the chorister, and the result is green, red, black, white, tan, and various mixtures—all shades that are generally seen in the month of August.

The Baxley choir always takes high rank, and it especially appeals to those who are more or less in the realm of the new sophisticates. Yet for sheer driving power and primitive, unleashed emotional surge, there is nothing quite like the Bill Edwards choir from Americus, Georgia. In the first place, Edwards is certainly one of the most powerful singers in the world. This power is combined with a native comedy and fervent dignity. He is a great master of pantomime and innuendo. He makes faces at the audience and at his singers without being aware of it. He directs his singers from the end position by heaving and throwing his great barrel chest. Sometimes he lifts a foot for a note or just squints an eye. Often he will lift his eyes above the audience and point his finger as though directing an invisible choir. Then with a deft motion he will lower his head, laugh with ecstasy, and rub his face as if to reawaken his earthly consciousness. The singers and the audience catch his powerful spirit and rejoice in it. When Edwards sings "Yo' Caint Hide!" the images are as the real visions in the Day of Judgment. The song itself finds the "real self" of everyone present and reveals it.

Other groups with striking originality and folk dynamics are present with original songs and techniques. High among these are the following from Georgia:

Organization	Leader	Location
New York Choir	Mrs. Mammie Clark	New York
Golden Jubilee Singers	Mr. Marvin McCrary	Dooling
First Baptist Choir	Mrs. Beady Gay	Byron
Middle Georgia Singers	Mr. H. P. Purnell	Macon
Silver Moon Singers	Mr. Joe Brown	Macon
Pearly Gate Choir	Mr. Albert Scott	Roberta
Silver Moon	Mr. Sam Rucker	Fort Valley
Kennedy Brothers[2]	Mrs. Kennedy	Fort Valley

When the judges retire to make their decisions regarding the winners, the meeting is given over to the singers and the audience. Here one finds the most spirited singing of the entire session. By the time this happens, all of the people have become one large family. The leaders engage in a free-for-all, "catch-as-catch-can" singing tourney. The time has come for the final test as to who the "champ'n songster" is. The audience is the choir, except when some bolder soul yells out insistently for one of the leaders or organizations to take over the proceedings for the rendition of a favorite song previously sung or not included in the fare programmed for the afternoon. Nothing in the way of words can convey the sensory impulse generated by the event. It has to be witnessed to be fully understood. After the awards are announced, each singer is given a memento. Sometimes it is a souvenir brochure containing photographs of famous festival personalities and some scenes of the campus. In 1942 everyone was given a certificate of attendance.

While it is not possible, or even desirable, that all Negro colleges should engage in similar productions, it is desirable and possible for at least one such enterprise to be held annually in each of the southern states. Such experiences are of great educational value in the

2. The Kennedy Brothers are children trained by their mother.

sociological and artistic sense. They furnish a fertile laboratory for the folklorist and artist. They create a deep self-respect for people who need such recognition of their true worth.

How much could have been learned and preserved if the "Fort Valley Idea" had been realized at least forty years ago! W. C. Handy, John Work, William Dawson, Sterling Brown (the poet), and the Library of Congress have all become richer for their having been touched by this festival. The Fort Valley State College students have the richest benefits of all. Theirs is a vital membership in the actual, functional development that takes place from year to year.

The Counterbalance

One of the strange developments of this age are the spectacular singing circuses held by various quartets in the larger cities of the country. Perhaps nowhere do these occasions find a fonder public than in Atlanta, Georgia. There is little to commend in these pseudo–folk festivals, and much to regret and wonder about. The singers come dressed in costumes similar to those found in the old minstrel shows. Here and there one does happen to strike a formal and accepted attire, but the general tone of the entire performance is theatrical and cheap.

The music is commercial and generally of poor quality. Here and there a significant song may be sung, but the ballad-type songs, which are saturated with secular idioms that appeal to the emotions, constitute the main fare. The whole enterprise is developed around monetary considerations. Not one of the singers is there because he loves what he is doing and wants to express himself as best he can in his own way. At the intermission the various organizations send books and pictures through the audience, which is virtually set upon by these vendors who prolong the intermission as long as business seems good.

The promoters are master showmen who exploit various occasions, such as Mother's Day and others that they develop. One of these latter is the candlelight service, which I believe was adapted from the Spelman College annual Christmas carol concert. If anyone is dismayed because I have not given a more vivid description of these travesties, I hope to console him by assuring him that the devices and characteristics common to them forbid any one description. It is enough to remember what has been said here as a reminder of what takes place when there is no one present to direct the would-be folk expression. These singing circuses are among the most pathetic of all Negro institutions in existence, and yet their audiences range into the thousands and some people even shout in the aisles to the singing. All pay a minimum of seventy-five cents' admission.

To further my argument, I will cite two articles from the *Atlanta Daily World*, June 1946. The first one is entitled "Music Festival Slated at Auditorium June 30." It is written by the sponsor, Bishop T. M. Mabry, and it reads:

> Coming on June 30 to the Atlanta City Auditorium, "Maceo's Divine Heaven." The public is more than welcome. This will be the greatest music festival ever presented in the city of Atlanta. The world's wonder child pianist, little Maggie Mabry, will be present, also Prof. L. B. Byron, the man who makes you dream at night, Mrs. Malana Banks, vocal soloist, and Mrs. Mary Paterson, vocal soloist. The Rising Eight Gospel Singers. One of the greatest quartet contests ever heard will be presented on this day at 3 P.M. Special features: Little Louise Harris will go away into a deep trance. God will appear before me. Come and see the man that talks with God daily and also the man that fasted 21 days; Bishop T. M. Mabry. He will tell you what happened. Bishop T. M. Mabry's sermon will be: "Just Go Back to God, When the Shadows of Death Roll Away." The phenomenon of any natural fact. I will be glad to meet you all at the City Auditorium June 30 at 3 P.M. This program will inspire you intellectually and spiritually, so come out that you might be able to receive the good things that await you. Many other groups will appear on the program.

The second article in the paper is by J. Richardson Jones, who writes:

> Tonight at the City Auditorium 8 P.M., Bishop E. D. Crockett will offer a most unique musical presentation, a battle of song

between the National Independent Quartet of Atlanta, and the Heavenly Gospel Singers, of Miami, Florida.

Supporting the contesting groups will be the R. S. B. Trio, Echoes of Zion, and the National Independent Juniors. For those who have not heard the National Juniors a real treat is in store.

Several weeks ago the Heavenly Gospel Singers were heard here, and they electrified the audience with their unique method of presenting their songs. The tenor, a diminutive, high-stepping individual, brought vociferous applause.

Atlantans know the superior style of the inimitable National Independents, and the boys from Florida will have to strut high and sing plenty to contest Bishop Crockett's group. Music lovers are in for a grand evening, and you are urged to be on time for a good seat.

Bishop Crockett announces he will introduce and demonstrate what he terms, the most amazing discovery of the Atomic Age. He has revealed very little information anent his Atomic Age discovery, and his followers are very anxious to know the details.

It is noteworthy that both of these events are sponsored by "bishops," whose most active interests seem to be these "battles." Could it be that these "bishops" represent their own proclamations of high office? Do they by any means realize what a bishop is supposed to do? Several years ago I went to see one of these "bishops" and asked if any of his quartets would be available for the festival at Fort Valley. I explained the "Fort Valley Idea" to him and gave him one of the handbills. Because the event did not offer sufficient financial surety, however, no quartet from Atlanta participated. I wonder, though, if my visit gave the "bishop" some ideas.

Chapter 13

Urban-Rural Cycle

I

When considering Negro folk music, one automatically thinks of rural folk, and rightly so. The legend of Negro folk music has developed around primitive people. The store of tales, true and imagined, which have been current in recent years leaves the common impression that all Negro folk music was of the past. The bald fact is that Negroes in the city and the small town are forced always to create a city-within-a-city, a town-within-a-town. Being in a segregated area in most cases, Negroes live in a condition that is not a true representation of the general life found there. It is Negro life in the city. The Negro area is made up of the usual three socioeconomic classes—lower, middle, and upper. For this study, it is very important to look upon these divisions as being folk level, semi-folk level, and super-folk level. Working together, these groups continue to bring about an exchange of songs, back and forth among themselves, which is one of the most interesting and far-reaching developments of which I have taken note.

In making extensive tours of the Deep South for the purpose of studying Negro folk music, I have noticed that the Negroes who live in rural areas generally do not sing the songs that are often looked upon by urban people as being the very essence of Negro folk song. These rural Negroes seem to have forgotten the songs that are commonly looked upon as spirituals or jubilees. To go further, it is safe to say that, except for the older generation, rural Negroes do not even know most of the songs found in our earlier anthologies, and they know a surprisingly small percentage of those in active use today. It is almost a thing of the past to hear even such favorites as "Swing Low Sweet Chariot," "Go Down Moses," "Lord, I Want to Be a Christian," "Ev'rytime I Feel de Spirit," and "Deep River." I have never even heard the latter except in urban places. When vestiges of these songs are heard on rare and far-flung occasions, they in fact represent new songs.

This situation indicates a condition that may call for a separate study, but in this chapter enough may be gained by the reader to realize the events taking place in the realm of Negro songs. In going ahead with this limitation in mind, we can thus say that the city has become the refuge of a series of Negro songs which Negroes on the folk level no longer feel called upon to maintain. These songs fall into two classes. The first class comprises the songs that city people (Negroes and whites) use as a means of entertainment and worship. The second class comprises songs that are safely and, may I say, sadly entombed in the various libraries, public and private (this latter being used only by music curio seekers or by scholars). Be it quickly said, though, that many songs lie thus buried which are more deserving than many in active use. With regard to song, then, there needs to be an actual "spiritual awakening." Some organized effort should be inaugurated to give a hearing to these fine songs, in most cases religious but combining some seculars of value. This is the responsibility of the city musician and scholar.

Now, here is the paradox. The folk-level Negro in the city and in the country purchases what is already his in the form of composed "ballads." These songs are developed in about three ways, with variations taking root in all three. This type of ballad is a brief song of high emotional content, colored with all of the various Negro musical types, from blues to boogy woogy. These songs are assigned to the familiar sheets that have been used by song and poem vendors for ages: (1) They are made by transforming genuine Negro songs into more modern, catchy rhythms borrowed from jazz dance idioms and dance styles of the past. (2) The texts of old hymns are colored with the feeling of Negro blues and given new settings often developed from hymn motifs or even whole phrases. (3) The deliberate confusion of motifs from blues, spirituals, jubilees, boogy woogy, and whatever else may be desirable from hymns produces songs that are loved by most adherents. These songs are indeed the poorest product of the Negro as a music maker.

It is strange how great a following these inferior songs have acquired among the people whose genius at song making always produces something infinitely fine. These urban gifts to the folk-level Negroes are rapidly wreaking the destruction of genuine folk music among the Negro masses. It is to be noted that many Negroes above the folk level, including the clergy, prefer these mongrel songs to real Negro music. This can only be explained in terms of the radio and record-playing machines, which have so much saturated us with jazz and its derivatives that the tastes Negroes once possessed in music are becoming amalgamated.

There is another source of musical infection making the rounds in this regard. This source is not as far removed as the others, and so is more sinister. This sinister source of musical infection is the type of Negro teacher who goes from the city into the rural areas to teach. Too often we find the children in these areas singing blues songs with religious words and jazz songs with hymn texts. When one considers that this is being done with mere children at the most impressionable stage of their lives, the situation becomes serious. Again, may it be said that much of this condition stems from the failure on the part of urban Negroes to make active use of the songs that have been given to them in collected form. The perpetual use of a few songs gives the ballad song maker a chance to bring a novel-type song into use as a welcome experience for those Negroes in cities who do not really know the spirituals anyway. This backfires into the rural areas and into the less developed urban areas, where the music is considered excellent. In turn, more developed Negroes and white people, who do not know the true nature of Negro folk art, accept these songs as being authentic Negro pieces.

II

During the last twenty years a vogue of singing has mounted in the South and spread to all parts of the nation through the aid of the radio and the phonograph record. This species of ensemble is the common Negro gospel quartet. These organizations are the result of the old authentic Negro groups that sang in the barbershops and on street corners throughout the South. Formerly these groups sang in a manner that may not be described accurately here due to the lack of comparison. However, it is fair to say that with few exceptions they were musically superior and more interesting in every way than those that are heard today. The rise of these old quartets resulted from the example of the white man's singing in the early minstrel shows and in the traveling show quartets that played under tents throughout the South (and in rather rare cases still do).

For fifty years, roughly speaking, the Fisk Singers sang in America and Europe, both as a mixed group and as a male quartet. It was only natural that other schools would take up the art of singing spirituals in a general sort of way. Therefore, it was not long before there were scores of Negroes in schools forming quartets (there were only a few colleges in those days) singing all over the country for the cause of Negro education. Since the schools had to depend upon unreliable travel conditions, it was easier to have an all-male organization than a mixed one, and a quartet was cheaper than a glee club would be. Hence there arose the vogue of singing spirituals and jubilees in quartet form, unnatural though it is from a musical as well as a sociological point of view.

The students of schools that had the more famous and best-developed quartets—such as Fisk, Hampton, Tuskegee, Florida Baptist Academy, and the Atlanta group—went forth to spread the influence of Negro folk songs. This caused the folk-song quartet to spread among schools in the rural areas, more as a means of entertainment than as a means of education or financial survival. Since the quartets were called upon to sing for local white audiences and for Negroes as well, care was taken to sing only songs that would be pleasing and create goodwill, if nothing more. The white people in the communities of the South and North where Negro quartets appeared selected the songs they liked best and demanded that they be sung over and over again, so that these songs remain to this day the best-known and most used of all Negro songs. In most cases these special songs do not turn out to be as typically Negro as some that are less familiar, for the white man naturally took to the songs that were closest to his conception of what a song should be (which is not to say that these songs were his own). In other words, the songs the white man preferred were ones that were more satisfying to his taste based upon his culture and racial feeling.

As for the Negro listener at the folk level, he preferred the novel songs or theatrical effects added to them. The singing of his traditional songs in a manner developed by the schoolteacher did not interest him. Finally, at the beginning of the last twenty years, Negroes on the folk level generally began to make quartets of their own in large and ever-increasing numbers. These were the organizations heard on the records of the Paramount and Okeh trademarks. Since the only place these Negro men had learned to sing together was in work camps, with section gangs and longshore gangs, and on street corners, they brought this strange folk harmony into the realm of religious song and further developed it by making it adaptable to four men, blending the qualities of the urban and the rural Negro harmony styles.

In the twenties, the phonograph companies exploited blues to the fullest. There were companies like the two previously mentioned which operated entirely on the "race record" market. Indeed, in several instances these companies rose and fell with the vogue that built them. It was customary for these companies to go into the South and find talent in the Negro sections of the southern cities. This general search for talent uncovered the Negro folk quartet, and the record companies helped popularize it. The popularity of these records forced the more conservative companies to go into the field of making "race records." The connection of these companies with radio brought further popularity to the folk quartet.

A band of brothers answering to the name of Mills caught on to the vogue. But being more sophisticated in all respects than their predecessors, they entered the realm of imitating instrumental sounds. This was the great period of the Negro jazz band, so these Mills Brothers took the example set by these bands and imitated with their voices what the Negro jazz orchestras were doing with their instruments. These boys (for boys they were) created a sensation. They "stopped" the radio show, so to speak. It was not long before everyone in radio-listening America, whether they were sympathetic or not, knew and listened to this new quartet. They were imitated then, as they are now, by Negro men and by white men. However, the most significant effect of their singing is that it influenced today's Negro folk-quartet singing all over America. No other Negro quartet had ever been presented on a program that so completely caught the fancy of these people of lower life. Here was a group of Negroes not singing as schoolteachers or big-city teachers had taught them; they were singing in a new language. It rather reminded them of their old jug bands and string bands rolled into one, with a dash of Duke Ellington thrown in for good measure. Now these quartets were saying, as I imagine: "Dem Mills Brothers sho is de bes' singin' thing I ever come 'cross. How come we can't sing like 'em? I kin make ev'y sound dat basser make, if yo' all kin make de rest. Come on, we go' see."

The trouble was that these Negro folk quartets had brought themselves up on religious songs, since they had gotten that idea from their city brethren. Also, when singing in public, which really meant singing in churches, they had no adjustments to make with respect to conventions; nor did they forget white patronage. However, when they took up the style of the Mills Brothers, they unknowingly did what they had tried to avoid. They brought jazz orchestras and spirituals into the same fold and into the church. No longer relying on their own talents, these Negro quartets that were once the most interesting of all Negro quartets have sunk into a singing pattern that is disagreeable even to a callous listener. They go all over the country giving concerts and appearing on the radio, combining the ridiculous with the sublime in an unsurpassable manner.

If this singing style is mentioned more than once in this book, it is only because it is necessary. To ignore these groups is to make a very serious blunder, for what they sing and the way they sing are two different things. Many a beautiful spiritual or jubilee may be found beneath the sheer noise of the accompaniment of the singers in the quartet, who at times do not sing any words at all but engage themselves in producing the Mills Brothers' orchestral effects. Urban and rural Negro music find their truest fusion in this most untrue representation, which is passing for authentic religious music created by the Negro race as a whole.

Three quartets have come to the fore as exponents of Negro songs of this manner. They are the Southernaires, the Charioteers, and the Golden Gate Quartet. Of these three, the Golden Gate Quartet holds the palm for authenticity. They possess a leader who is surely one of the great Negro song leaders in the world. If at times their style is questionable, that questionable aspect can be traced to their great demand as radio performers and to their urban associations. The Southernaires sing in the old vaudeville manner, while the Charioteers tend toward the jazz idiom.

III

The choir is a very old institution among peoples. It is the only natural folk way of singing, particularly the mixed choir. Man is musically at his best when men and women sing as they were intended to live—together. One may see at once that a choir of this nature is nothing more than a select portion of a normal congregation of human beings. It is for this reason that I say consistently that the male and female quartets are the most unnatural of all organizations that sing spirituals. Despite the pleasing tone quality of the quartet, the choir remains the symbol of congregational singing in the small church in the city, town, and country. No music ever belonged to any instrument more than a spiritual or jubilee belongs to a group of Negro men and women singing together.

In view of this truth, one may ask why we waited so long for the age of the Negro folk choir. True, there were many choirs among schools and colleges that sang an occasional spiritual or sang spirituals in an "extra" sort of way, but there was no recognized folk singing group in past decades which devoted itself to the singing of Negro music as did these quartets. The choirs in colleges felt that the quartet had priority when it came to spirituals, and modestly moved aside.

It is not overlooked here that the original Fisk Singers were mixed, that the entire student body sang spirituals together, and that special mixed groups were used at various times for special occasions. The point here is simply that the rise of the Negro choir as an outlet for Negro music had to await the arrival of Hall Johnson. It was this man who made people realize the potency of a group of Negro men and women singing spirituals and all classes of Negro music together. When Hall Johnson came along, the ideal set by the early Fisk Singers was lost. John Work, Sr., was no longer at the helm, and the Fisk Singers had emerged as a male organization. Also, their method of singing Negro songs had changed from an authentic style into a rather polished and sophisticated style. The spark had flickered and the spontaneous fire had all but died.

The story of Hall Johnson's rise as a choral director began when he was playing violin in the orchestra of the Negro play *Running Wild*. In this show there was a quartet singing spirituals in the stage manner. Sitting there in the orchestra pit, Johnson realized the tremendous power this singing had over the audience and resolved to organize his own group. Though the idea was born from his observing a Negro quartet, it found its expression in a more perfect medium— the Negro choir. Perhaps Johnson remembered his school choir and its potential.

The Hall Johnson Choir came along the hard way, which was a good thing, too. Their experiences welded a bond among these people which was an indispensable factor in their group's artistic feeling, comprehension, and action. This group of singers caught the folk spirit and fashioned their singing to it. No effort was made to create the impression that the choir was itself a primitive organization, but the very essence of the group's singing style took its model after the spirit of Negro folk singing. The choir possessed artistry of a high order, which it submerged, as it were, in a solution of Negro folk rhythms, melodies, cries, and harmonies. The Eva Jessye Choir gave emphasis to the Johnson vogue and supported it in a representative manner, further enhancing the folk choir growth.

The urban musician was needed to bring about this phenomenon. The rural or folk-level musician was too near the scene to produce this type of singing group. He preferred singing in the congregation or leading the singing from his seat on or near the front pew. The Hall Johnson Choir provided the exact means of getting the Negro folk song into the channel that would lead from Harlem to the outside world through the matchless distributing power of New York City. In fact, the sensational success of *The Green Pastures* was enhanced largely by the singing of the Johnson Choir. Anyone who has heard the choir sing "Lord, I Don' Feel No Ways Tired" realizes the difference in power, beauty, and imagery achieved here from that ordinary, urban spiritual singing. As Negroes became aware of this fact, other Negro choirs that sang spirituals began to emerge all over the United States. This was caused by the frantic competition among

Negroes for mere existence in the large cities and by their inherent love for singing itself. Thus the age of the Negro choir was born. The quartet was not supplanted but was merely artistically outdistanced as a singing medium. What had been held in leash on Negro college campuses was now given to the public in a new and vital singing style, for there is a great difference in what the college choir produces and what these newer groups achieve.

When the Works Progress Administration (W.P.A.) came into being during the Depression, there was seemingly no end to the creation of Negro choirs. The vogue was at its height, since the opportunity was given for compensation and enjoyment at a time when both were at a premium. It was also natural that people nearest the folk level would be hardest hit by the Depression. These people were the ideal timber for making folk-song choirs. The radio was called upon to dispense the accomplishments of these choirs, thereby carrying the idea of the choir principle to the entire rural population as well as to the urban. Soon churches, where choirs had never been anything more than a sort of dressing for the service, especially in the most rural areas, began having choirs. These organizations became true folk creations in that they sang in no definite vocal relationship or balance. The shape-note singers, who had functioned separately from the church, became interested in "de gospel choir."

Again, the influence of the rural schoolteacher took effect. In style and principle choirs became imitators of those more famous choirs on records and the radio. As was the case with the quartets, the rural people took up their principle but not their policy. Their organizations were used to sing very much like the rural congregation but with "improved" versions of the songs. There was little attention given to the matters of style and delivery. Among the urban Negroes at the semi-folk level the same principles were at work. Gospel choirs that sang ballads and spirituals came into being. Often these choirs were special organizations functioning not with the regular choir but really in contrast to it. The introduction of these choirs fitted neatly into the programs of many pastors and appealed to their church memberships.

The famous Wings Over Jordan Choir, perhaps the most-followed choir ever organized in America, is a direct product of the situation just described. Whereas this choir is generally looked upon as a Negro choir of authentic Negro folk expression, quite the contrary is true. The fame of this organization rests on a combination of disguised traditional spirituals, "ballads," the use of blues and jazz for motifs, and the personal touch that comes from the urgent desire to please the masses. Their following is large because their singing has some of all the popular types of music rolled into one—blues, boogy woogy, jazz, hymns, spirituals, and jubilees.

The Wings Over Jordan Choir, placed as it is on a consistent network program backed by a continuous procession of the most prominent Negro speakers, catches the fancy of many people decidedly removed from it in cultural tastes. Its exceptional position as the most famous of all Negro choirs has led its method to be adopted by a large percentage of other choirs. Even some colleges and schools have taken up the style of the Wings Over Jordan Choir. This completes the cycle. However, the singing of these more sophisticated college choirs is likely to become in time a representation more of the spontaneity found in the method than of the singing itself. There can be no danger that the rank and file of Negro college choirs will adhere to the style of the Wings Over Jordan Choir, so long as we have the traditional leadership of the choirs at Fisk, Hampton, Atlanta, Talladega, and the many exceptional state institutions.

The influence is sure to remain. The urban and rural Negro must keep the cycle in operation, giving and taking and repeating the process infinitely. It is also important that scholars keep themselves posted as to the trend of things. This will enable them to serve as guides in the paths leading from the past to the present and the future.

IV

There is one phase of singing that remains essentially urban—the solo version of the spiritual and jubilee with piano accompaniment. The folk-level singer, in the towns as well as in the country, does not seem to prefer this strange adaptation of his music. True, one finds a blind beggar on the streets singing spirituals, but this is not sufficient to make a difference in my statement that the folk-level singer does not prefer solo versions of the spiritual. The communal nature of the spiritual is understood and preferred by the folk-level singer in its correct, natural setting. My point can also be made with the blues. One finds that the folk singers who have achieved distinction have all been blues singers. With this form of folk song the natural mode of rendition is soloistic and is therefore preferred. These two illustrations serve to prove the inherent understanding of the folk for what they create.

Harry T. Burleigh created the vogue of the solo spiritual in the first part of the century. Being a great singer as well as a composer-arranger, he found it worthwhile to set his own folk music so that the concert-stage singer could claim it as a new medium. He also may have been thinking of his own needs, just as artists such as Fritz Kreisler, Percy Grainger, Pablo de Sarasate, and Henri Wieniawski have done in the past where their native music was concerned.

It was left for the incomparable Roland Hayes to give the Negro spiritual and jubilee the place they presently hold on all recital programs. Having every power necessary, Hayes made people realize the greatness of these songs, even when used with piano accompaniment in Carnegie Hall. His stature as a singer in general put authority behind this type of art, which gave it an immediate following among fine artists. Indeed, Hayes's practice of placing the spirituals at the end of his programs is one that has been imitated by practically all Negro singing artists, even when they do not sing them as well as they sing other works.

Paul Robeson became famous as a specialist on Negro songs. Marian Anderson and Dorothy Maynor have given further security to this tradition by their performances, as well as by their artistic stature. Consequently, many educated Negroes are more willing to accept Negro songs as real art now than before these aforesaid developments. If no response has come from the rural Negro in the form of imitation, it is a good thing for all concerned, since the very nature of the solo spiritual is contrary to the rich and beautiful singing tradition one hears only from the lips of people who are on the folk level.

V

R. Nathaniel Dett has been the most successful arranger of spirituals. He is the joy and the despair of the average Negro choral conductor, be he in college or rural school. The fact that Dett was a genius is not to be denied. His music for choir has a peculiar folk-like charm, despite his use of original melodies in profusion. For the past twenty years, the vogue of singing Dett's songs has become a standard concert custom in most Negro colleges and high schools. This ultra-urban music has caused many students to lose their appreciation for the regular traditional forms, and to look upon these powerful forms as being old-fashioned. It is unfortunate that when these students return to or go to the rural districts to teach, they are often put in charge of the singing. The students in these schools are too frequently forced to "sing" these difficult anthems by composers such as Dett. I have often sat in a whirlpool of pity, anger, humor, grief, and resignation when listening to some of these sessions. These youths, who are in the very vineyard of the "songs of their fathers," are given the distilled fruit and denied the vine—their birthright. This is very unfortunate.

When these youths reach maturity, there is a slight chance that they will find the balance point between the traditional form of the spiritual and the anthemic form. However, it is more than likely that unless they are brought into a knowledge by the understanding efforts of some college teachers, they will never arrive there. Alas, the example of Dett has bred scores of "arrangers." Almost everyone in charge of a group now "arranges." In one respect, this is a good thing, for out of this is bound to come some real talent. However, this trend leads away from the traditional. One should first know the traditional form of the spiritual, which is too frequently not the case. So, the years to come may not offer the students in many colleges the true understanding of the greatness of Dett, because they may not realize the greater source of Dett's power.

Forty Religious Negro Songs
Most Used by Congregations in the South

The two lists given below are the result of my years of observation as a researcher in the Deep South, as a director of folk festivals, as a director of folk choirs, and as a teacher of music in Negro colleges in Louisiana, Georgia, and Alabama. Moreover, song collections and hymnbooks have been used on a comparative basis and in comparison with the primary source—the folk themselves.

The songs are arranged in an order based on those considered to be favorites, which means the order is necessarily an approximation. The songs are limited to twenty in each list, a limitation that was undertaken with the hope of forcing a rather restricted and therefore more authentic compilation. It will be noticed that the difference between the two lists is striking. For instance, the percentage of songs in use in the city is far smaller than the percentage in use in the country. My purpose is to give a picture of the different song preferences held by the rural and urban people. Of course, one should not think that this distribution will hold in every situation, since certain areas have their own songs—the Georgia Sea Islands, for instance. Nevertheless, the overall picture I give is very reliable as regards the principle and to a large extent the practice.

Rural Songs
1. "I'm Go' Live So God Can Use Me"
2. "Guide My Feet, While I Run Dis Race"
3. "I'm Working on a Buildin'"
4. "Keep on to Heaven Anyhow"
5. "Git Right, Stay Right"
6. "Calvary"
7. "Lordy, Won't You Come by Here"
8. "De Sign o' de Jedgment"
9. "May Be de Las' Time, I Don't Know" (Communion)
10. "I Know It Was de Blood" (Communion)
11. "God's Gonna Straighten 'Em"
12. "I Ain't No Stranger Now"
13. "My Jesus Is a Rock"
14. "De Fault in You"
15. "De Blood Done Sign My Name"
16. "Gonna Stan' Dere Anyhow"
17. "I'm in a Strange Land"
18. "D'ain't But Me, One"
19. "Don't Be Bound, I'm Yo' Heart"
20. "I Know He'll Bring You Out Alright"

The following list is far more difficult to adhere to than the previous one, due to the tendency toward changes in the rural taste and style over a period of ten years. The selections given above should be looked upon in this light. The urban list will vary but little, if any, if the present trend is continued—mainly, that of using what is already known rather than learning other fine songs.

Urban Songs
1. "Swing Low Sweet Chariot" (two versions)
2. "Steal Away"
3. "Lord, I Want to Be a Christian"
4. "Down by de Riverside"
5. "Ev'rytime I Feel de Spirit"
6. "We Are Climbin' Jacob's Ladder" (two versions)
7. "I'm Goin' Down to de River o' Jordan"
8. "Calvary"
9. "He Rose"
10. "Go Tell It on de Mountain" (Christmas)
11. "Couldn't Hear Nobody Pray"
12. "Roll, Jordan, Roll"
13. "Dere Is a Balm in Gilead"
14. "In Bright Mansions Above"
15. "Nobody Knows de Trouble I See"
16. "Were You Dere"
17. "Walk in Jerusalem Jes Like John"
18. "Great Day, de Righteous Marchin'"
19. "My Lord, What a Mornin'"
20. "Plenty Good Room"

Songs such as "Deep River," "Go Down Moses," "Sometimes I Feel Like a Motherless Chile," and "Bye and Bye" are famous and generally better known than some of the songs listed above. However, they are sung in a special manner by groups and soloists. For instance, "Listen to de Lambs" is very famous but is seldom ever sung except in Dett's arrangement and therefore by a chorus.

It is natural that a race that produces its own folk music in quantity and quality would also produce composers, authors, poets, singers, and instrumentalists who distinguish themselves in the idiom of the race. It is also natural that this idiomatic expression would be on a plane far beyond the folk concept and therefore beyond the reach and even the comprehension of the masses of the race. These are the "chosen few" whose privilege it is to serve the final purpose of the creative urge in man. Theirs is beyond but not apart from the subject at hand, so that a treatise such as this must take their work into the scope of its consideration. Their contributions, based upon Negro folk art, form a great and enduring fantasia wherein the voice, the written word, the piano, and the orchestra are used. Some of the personalities treated herein have been partly appraised in previous chapters. If they are mentioned again, it is because a more detailed characterization is sought with regard to their work and its relationship to that of others.

Samuel Coleridge-Taylor (1875–1912) was the greatest of the Negro composers. He was the first and remained one of the few world composers of his race. Born to an English mother and an African father, it has been said that Coleridge-Taylor was incidentally English and essentially Negro. His genius was always directed toward the music of African and Afro-American Negroes. Negro music was the inspiration of almost all of his music, even when it professed purposes different from the portrayal of Negro racial feeling. His rhythms, tonal sequences, and warm orchestral colors give proof to the previous statement. Above anyone else, Coleridge-Taylor gave Negro music its first serious compositional treatment and set the pace for those who came after him. His *Bamboula, Dance Negre, The Violin*

Concerto, and *Symphonic Variations* are all outgrowths of strong racial feeling, but his attitude toward Negro songs is best related in his own words:

> There is a great distinction between the African Negro and the American Negro melodies. The African would seem to be more martial and free in character, whereas the Americans are more personal and tender, though notable exceptions to this rule can be found on either side. One of the most striking points regarding this music is, in the author's opinion, its likeness to that of the Caucasian race. The native music of India, China and Japan, and in fact all non-European music, is to our more cultivated ears most unsatisfactory, in its monotony and shapelessness. The music of Africa (I am not thinking of American Negro music, which may or may not have felt some white influence) is the great and noteworthy exception. Primitive as it is, it nevertheless has all the elements of the European folk-song and it is remarkable that no alterations have had to be made before treating the Melodies. This is even so with the example from West Africa—a highly original number. One conclusion may be safely drawn from this—the Negro is really and truly a most musical personality. What culture may do for the race in this respect, has yet to be determined, but the underlying musical nature cannot for a moment be questioned.[1]

In regard to his treatments of Negro themes, it must be said that they are more European than is desirable in this day. The piano works are variations on the themes and are not always highly pianistic. However, the scholarship and the purpose of his music are of such a high order that the end reaches far into the future. Coleridge-Taylor is the "wheel-of-fire" in the music of the Negro in Africa and in the United States. Alas, the fire burns all but unattended.

Harry T. Burleigh (1866–) is recognized as one of the greatest songwriters and music scholars ever identified with Negro song. As music

1. London, England, December 17, 1904. This statement would seem to answer some present-day questions regarding Negro music in America.

arranger, composer, singer, and editor, Burleigh stands unique in the realm of Negro folk songs. No other person has been more fundamental to the general acceptance of the Negro folk song than has this man. It is to him that we must turn as the source both of the concert solo version of the spiritual and of the choral arrangement form. No significant work in these two fields may be said not to have been influenced by Burleigh. His advice and judgment as a scholar are constantly sought on matters concerning Negro music—its origin, nature, and authenticity.

Will Marion Cook (1865–1944) is the forerunner of all American composers who have specialized in the secular idiom of the Negro during the last forty years. It is not going too far to say that the "Cook idiom" is being heard today in many unsuspected places. He was sought by composers of both races as a "finisher." His works were sold outright in some instances, so that his name never appeared on the title pages. The exhortation song was developed by Cook. It has been used by many composers and was used by George Gershwin in *Porgy and Bess*. The most famous of all of his songs, "Swing Along," represents a turning point in the choral conception in the United States. Here we have the spirit of the "buck dance" and the cakewalk lifted to the realm of the choral art song. The final testament to his service to Negro music rests in his masterful use of exotic dance rhythms and the subjugation of these rhythms to the more subtle feeling Negroes are noted for possessing. Cook was a genius, expertly trained, who chose from his race that which was considered trite by those less endowed than himself. He was master of the Negro secular idiom as it was known in his day, and he did much to bring the Negro's songs and dances into the unique position they occupy in the present day.

R. Nathaniel Dett (1882–1943) occupies the most generally accepted position of any Negro composer yet. He created the "spiritual anthem" in such works as "Listen to the Lambs," "I'll Never Turn Back No More," "Oh, Holy Lord," and many others. No Negro has been able to achieve comparable distinction as a choral writer of Negro songs. His piano works are equally famous and are constantly performed by students and established artists. "Juba" has been performed in arrangement by several of the major symphony orchestras.

His solo versions of spirituals have not fared so well, because they are too ornate or too personal for general acceptance, but even here there is much to be found of value. The *Ordering of Moses* is the crowning event of Dett's musical life. It has been performed by major organizations throughout the country and has been acclaimed by critics. The themes are derived from Negro folk music, and the treatment is harmonically advanced as compared to Dett's other works. Dett is the founder of the modern concept of choral adaptations and derivatives based on Negro songs. His imitators are legion. His equals are rare. He is the choral master in full stride.

James Weldon Johnson (1871–1938) and J. Rosamond Johnson (1873–) are brothers thought of almost as one when Negro music is considered. The two worked together as lyricist and composer for almost the entire life of their productivity. This relationship was terminated by the tragic death of James Weldon a few years ago. From my point of view, it seems that these two men did the most for Negro folk music when they took the Negro folk idiom and worked it into art song. By way of illustration, "Since You Went Away" is a combination of blues and the spiritual from the viewpoint of the music, and it ranks with true folk poetry from the viewpoint of the text. The Johnsons created the true medium of Negro folk art song expression. James Weldon has written a very able treatise on Negro music in his introduction to *The Book of American Negro Spirituals*. The arrangements by his brother are not uniform in their acceptability. At times there is a tendency toward showiness and the theatrical. "The Negro National Anthem," which is in reality "Lift Every Voice and Sing," is not done in the Negro idiom. This is strange. In addition, it is the most famous of the works done by the two Johnsons, yet it is not among the best. The shows and idiomatic songs are their masterpieces.

W. C. Handy (1873–) has been spoken of here in connection with the blues. It is now necessary to speak of his larger contribution to the cause of the Negro. During his later years he has become more and more interested in promoting Negro music in general. His publishing house is now more devoted to the spiritual than the blues. Many Negro composers who otherwise would not get a hearing at all are being given their chance. Some of these artists are not good, others show promise, and some demonstrate real power. Handy is the only Negro to be in a position to promote firsthand the musical creative talents of his race. If Handy could obtain the help he needs and so greatly deserves, his company could become epochal. He deserves a scholarly editor and the works of our best Negro composers. Handy, the blind researcher, composer, arranger, founder, publisher, and cornet virtuoso, is the most popular person connected with Negro folk music.

Edward Boatner (1897–) has been very active as a conductor and arranger of Negro music. His works have a very human quality and have consistently been performed by the greatest Negro singers. Boatner is one of the half dozen Negroes who have been able to achieve a style in their arrangements that has gained the favor of the finest publishers, artists, and critics alike. He is giving folk music a high and merited place in the musical life of the Northeast—Brooklyn, New York, in particular.

Zora Neale Hurston (1903–) is one of the ablest folklorists in America. She has written copiously of the ways and folk products of her race. Her *Mules and Men* may be one of the finest works on folklore yet. Hurston has collected excellent folk songs and given them the benefit of her great knowledge of the background of the American Negro. She is the most prolific writer and one of the most authoritative scholars of Negro folk culture. The music she uncovers always proves to be new to the ears of folklorists and valuable to the total corpus of Negro songs.

Clarence Cameron White (1880–) has become recognized as the foremost adapter of Negro folk song for violin. Famous as a violinist, he toured the South as well as other parts of the country. While at Tuskegee Institute, he heard the students sing spirituals and was moved to adapt some of them, very successfully, as solos for violin. Fritz Kreisler and Jascha Heifetz, among others, have given his arrangements splendid hearings. The Boston Symphony Orchestra has rendered arrangements of his *Bandanna Sketches* with distinction and pleasure. White has been the most consistent developer of Negro violin music in America.

William L. Dawson (1898–) has achieved the distinction of writing one of the few major works based on Negro folk song. His symphony on Negro themes was first performed by Leopold Stokowski and the

Philadelphia Orchestra and, later, other symphony orchestras. Being highly gifted and well trained, Dawson has kept the high musical tradition of Tuskegee Institute secure and advancing. His choir at Tuskegee is famous for its great facility with Negro music. As a choral writer, Dawson has followed the example of Dett, but he has also been able to develop his own style.

The Work family has justly been called the most unique family of its kind in this country. The late John Work, Sr., Mrs. Agnes Work, Frederick J. Work, Elnora J. Work, and the contemporary John Work, Jr., have all lived lives of involvement in Negro music. Being identified with Fisk University, they did much to create the distinctive place Negro music holds at that great university. John Work, Sr., was one of the great Negro singers of all time. His voice was golden, and in the field of Negro music he engaged in scholarship of rare quality. His book *Folk Song of the American Negro* is of great value, and he led the Fisk Singers to their greatest artistic heights. His wife, Agnes Work, was a rare singer and a keen student of the spiritual. Her contralto voice made many people who had no appreciation for Negro folk song realize the power of the music. Frederick Work has been highly valuable as a teacher, composer, collector, and singer with the Fisk group. John Work, Jr., is among our most able folklorists and composers. He is the most highly trained musician in the Work family. His illustrious parents found in their son excellent fruition of their powers. The book *American Negro Songs* is one of the finest collections of its kind. It has enriched the status of Negro music in general. Thus, more than any other family, the Works have institutionalized Negro music in America.

Hall Johnson (1888–) is best known as a choir director, but he is more valuable as a composer, collector, and arranger. The high scholarship of Johnson does not destroy his spontaneity but rather seems to enhance it. The spirituals he arranged for the musical *The Green Pastures* rank among the most able and authentic solo settings of Negro songs ever achieved. His choral settings are forceful and simple in design. Their main power lies in rhythm and dynamics. Johnson also pioneered the professional Negro folk choir and gave Negro music a freshness as arranger, collector, and director. He is one of the greatest handlers of folk music, sung or written.

William Grant Still (1895–) is considered by many the most gifted of the American symphonists. Still is another combination of rare Negro musical feeling and scholarship of a high order. One of the apparent reasons for his existence is to expand a musical philosophy on the conditions of the Negro in America. Still is recognized as one of the greatest of all modern orchestrators. He is gifted with a subtle Negro idiom that borders on jazz at times and on the spiritual at others, without becoming either. Still seems to have caught the torch from the fallen Samuel Coleridge-Taylor, but it is too soon to judge the result at this time. When Still has undertaken to do arrangements for voice, he has not seemed quite so happy. His predilection for larger forms has apparently made it difficult for him to rise to expressive heights in a matter of seconds. There is a strong tendency in his work toward the modern feeling, which does not always fit the nature of Negro song. Still is the musical embodiment of the feeling of the urban, sophisticated Negro of today. His music is of the folk who have become "new"—those who work and think American but live, by force, Afro-American.

Nicholas George Julius Ballanta (1897–) is a native African who has lived in America only a short time, but it must be noted that he has done a remarkable service for Negro music. Ballanta visited the Penn School and compiled a valuable collection of 103 Negro songs, some of which are indigenous to St. Helena Island, where the school is located. The introduction to his book is a rare document indeed. The rhythms of the Africans as well as their melodies are given a scholarly discussion. The book is one of the most valuable in the whole realm of Negro song literature. Ballanta has narrowed the gap between African Negro and American Negro music with more authenticity than any other person heretofore.

Carl Diton (1886–) has made several arrangements of spirituals for choral rendition. His work won high favor at one time but has not fared so well recently. At the time of his greatest popularity as an arranger of Negro music, he was a concert pianist of considerable recognition. This fact evidently lent prestige to his written expression. In spite of the apparent decline of interest in his choral works, Diton must be recognized as one of the first Negroes to gain favor and fame for the formal expression of Negro music in choral form.

He was also one of the first Negroes to gain recognition as an organ composer who based his work on Negro themes.

W. E. B. Du Bois (1868–) wrote a chapter in his book *The Souls of Black Folk* in which he paid tribute to the Negro's songs. While no musician, Du Bois is a rare scholar. His love and respect for the songs of his people inspired a general appreciation and consideration of them among many people, white and Negro, who were previously unable to make up their minds about the music. Du Bois gave more vigorous, scholarly support to Negro music than any earlier Negro scholar. In doing this, he contradicted many of his colleagues.

Paul Laurence Dunbar (1872–1906) took his cue from Negro secular folk songs and folk language. He collaborated with Samuel Coleridge-Taylor by writing lyrics, which made him a recognized songwriter. However, Dunbar's "The Corn Song," "At Candle Lighting Time," and "African Romances" were music in words long before Coleridge-Taylor actually set them to music. In 1898 Dunbar and Coleridge-Taylor wrote the slender operetta *The Dream Lovers*. Dunbar gave Will Marion Cook the inspiration to write his great success, *Clorindy*. The rhythm and the color of the old Negro dance is found in Dunbar's poetry as it is in no other literature.

Booker T. Washington (1859–1915) wrote an introduction to Coleridge-Taylor's *Twenty-four Negro Melodies*. His great stature as an American citizen, educator, and Negro leader caused the work of Coleridge-Taylor to be of immediate interest to Americans as well as Englishmen. Washington also regarded it as a sacred duty to maintain a faith in the songs of his people. Due to the interest and spirit of Washington, the students at Tuskegee Institute were taught an appreciation for Negro music that was rare. Washington was among the first great Negro educators to champion the cause of Negro folk music before the world.

Alain L. Locke (1886–) has written of the Negro arts in a most vivid and scholarly manner. His greatest effectiveness has been between 1925 and the present. *The Negro and His Music* is one of the most interesting and unique creations to come from this scholar. In addition to this, Locke contributed a lecture in connection with the "Seventy-five Years of Freedom" celebration sponsored by the Library of Congress. The publication of this lecture constitutes one of the more important events in the progress of Negro music and its being understood from a philosophical rather than an analytical viewpoint.

Sterling A. Brown (1901–) is closer to the heart of Negro folk music than any Negro poet has ever been before. He is not only conversant with the spirit of the musical text, but he has acquired a splendid knowledge of the secular music as a whole. His lecture during the "Seventy-five Years of Freedom" celebration, his *Southern Road*, and his collections and papers represent some of the unique contributions pertaining to and stemming from Negro music in this age. Brown has glorified the Negro folk song text as has no other poet.

Mr. and Mrs. J. A. Myers have given years to the promotion of Negro music, both as members and successive directors of the Fisk Singers. Mrs. Myers is the present director (1945) of the famous organization, having succeeded her late husband. Without doubt, the work of these two people has had a great measure of influence on the development of the "Fisk Tradition," even though the golden age must be assigned to the tenure of John Work, Sr. For years J. A. Myers sang in the quartet alongside Work, the master.

The following three people deserve mention on the basis of creative teaching. Sidney Woodward (1860–1924) was considered the finest Negro tenor when in early manhood. His best teaching was done in Jacksonville, Florida, where he led one of the greatest Negro quartets ever heard in America—the Florida Baptist Academy Quartet. The activities of this organization were confined to the rich eastern coast of Florida. Their singing is the first musical experience I can remember from my youth. Woodward was my first music teacher.

Jennie Lee (deceased) was for years the teacher of singing at Tuskegee Institute. She developed what was at the time the finest and the largest choir in the Deep South. Her ideals were such that the students entrusted to her care were held to the highest standards in Negro folk singing. The fame that comes to Tuskegee as a singing school is largely due to her. William Dawson and James Dorsey came under her influence, as did many other creative Negro directors and teachers of singing in America.

Kemper Harreld (1886–) is the youngest of the group. He came to

Morehouse College in 1911 and has remained to develop the music in the present university system, which comprises Spelman College, Morehouse College, and Atlanta University. Harreld's attitude toward Negro music has always been that of the purist. He has taught Negro music to thousands of Negro students, students who have gone out to teach in Negro colleges and high schools with distinction. Frederick Hall (teacher-composer), Herbert Mells (teacher-composer), and I were brought under Harreld's influence in college as quartet and Glee Club singers.

It must be mentioned that a number of others, Negro and white, have also been of great value to the study and progress of Negro folk music. Without them the status of Negro folk songs would be far different than it is today. Among those who have done exceptional service are Emily Hallowell, with *Calhoun Plantation Songs*; Williams Arms Fisher, with *Seventy Negro Spirituals*; and Noble Cain, with certain of his arrangements. The magnificent work of William Francis Allen, Charles Pickard Ware, and Lucy McKim Garrison has already been mentioned in an earlier part of this book. Now, special tribute is given to the following.

Antonín Dvořák (1841–1904) came to America and was fascinated by the music of the Negro. He set to work upon a study of the subject and as a result wrote his most famous work in large form, the *New World Symphony*. His string quartet is also strongly influenced by the music of the American Negro. His stature as a musician gave Negro music its first great boost in the realm of serious music developed in this country. Dvořák pointed to the songs of the southern black man as a rich source of America's future musical greatness. This prophecy is being steadily fulfilled by composers of both races.

Henry E. Krehbiel (1854–1923) produced what has become one of the most interesting and helpful books ever written about Negro folk songs. There is a wealth of information in *Afro-American Folk-Songs* which places it in a unique position. At a time when Negro folk songs were being attacked by Richard Wallenschek, some scholars were needed to answer him in kind. Krehbiel undertook the cause and wrote his great book. The wisdom, honesty, scholarship, and sympathy found in the book deserve the continual gratitude of all Americans who wish to know more about our collective culture.

John A. Lomax (1870–) is one of the outstanding collectors of Negro song, just as he is one of the outstanding collectors of American song. Traveling throughout the South, Lomax and his son, Alan, have distinguished themselves with their unique acquisitions and their constant interest in the field. Their approach is enhanced by their writings and lectures. Alan's work has been consistently of a high order, and his lecture at the "Seventy-five Years of Freedom" celebration was a compact and enlightening digest of two rare phases of Negro folk music—reels and work songs.

George Gershwin (1898–1937) during his short lifetime became one of America's most beloved composers of all time. Much of his success was due to his great gift of melody and his understanding and use of the Negro idiom. The blues haunted him day and night, so it is natural that his most famous piece would bear this stamp—*Rhapsody in Blue.* If the mastery of musical form is the criterion, then Gershwin carried secular Negro music to a higher plane than anyone had before him. It seems that Gershwin would have created a better opera (*Porgy and Bess*) if he had called upon the religious as well as secular music of the Negro. His own "spirituals" proved to be too much like the blues. The beautiful song "Summertime" is reminiscent of "St. Louis Blues." This idiom suggests moving feet and a dingy hall tinged with tobacco and alcohol rather than a sleeping child. "It Ain't Necessarily So" is strange to the ears of those Americans who are acquainted with the Negro's religious feeling. The words are profane, and the musical style is rooted in the blues. In fact, the whole opera is blues. Nevertheless, the music is beautiful in itself. Gershwin was happiest in *Rhapsody in Blue.* Here no proposition of stage and orchestra had to be considered. He could revel in his own inventiveness and give out what he felt, with obligation to no one. That in itself is the spirit of folk music, and that is where Gershwin excelled. Gershwin is the greatest genius to develop Negro blues music up to this day.

Lydia Parrish has produced a remarkable book, *Slave Songs of the Georgia Sea Islands.* Although I do not agree that all the songs in the book belong under its title, that all of the "work songs" are properly identified, nor that "slave songs" is an advantageous name, the book is of great importance and was done most painstakingly. Viewed from a sociomusical point of view, the text is invaluable. The photography and many of the songs should be cherished by all folklorists and people of culture generally. The section entitled "An Explanation" is the result of very keen observation and carefully selected reading. Thus, Parrish's *Slave Songs of the Georgia Sea Islands* is one of the most interesting and artistically designed books produced about the folk music of any people in so small an area. Creighton Churchill and Robert MacGimsey reproduced the musical examples faithfully and in the spirit of tradition. The book is further enhanced by an introduction by the great Olin Downes. The general tone of the book bespeaks the author's and contributors' most sincere respect for the people who produced such a wealth of song.

Robert Russa Moton (1867–1940) was the leader of spirituals at Hampton Institute during his tenure there. His rich baritone voice helped the students catch the spirit of his truly folk being. Moton remained one of the folk as long as he lived. It was his custom to "raise" a spiritual during the course of his speeches from time to time, especially if the audience happened to be Negro. The Tuskegee Institute choir reached its greatest heights as spiritual singers during his presidency. He lived and worked by the inspiration that lies behind the creation of Negro folk song. He loved, sang, led, and talked the Negro folk song as no other eminent Negro outside music has done.

Lorenzo Turner (1895–) is generally considered the first scholar in the fields of Negro dialect and African survivals in America. More than that, he has also made many remarkable records of the African tribes in Brazil and the people in the Gullah regions of the South Atlantic Seaboard. His scholarship was of great help to me in the preparation of the statements that address the relationship between Negro music in our country and that of Negroes in Africa and other countries throughout the world.

Maud Cuney Hare (1874–1936) was one of the greatest spirits privileged to work in the furtherance of Negro folk music. Throughout a long career she held steadfast to the firm traditions of scholarship and honest performance generally accredited to her. Indeed, Hare remains the most widely read historian in the field of Negro music. As a composer, arranger, artist, and lecturer, she carried her obsession—Negro music—into all that she did.

Finally, everlasting gratitude must be given to those white people who came south and taught Negroes in the fearful days of Reconstruction and thereafter. It must be remembered that the Negro was not in a position to realize his gifts by himself. He needed friends whose eyes were critically trained and sympathetic. The schools that gave the world its first real knowledge of Negro American music— though in a very restricted sense, limited to the religious—chose the noblest part of that music. These schools were founded by white people and were headed by white people. Fisk University, Hampton Institute, Calhoun College, Talladega College, and Atlanta University have been instrumental among these schools in the preservation of these songs. There are scores of smaller schools and colleges engaged in the practices established by George White and Erastus Cravath and their successors. Spelman College, founded by Sophia Packard and Harriet Giles, has maintained a love and appreciation for Negro religious songs over the years. Under Florence M. Read, its present head, Negro folk songs have come into their greatest active sponsorship. This book is largely a result of encouragement from this direction.

The famous singing done in Negro music at Tuskegee Institute, Morehouse College, Spelman College, and now at Howard University under Warner Lawson must be considered the continuation of the above-named institutions' traditions. The future of Negro song is rooted in the past, and the past has been a bountiful and beautiful one. Future generations must not be content to rest upon these laurels. The Negro himself must find the same pride and great force in his music that was heretofore largely discovered and sustained by his friends, white men and women who "faced de risin' sun." To this end and in this hope and belief was this book humbly written.

Appendix of Negro Songs

In making these additional songs part of this book, I have been interested in enriching the quantity of Negro songs with rare and, in most cases, heretofore unknown versions. The seculars are very rare, because seculars generally are the least known. Thus I am especially proud of placing them here. In fact, more great work songs and calls are placed here than may be found in any previous volume. The following items are presented for a better understanding of what follows.

1. The songs are not harmonized, for this book is designed not for choral groups but for seekers. Nowadays conductors do not follow the hymn-type harmonizations found in many books anyway. Also, I do not wish to stereotype the songs with my own taste.

2. The songs have not been too fully annotated, since I believe that this book has given sufficient background for an understanding of the songs. Moreover, a good folk song is its own best document. Yet, where clarity is concerned, the matter of annotation has been dealt with.

3. If too few songs have been assigned to definite areas or personalities, it is because I have thought it best not to be too arbitrary in assigning them. As I have mentioned before, folk songs travel continuously, and personalities change and claim them.

4. If composers and arrangers draw from these sources, a statement of acknowledgment in their works would be humbly appreciated. The songs are placed here to serve those who desire and need a new fount of inspiration and knowledge, as well as to contribute to a better understanding of the preceding discussions.

5. The songs were not set in the original styles of folk harmony because the quaint progressions in two and three parts would be mere strangers to the laity and to some musicians, unless they were

familiar with the folk idiom as it pertains to Negro harmony. This is best understood when listened to again and again firsthand or from reliable recordings. The harmonic principles illustrated in chapter 1 may be applied in a general way to most songs in this text. For those who wish to examine Negro folk harmony as it is set in books, I suggest that they make a survey of the harmony in *Calhoun Plantation Songs* by Emily Hallowell and *Slave Songs of the Georgia Sea Islands* by Lydia Parrish.

Outline of Negro Songs

I. *Secular songs*
  1. Song cries
  2. Dance songs (social songs and game songs)
  3. Blues—folk, vocal-instrumental
  4. Ballads and ballad types
  5. Work songs
     a. Road songs (railroad and construction)
     b. Water songs (loading and boat songs)
     c. Field songs
     d. Camp songs
     e. Hammer songs
     f. Work songs—cries (liberally considered)
  6. Slave songs
  7. Lullabies
  8. Satire songs

II. *Religious songs*
  1. Spirituals
  2. Jubilees, song sermons
  3. Morality songs
  4. Humorous, Bible character songs
  5. Folk hymns (derivatives, words and tunes)
  6. Folk meters (derivative tunes, words not changed)

Dis Ol' Hammer Kill' John Henry

This is a rare version of the best-known Negro work song among Negroes themselves. On every third beat the hammer falls and the "driver" emits "hanh" or some other sound akin to it. This is to be remembered in all subsequent hammer songs in this book.

Dis ol' hammer (hanh) kill' John Henry,
Dis ol' hammer kill' John Henry,
Dis ol' hammer kill' John Henry,
Dis ol' hammer won't kill me.

Dis ol' shovel buried John Henry, (3x)
Dis ol' shovel won't bury me.

Lay mah head on de railroad track, (3x)
Train come along, snatch it back.

Dis Ol' Hammer Kill' John Henry

Rests represent hammer-falls.

Hammer Song

Pay Day

Surely if I stay all day, I may be able to get my money. Don't think I am going to get tired of waiting.

> De day is pay day,
> De day is pay day,
> De day is pay day,
> All day, day long.
> Gimme, O gimme,
> What to me b'long.[1]

Pay Day

Rests represent hammer-falls.   *Hammer Song*

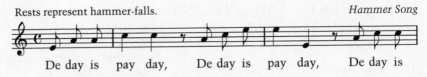

De day is   pay day,   De day is   pay   day,   De day is

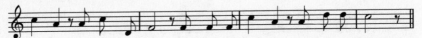

pay day, All day, day long. Gim-me, O gim-me, what to me b'long.

Gwine Ter Gawjay (Georgia)

This is a hammer song. It is one of the few that have no hint of resentment. The bragging is done on a personal basis, entirely without comparisons. Can it be that the Stetson hat mentioned was obtained by devices other than outright purchase? Perhaps the answer is found in stanza 3. As in all hammer songs, the rests signify the hammer fall and the grunts of the driver.

> Ah feel lak gwine, lak gwine ter Gawjay,
> Ah feel lak gwine, lak gwine ter Gawjay,
> Ah feel lak gwine, lak gwine ter Gawjay,
> But ah can' make it up in mah min'.

---

1. A stranger song in two modes at once.

Now, ah done got me a Stetson hat,
Now, ah done got me a Stetson hat,
Now, ah done got me a Stetson hat,
Ain' gwine tell you where I got it at.

Don' never fool 'round no gamblin' game,
Don' never fool 'round no gamblin' game,
Don' never fool 'round no gamblin' game,
Take all yo' money an' steal yo' name.

Go to de train track an' flag de train,
Go to de train track an' flag de train,
Go to de train track an' flag de train,
A job wid me ain' no ball an' chain.

Everytime dat I goes ter town,
Everytime dat I goes ter town,
Everytime dat I goes ter town,
De pretty wimmens all run me down.

Gwine Ter Gawjay (Georgia)

Hammer Song

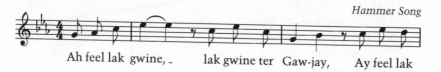

Ah feel lak gwine, _ lak gwine ter Gaw-jay, Ay feel lak

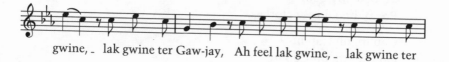

gwine, _ lak gwine ter Gaw-jay, Ah feel lak gwine, _ lak gwine ter

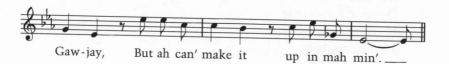

Gaw-jay, But ah can' make it up in mah min'. ____

Lay 'Em Up Solid

Lay 'em up solid,
Lay 'em up solid,
Lay 'em up solid
So dey won' come down.

Lay 'Em Up Solid

Rests represent hammer-falls.

Hammer Song

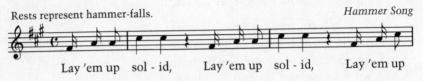

Lay 'em up   sol - id,   Lay 'em up   sol - id,   Lay 'em up

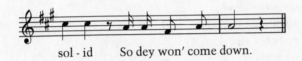

sol - id   So dey won' come down.

Cap'm, Time Done Come

Cap'm, oh Cap'm,
Oh Cap'm, oh Cap'm,
De time done come,
De time done come,
De time done come
To take my baby
Pretty brand new clothes.

Cap'm, oh Cap'm
Oh Cap'm, oh Cap'm,
De time done come,
De time done come,
De time done come
To take my baby
To New Orleans.

Cap'm, oh Cap'm,
Oh Cap'm, oh Cap'm

De time done come,
De time done come,
De time done come
To take my baby
Some pork chops brown.

Cap'm, oh Cap'm,
Oh Cap'm, oh Cap'm,
De time done come,
De time done come,
De time done come
To take my baby
Some frog skin pie. ["greenbacks"]

Cap'm, Time Done Come

Rests represent hammer-falls.

Hammer Song

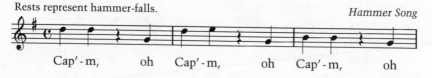

Cap'-m,   oh   Cap'-m,   oh   Cap'-m,   oh

Cap'-m,   De time done come, _ De time done come, _ De time done

come _   To take my bab-y   Pret-ty brand new clothes.

Jonny Joe Green

This is one of the most rhythmic songs one may ever hear. It is a rebuke, in the cruelest manner, to the stool pigeon. It is also a most original piece of rhythmic invention. Try to find another like it. The search may prove fascinatingly disappointing if not futile.

Jonny Joe Green,
I seed yo' talkin', talkin',
To de Capt'in, to de Capt'in.
Yo' mus'a, yo' mus'a been talkin', been talkin' 'bout,
Talkin' 'bout me, 'bout me, 'bout me,
Been talkin' 'bout me, 'bout me.

Jonny Joe Green
I won't be worried, worried,
Wid yo' long, wid yo' long.
I got jes, I got jes six months, six months,
But yo' got yo' life, yo' life,
But yo' got yo' life, yo' life.

Jonny Joe Green

Rests represent hammer-falls.   *Hammer Song*

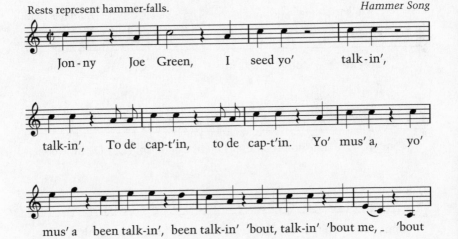

Jon-ny   Joe Green,   I   seed yo'   talk-in',

talk-in',   To de cap-t'in,   to de cap-t'in. Yo' mus'a,   yo'

mus'a   been talk-in', been talk-in' 'bout, talk-in' 'bout me, _ 'bout

me,   'bout me,   been talk-in' 'bout me,   'bout me __

Soun' Like Thunder

I'm a man, tall lak a mountain,
I'm a man, steddy lak a fountain,
Folks all wonder what makes it thunder,
When dey hear, Lawd, my hammer fall.

Did yo' read it in de paper
'Bout de gov'nor an' his family,
Dey am 'cided to come to de new road
Jes to hear, Lawd, my hammer fall.

Boss got money—mo den de government
Come to town ridin' a chariot
Drivin' forty big fine race horses
Jes to hear, Lawd, my hammer fall.

Chorus
An' hit soun' like thunder
Lawd, hit soun' like thunder
When my hammer fall.

Soun' Like Thunder

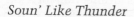

Rests represent hammer-falls.

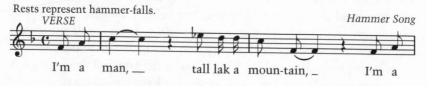

I'm a   man, ___   tall lak a moun-tain, _   I'm a

man,   sted-dy lak a foun-tain. _   Folks all wond-er   what make it

thund-er,   When dey hear, Lawd, my ham-mer fall.   An' hit soun' lak

thund-er   Yes hit soun' lak thund-er   When mah ham-mer

fall,   When my ham-mer fall.   Yeah, hit soun' lak

thun-der   Lawd, hit soun' lak thund-er,   When mah ham-mer

fall, _____   When my ham - mer _ fall!

De Railroad Line's Mah Home

It seems to me that the title of this song expresses an affection for a job and occupation far beyond what is generally expected to be found in the hearts of steel-driving men. The sincerity behind the song never varies for an instant. "De big 'Hot Shot' come rollin' down lak de mountain top" is a figure of power and majesty that seems to gain in momentum upon each successive reading. This is one of the rarest of work songs. It is a reminder of the kind of work songs that have passed away.

Oh Cap'in come
See what I done,
I laid de track
So de train can run.
De railroad line's mah home, mah home,
De railroad line's mah home.

Oh Cap'in Bob,
De big "Hot Shot"
Come rollin' down

Lak de mountain top.
De railroad line's mah home, mah home,
De railroad line's mah home.

De fastes' train
I ever seen,
Was stretch' f'om
Georgia to New Orleans.
De railroad line's mah home, mah home,
De railroad line's mah home.

Oh partner Joe,
Ah'm ready ter go,
Ter see de woman
Dat grieve me so.
De railroad line's mah home, mah home,
De railroad line's mah home.

De Railroad Line's Mah Home

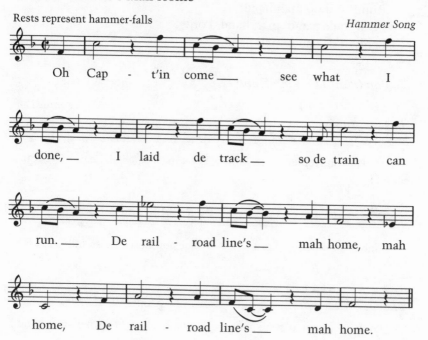

Rests represent hammer-falls

Hammer Song

Oh Cap - t'in come __ see what I done, __ I laid de track __ so de train can run. __ De rail - road line's __ mah home, mah home, De rail - road line's __ mah home.

De Pan (Palm) O' Mah Hand

Fortune teller come, Lordy,
Look in de pan o' mah hand.
Say dere's one thing dere, Lordy,
She don't understand!
Look in de pan o' mah hand, Lordy,
Look in de pan o' mah hand.

Fortune teller say, Lordy,
Look in de pan o' mah hand.
Got a line thoo dere, Lordy,
Ain't lak no natchel man!
Look in de pan o' mah hand, Lordy,
Look in de pan o' mah hand.

Go an' tell de Cap'm, Lordy,
Look in de pan o' mah hand.
Got de seaboard line, Lordy,
Runnin' thoo mah hand!
Look in de pan o' mah hand, Lordy,
Look in de pan o'mah hand.

De Pan (Palm) O' Mah Hand

Railroad Song

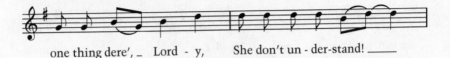

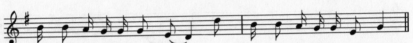

For-tune tell-er come, Lord-y, Look in de pan o' my hand. Say dere's

one thing dere', _ Lord - y, She don't un - der-stand! ____

Look in de pan o' mah hand, _ Lordy, Look in de pan o' mah hand.

Rollin On De Y. & M. V.

Here come de big wild-wagon,[2]
Gwine to Buffalo.
Ef I git whar she's gwine,
Ain't never comin' back no mo'.

She got a great big fir'man,
A hundred inches tall.
She soun' lak de panter [panther] squall,
Run lak cannon ball.

Chorus
Rollin on de Y. & M. V.,
Rollin on de Y. & M. V.
Here come de big wild-wagon,
Rollin on de Y. & M. V.

Rollin' On De Y. & M. V.

Here come de big wild wag-on, Gwine to Buf-fa-lo. Ef

I git whar she's gwine, _ Ain't nev-er com-in' back no mo.

2. A fast train of empty freight cars.

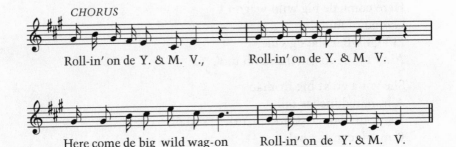

CHORUS

Roll-in' on de Y. & M. V.,   Roll-in' on de Y. & M. V.

Here come de big wild wag-on   Roll-in' on de Y. & M. V.

Pity a Po' Boy

This song typifies a strong and unique sense of suggestivity on the part of the Negro. Where the word "Lawd" comes it must not be taken as a sign of religious feeling. It is more an expression of serious meditation. However, often Negroes will say "Lawd Lawd" with only a feeling of reflection, amazement, or surprise behind the statement, only to make subsequent statements using the word with religious feeling. "Can't git a toe holt" comes from the mule driver's lexicon. Having watched the mules struggle to pull in muddy ground, the singer applies the figure to his own precariousness.

> Pity a po' boy,
> Pity a po' boy,
> Pity a po' boy, Lawd,
> Pity a po' boy,
> Pity a po' boy,
> Pity a po' boy, Lawd.

> Can't git a toe holt,
> Can't git a toe holt,
> Can't git a toe holt, Lawd,
> Can't git a toe holt,
> Can't git a toe holt,
> Can't git a toe holt, Lawd.

Pity a Po' Boy

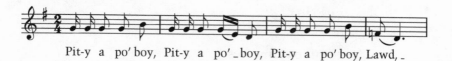

Pit-y a po' boy, Pit-y a po'_boy, Pit-y a po' boy, Lawd,_

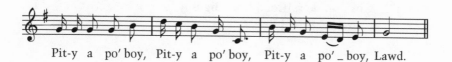

Pit-y a po' boy, Pit-y a po' boy, Pit-y a po'_boy, Lawd.

Lis'n, Big Boy

This is one of the rather few (five or six) work songs I have taught to male glee clubs. It was one of the most popular at the State Teachers' College in Montgomery, Alabama. Andrew Branche, Winston Jones, Joseph Paige, and Andrew Fair, who were students there and who later taught music in the state schools, made it very popular by teaching it to the children in their schools. However, the versions changed here and there due to transition by word of mouth. This version is the original one, with the exception that the call at the beginning was repeated at the end by Joseph Paige, who sang the verse.

> Hey Big Boy, Big Boy! (call)
>   (song)
> Lis'n, Big Boy,
> Ef yo' wanna be a man,
> Work de railroad line.
> Swingin', Big Boy,
> Wid a hammer in yo' han';
> On de railroad line.
>
> (call omitted second time)
> Lis'n, Big Boy,
> What I heered de people say,
> On de railroad line.

Yo' gal gwine quit yo'
'Cause yo' never git no pay;
On de railroad line.

Refrain
Work on de railroad line, yes,
Work on de railroad line.
Oh, work on de railroad line, Big Boy,
Work on de railroad line.

Lis'n, Big Boy

Hey ___ Big Boy, ___ Big Boy! _ Lis'n, Big Boy, ef yo'

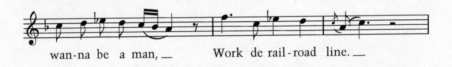

wan-na be a man, _ Work de rail-road line. _

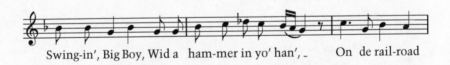

Swing-in', Big Boy, Wid a ham-mer in yo' han', _ On de rail-road

line. Work on de rail - road line, Yes,

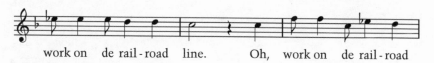

work on de rail - road line. Oh, work on de rail - road

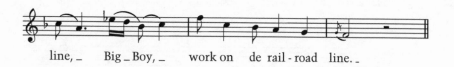

line, _ Big _ Boy, _ work on de rail - road line. _

Col' Iron

This song was sung for me in a dormitory room at Leland College one winter's night by my fine friend Kimuel Huggins. The furnace boiler had burst and the building was cold. As we sat around a contrary oil stove, Huggins began to proclaim his preference for the guitar above all instruments. To prove his point he began singing this song and relating how wonderful it was when heard with a guitar. Though I never wrote it down until now, it has remained in my head all of the intervening years.

Have yo' ever seen col' iron
Run lak lead, buddy, run lak lead;
Have yo' ever seen col' iron
Run lak lead, run lak lead?

Did yo' ever see de Capt'in
Standin' 'lone, buddy, standin' 'lone;
Did yo' ever see de Capt'in
Standin' 'lone, standin' 'lone?

He was scared to face de bossman
'Bout de pay, buddy, 'bout de pay;
He was scared to face de bossman
'Bout de pay, 'bout de pay.

Ef I ever see "De Special" [train]
Run mah way, buddy, run mah way;
Ah'm go' take de big road goin',
An' go' stay, an' go' stay.

Col' Iron

Railroad Song

Have yo' ev - er seen col' i - ron run lak

lead, bud - dy, run lak lead; Have yo'

ev - er seen col' i - ron run lak lead, run lak lead?

Sweet Water Rollin'

There is a version of this song in *St. Helena Island Spirituals*. It is religious and is possibly older than the version given here.

Verse
Roll me to de shore,
Roll me to de shore.
If I can't leave when you go,
Tell my best gal don't fool wid Joe,
Sweet water roll.

Chorus
Sweet water rollin',
Sweet water rollin',
Sweet water rollin',
Sweet water roll (Oh)

Sweet Water Rollin'

Sweet wat-er roll-in', Sweet wat-er roll-in', Sweet wat-er roll-in',

Sweet wat-er roll. _ (oh) Roll me to de shore, Roll me to de shore. If

I can't leave when you go, Tell my best gal don't fool wid Joe, _

Sweet wat-er roll. __

Got Mah Head Under Water

Got mah head under water,
So ah ain't go' swell mah chest.
Ah'm go' keep on trav'lin',
Let de good Lord do de rest,
Let de good Lord do de rest.

Got Mah Head Under Water

Pure Blues

Got mah head ___ und-er wat-er,   So ah ain't go' swell mah

chest.   Ah'm go' keep _____ on   trav'-lin,   Let de

good Lord do   de   rest,   Let de   good Lord do   de   rest.

I'll Wait for Sundown

Ain't but one thing on my min',
Dat I know can start my cryin',
Jes a li'l' gal 'bout five-foot fo',
But where she gone to I don't know.

Ain't but one thing in dis lan',
Dat can make me a worl' farin' man,
Jes a li'l' gal 'bout five-foot fo',
But where she gone to I don't know.

Chorus
So, ev'ry day, I'll wait for sundown,
Oh, ev'ry day, I'll wait for sundown,
Yes, ev'ry day, I'll wait for sundown,
To see if tomorrow will bring me back my love.[3]

3. See chapter 3 for other examples of blues.

I'll Wait for Sundown

Ain't but one thing on— my— min', Dat I know can

start— my cryin', Jes a li'l'— gal 'bout five - foot fo', But

where she— gone to I— don' know _____ So, ev' - ry

day, _____ I'll wait for— sun-down, _____ Oh ev' - ry

day, __ I'll wait for sun-down— Yes, ev'-ry day __ I'll wait for —

sun-down, — To see if to-mor-row will bring me back my love. __

Creepin' Midnight

Creepin' Midnight was a low down man,
Creepin' Midnight was a low down man,
Things he done couldn't no one understan'.

Creepin' Midnight bought hisself some shoes,
Creepin' Midnight bought hisself some shoes,
Paid de man in ones, but de po' man thought dey's twos.

Creepin' had him dozen wimmens or mo',
Creepin' had him dozen wimmens or mo',
Dey couldn't tell whether Creepin' was wid 'em or no.

Rascal went down to de com'sary sto',
Rascal went down to de com'sary sto',
Took all he want, den faded out de do'.

Dey put him in de penotensher jail,
Dey put him in de penotensher jail,
His black cat bone was all he need fer bail.

Creepin' walk on down de jailhouse stairs,
Creepin' walk on down de jailhouse stairs,
De key boss jumped an' high tail 'way f'om dere.

Creepin' died, but I can't tell yo' how,
Creepin' died, but I can't tell yo' how,
Truth is, he mout be still walkin' 'bout now.

Bur'ed him by col' iron railroad track,
Bur'ed him by col' iron railroad track,
So he could hear de runnin' o' de southbound Jack.

Refrain
Go down de line.

Creepin' Midnight

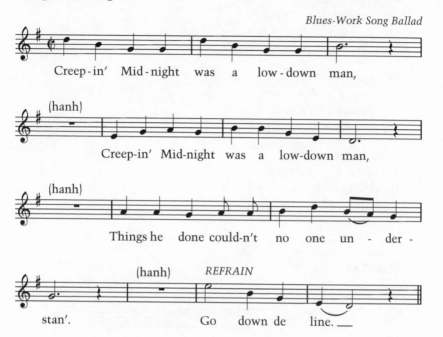

Blues-Work Song Ballad

Creep-in' Mid-night was a low-down man,

(hanh)

Creep-in' Mid-night was a low-down man,

(hanh)

Things he done could-n't no one un - der -

(hanh)   REFRAIN

stan'.   Go down de line. __

Nassau-American Song
Mosquito Bite Me

When I was a small boy in Jacksonville, Florida, it was customary for a group of Nassau Negroes to come to the Florida Baptist Academy each year as students. Among these were a few who did not have the complex that forbade them to sing and talk of their past. This song was one of the few I remember having heard. The boy I heard singing it was Arnett Mitchell, who was not a Nassau Negro but had learned it from the Negroes.

Mosquito bite me las' night,
De san' fly come ter see;
De monkey dance by side o' mah bed,
Said glad dat ain't a bee.

Mosquito sing me las' night,
De san' fly sing me too;
De rat coon [raccoon] heard what dey sing,
Said when yo' gwine git through?

De rabbit he don' dance,
De squir'l he dance fine;
De 'gator he so shame hisse'f,
He make lak he gone blin'.

I wish I was a lark,
De one what in de fiel';
De day I git through workin',
I would not have ter steal!

Nassau-American Song
"Mosquito Bite Me"

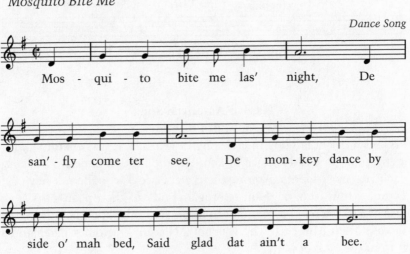

Dance Song

Mos - qui - to bite me las' night, De
san' - fly come ter see, De mon - key dance by
side o' mah bed, Said glad dat ain't a bee.

Sally Brown

Many songs of Negro origin have a peculiar sparkle that is very unlike the great majority of Negro folk songs. "Sally Brown," a dance song that has a tinge of jazz in it, seems to belong to the present as much as it does to the past. When this song is combined with foot-pats and hand-claps, the effect is to bring the dancer to the verge of frenzy.

> You ought to see Miss Sally Brown,
> Jes a-swingin' down de line,
> De dress she wear, it look so gran',
> I wish dat it was mine.

> Now here come sweet Miss Sally Brown,
> Folks all watchin' her pass by,
> She's sweeter den de sugar cane,
> An' better den peach pie.

> *Chorus*
> Shoo 'long, Sally Brown,
> Da, da, da, de o,
> Shoo 'long, Sally Brown,
> Da, da, da, de o.

Sally Brown

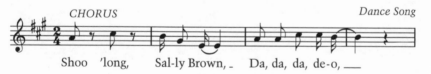

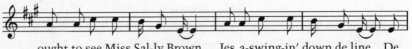

ought to see Miss Sal-ly Brown, _ Jes a-swing-in' down de line, _ De

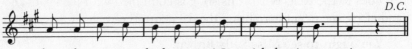

dress she wear, it look so gran', I wish dat it was mine.

O Me, Pity Po' Me

To my mind, this song is not as strongly Negro as some of the others, yet it is a product of Negro ingenuity.

> O me, pity po' me!
> I'm in dem ladies garden.
> O me, pity po' me!
> I'm in dem ladies garden.
> Bow to de ladies, Susan Gray;
> Bow to de gen'lmen, Susan Gray.
> Bow to de ladies, Susan Gray;
> Bow to de gen'lmen, Susan Gray.

O Me, Pity Po' Me

Dance Song

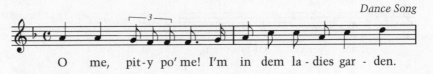

O me, pit-y po' me! I'm in dem la - dies gar - den.

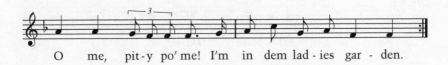

O me, pit-y po' me! I'm in dem lad - ies gar - den.

Bow to de lad-ies, Sus-an Gray; Bow to de gen'-l-men, Sus-an Gray.

Bow to de lad-ies, Sus-an Gray; Bow to de gen'-l-men, Sus-an Gray.

Cap'm Riley's Wagon

Meanness was perhaps never turned into mirth with more candor and good humor than in this song. To sing it is to dance. Negroes, always bitterly poor in the days gone by, had a hard time trying to pay the installments on the few pieces of furniture they bought. To be able to dance and sing amid such heartbreak is what has allowed the Negro to live in a situation in which many another race would have chosen fatalism and died.

Cap'm Riley, O Cap'm Riley,
Ah dunno yo' be so mean,
Yo' step all on mah baby corn,
Reachin' fo' de sewin' machine.

Cap'm Riley, O Cap'm Riley,
Yo' meanes' man I knows,
Jes git yo' big foots of'm dat dress—
Dems mah wife's Sunday clothes.

Cap'm Riley, O Cap'm Riley,
Yo' stayin' mouty long,
But yo' sho can't stay all night—
De beds is done all gone.

Chorus
Cap'm Riley's wagon been yar,
An' tuk all de furniture
An' car'ed um 'way.
Cap'm Riley's wagon been yar,
An' car'ed um, car'ed um 'way.

Cap'm Riley's Wagon

CHORUS   *Dance Song*

Cap'-m   Ril - ey's   wag - on   been   yar,   an'

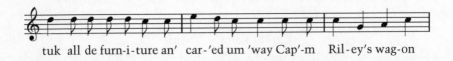

tuk all de furn-i-ture an' car-'ed um 'way Cap'-m Ril-ey's wag-on

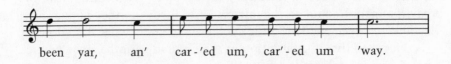

been   yar,   an'   car-'ed um,   car'-ed um   'way.

VERSE

Cap'-m   Ril - ey,   O   Cap'-m   Ril - ey,   Ah

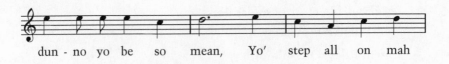

dun - no   yo   be   so   mean,   Yo'   step   all   on   mah

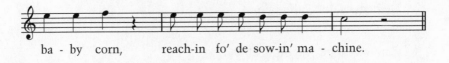

ba - by   corn,   reach-in   fo' de sow-in' ma - chine.

I'm Gonna Run to Town

"Ball de Jack" is an old dance that was never as popular in practice as it was in song. However, this particular song cast light on the fact that the dance was solo, which means that it was very primitive. The melody is odd and very fascinating.

> I'm gonna run to town,
> I'm gonna hurry back,
> To see my baby ball de jack.
> When she jump to de right,
> When she jump to de left,
> De folks all holler,
> Don't hurt yo'se'f.
> Da, da,
> Ball de jack;
> Da, da,
> Ball de jack.

I'm Gonna Run to Town

I'm gon-na run to town, I'm gon-na hur - ry back, To

see my bab - y ball de jack. When she jump to de right, When she

jump to de left, De folks all hol-ler, Don't hurt yo' - se'f.

Da, da, ball de jack; Da, da, ball de __ jack.

Go to Sleepy

This song in its various versions is familiar in some parts of the South. It seems to me that this is the most satisfying version that I have heard. One version was known by my mother-in-law, Rosa J. Fisher, in Hammer, Alabama, when she was a girl. She is now more than seventy years old. Some idea of the song's age is thereby given. Children like to sing it and use it as a sort of game song.

Go to sleepy little baby,
Ah'm go' give yo' pretty tea cake,
Big roun' tea cake,
Big red tea cake,
Big green tea cake,
Ev'y kind o' tea cake;
Go to sleepy little baby,
Bye-lo, bye-lo,
Bye-lo an' bye.

Go to sleepy little baby,
Ah'm go' give yo' pretty horses (etc.)

Go to sleepy little baby,
Ah'm go' give yo' pretty wagon (etc.)

Go to sleepy little baby,
Ah'm go' give yo' pretty ball (etc.)

Go to Sleepy

Play Song and Lullaby

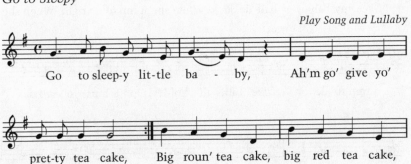

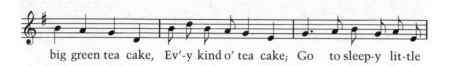

big green tea cake, Ev'-y kind o' tea cake; Go to sleep-y lit-tle

ba - by, Bye - lo, bye - lo bye-lo an' bye.

Dis Chile

Lullabies are perhaps the rarest of all Negro songs. Negroes usually sing to themselves as well as to children. This song is one of the most beautiful of all of these rare gems.

His mama do love dis chile,
His mama do love dis chile;
Jes cause he made so neat,
All over an' under his feet.
His mama do love dis chile,
His mama do love dis chile;
Love dis chile.

Dis Chile

Lullaby

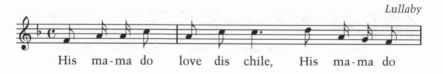

His ma-ma do love dis chile, His ma-ma do

love dis chile; Jes cause he made so neat, all __

ov-er an' un-der his feet. His ma-ma do love dis chile; His ma-ma do

love   dis   chile, _____   love   dis   chile _____

Many Thousand Gone

No more auction block for me,
No more, no more.
No more auction block for me,
Many thousand gone.

No more peck of corn for me (etc.)

No more driver's lash for me (etc.)

No more pint of salt for me (etc.)

No more mistress' call for me (etc.)

Many Thousand Gone

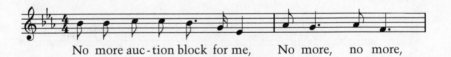

No more auc-tion block for me,   No more,   no more,

No more auc-tion block for me,   Man-y   thou-sand gone.

Is Master Going to Sell Us Tomorrow?

Mother, is master going to sell us tomorrow?
Yes, yes, yes!
Mother, is master going to sell us tomorrow?
Yes, yes, yes!
Mother, is master going to sell us tomorrow?
Yes, yes, yes!
Oh, watch and pray.

He is going to take us down to Georgia,
Yes, yes, yes! (etc.)
Oh, watch and pray.

Fare you well, mother, I must leave you,
Fare thee well! (etc.)
Oh, watch and pray.

Mother, don't you grieve after me,
No, no, no! (etc.)
Oh, watch and pray.

Is Master Going to Sell Us Tomorrow?

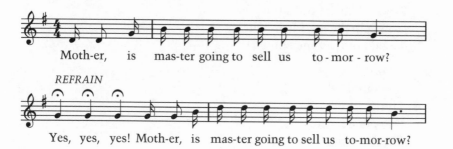

Moth-er, is mas-ter going to sell us to-mor-row?

REFRAIN

Yes, yes, yes! Moth-er, is mas-ter going to sell us to-mor-row?

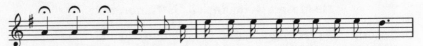

Yes, yes, yes! Moth-er, is mas-ter going to sell us to-mor-row?

Yes, yes, yes! Oh, — watch and — pray.

Stars in de Elements

Negro songs naturally speak of the sun more than of any other light in the heavens. However, the stars have enchanted the Negro as they have all men. The stars seem to be used mainly in religious songs, while the sun is used more generally. I know of comparatively few uses of the moon.

> When de storm is raging so,
> Good Lord, let me shine.
> Guide me to de peaceful shore,
> Good Lord, let me shine.

> Here's what Christians ought to do,
> Good Lord, let me shine.
> You help me an' I help you,
> Good Lord, let me shine.

> *Chorus*
> Stars in de elements,
> Shine, shine, shine.
> Stars in de elements,
> Shine, shine, shine.
> Stars in de elements,
> Shine, I want to shine,
> To shine like a star
> Dat's away in Glory;
> Good Lord, let me shine.

Stars in de Elements

Stars   in   de   el - e - ments, ___   shine,   shine, _ shine. _

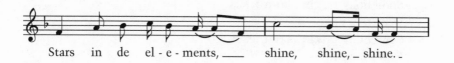

Stars   in   de   el - e - ments, ___   shine,   shine, _ shine. _

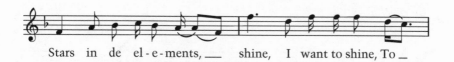

Stars   in   de   el - e - ments, ___   shine,   I   want to shine, To _

shine like a star dats a-way in Glo - ry;   Good Lord, let me shine. _

When de storm is   rag - in' so, _   Good Lord, let   me shine.

Guide me   to   de peace-ful shore, _   Good Lord, let   me shine. __

Ev'ywhere I Go

Ef I had a-died when I was young,
I wouldn't have dis race to run.

Chorus
Ev'ywhere I go,
Ev'ywhere I go,
Somebody talkin' 'bout Jesus
Ev'ywhere I go,
Somebody talkin' 'bout Jesus,
Ev'ywhere I go.

Ev'rywhere I Go

Ev'-y - where _ I go, Ev'-y - where _ I go,

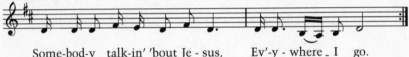

Some-bod-y talk-in' 'bout Je - sus, Ev'-y - where _ I go.

Ef I had a-died when I was young, _ I would-n't have dis race to run.

Some-bod-y talk-in' 'bout Je - sus, Ev'-y - where _ I go.

F'om Ev'y Graveyard
(As sung for me by Percy Stone of Savannah, Georgia)

I heard Jesus say,
Father these are they,
Come up through hard trials
F'om ev'y graveyard.

Blow out de sun,
Turn de moon to blood,
Loose de stars f'om heaven down
F'om ev'y graveyard.

Chorus
Oh what mournin',
Oh what mournin',
Oh what mournin',
F'om ev'y graveyard.

F'om Ev'y Graveyard

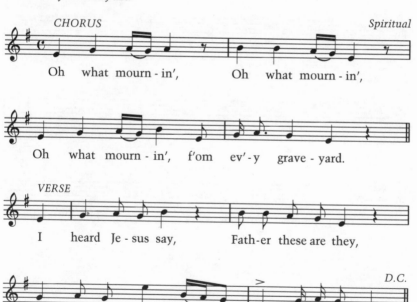

I'm Go' Stan'

I'm go' stan' right here,
Fo' mah Lord.
I'm go' stan' right here,
Fo' mah Lord.
I'm go' stan' right here,
'Til Shiloh come.
I'm go' stan' right here,
Fo' mah Lord;
Yes, fo' mah Lord.

I'm Go' Stan'

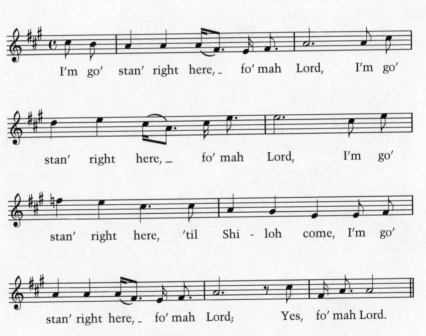

Through Dis Journey

As I go on through dis journey,
I will always take time to pray,
Time to pray,
Time to pray, pray, pray.
I will always take time to pray.

As I pray on through dis journey (etc.)

As I fight on through dis journey (etc.)

As I walk on through dis journey (etc.)

Through Dis Journey

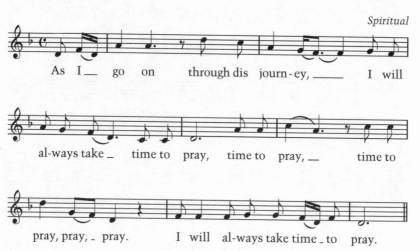

Ah'm Gonna Mek Mah Burden Easy

Ah'm gonna mek mah burden easy on mah knees,
Ah'm gonna mek mah burden easy on mah knees.
O, when ah git down on mah knees
An' say Jesus he'p me please—
Ah'm gonna mek mah burden easy on mah knees, on mah
     knees.

Ah'm gonna break de bread of mercy on mah knees (etc.)

Ah'm gonna mek mah peace in Glory on mah knees (etc.)

Ah'm gonna tell God how you treat me on mah knees (etc.)

Ah'm Gonna Mek Mah Burden Easy

Spiritual

Ah'm gon-na mek mah burd-en eas-y on mah knees, Ah'm gon-na

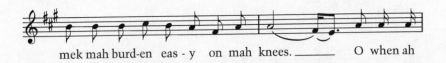

mek mah burd-en eas - y on mah knees. _____ O when ah

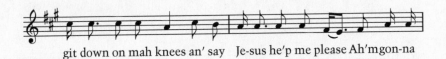

git down on mah knees an' say Je-sus he'p me please Ah'm gon-na

mek mah burd-en eas - y on mah knees _____ on mah knees.

Lord, Make Me

This is an unusual version of a familiar song, usually sung at Fisk University in six-eight time. It represents a certain amount of hymn influence.

Lord, make me mo' holy,
Oh Lord, make me mo' holy,
Oh Lord, make me mo' holy,
Untel we meet agin.

Lord, make me mo' loving (etc.)

Lord, make me mo' faithful (etc.)

Lord, make me mo' humble (etc.)

Lord, make me mo' trusting (etc.)

Lord, make me mo' righteous (etc.)

Lord, Make Me

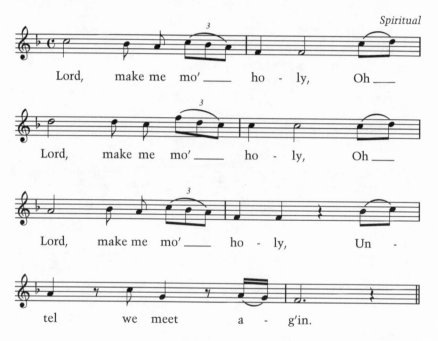

You Have to Pray Hard

Miss Emma, who was a combination of prophet, dreamer, and cook extraordinaire, sang this song for me one morning while she worked in the kitchen. She prided herself on dreaming things that were to happen rather than on her singing. This is the only time I remember hearing her sing. I would venture to say that her singing was superior to some of her other accomplishments. There is a strange melancholy to this song which defies mere musicological analysis.

Yo' have to pray hard to fin' Jesus,
Yo' have to pray hard to fin' Jesus,
Yo' have to pray hard to fin' Jesus,
An' yo' can't stay away.

Yo' have to bow low to fin' Jesus,
Yo' have to bow low to fin' Jesus,
Yo' have to bow low to fin' Jesus,
An' yo' can't stay away.

Chorus
Can't stay away,
Yo' can't stay away,
Yo' have to pray hard to fin' Jesus,
An' yo' can't stay away.

You Have to Pray Hard

Spiritual

Yo' have to pray hard ____ to fin' Je - sus, Yo'

have to pray hard __ to fin' Je-sus, Yo' have to pray hard __ to

REFRAIN

fin' Je-sus, An' yo' can't stay _ a - way.   Can't stay _ a -

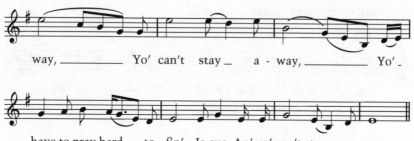

way, _____ Yo' can't stay _ a - way, _____ Yo' _

have to pray hard __ to fin' Je-sus, An' yo' can't stay _ a - way.

Keep My Commandments

Listen now my brother
I'll tell you what to do,
You better believe in Jesus
And stay on de journey too.

Listen now my sister
I'll tell you what I'd do,
I'd keep all the Ten Commandments
And believe on the Savior too.

The road is rough and rocky,
But you must keep to the right,
If you follow the narrow pathway
You'll surely come to light.

Chorus
Oh, if you love me keep my Commandments,
Oh, if you love me keep my Commandments,
Oh, if you love me keep my Commandments.
Oh, you better walk humble for my Lord
Everywhere you go!

Keep My Commandments

CHORUS   *Spiritual*

Oh,   if   you   love   me   keep my com-mand-ments, Oh, _____

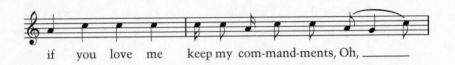

if   you   love   me   keep my com-mand-ments, Oh, _____

if   you   love   me   keep my com-mand-ments. Oh,   you

bet-ter walk hum-ble for my Lord _   Ev - ery-where you go!

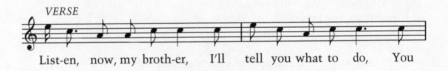

VERSE

List-en, now, my broth-er, I'll   tell you what to   do,   You

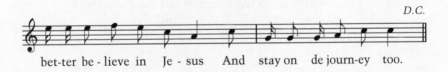

D.C.

bet-ter be - lieve in Je - sus   And stay on de journ-ey too.

Judgment Will Find You So

O brethren, brethren, watch and pray,
Judgment will find you so,
For Satan's round you every day,
Judgment will find you so.

The tallest tree in paradise,
Judgment will find you so,
The Christian calls the tree of life,
Judgment will find you so.

Oh! hallelujah to the lamb,
Judgment will find you so,
The Lord is on the giving hand,
Judgment will find you so.

Chorus
Just as you live,
Just so you die,
And after death,
Judgment will find you so.

Judgment Will Find You So

CHORUS · Spiritual

Just as you _ live, just so you _ die, And
af - ter death, Judg-ment will find you so. O

breth-ren, breth-ern, watch and pray, Judg-ment will find you so, For

Sa-tan's round you eve-ry day, Judg-ment will find you so.

I Been in the Storm So Long

I never shall forget that day,
Give me little time to pray,
When Jesus wash my sins away,
Give me little time to pray.

If ever I get on the mountain top,
Give me little time to pray,
I'll shout and shout and never stop,
Give me little time to pray.

Chorus
I been in the storm so long,
I been in the storm so long, children,
I been in the storm so long,
Just give me little time to pray.

I Been in the Storm So Long

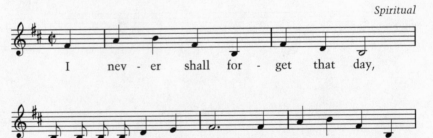

I nev - er shall for - get that day,

Give me lit - tle time to pray, When Je - sus wash my

sins a - way, Give me lit - tle time to pray.

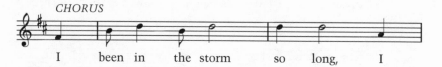

I been in the storm so long, I

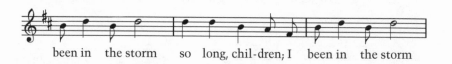

been in the storm so long, chil-dren; I been in the storm

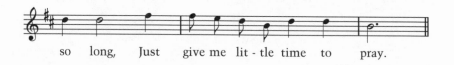

so long, Just give me lit - tle time to pray.

Read de Sign o' Jedgment

(See other verse version in poetry section)

Read de sign o' jedgment,
Aye Lord,
Read de sign o' jedgment,
Aye Lord,
Read de sign o' jedgment,
Aye Lord;
It drawin' nearer an' nearer,
Aye my Lord.

Read de Sign o' Jedgment

Spiritual

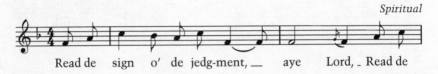

Read de   sign   o' de jedg-ment, __   aye   Lord, _ Read de

sign o' de jedg-ment, _   aye _ Lord, Read de   sign o' de jedg-ment, _

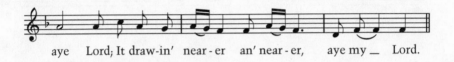

aye   Lord; It draw-in' near - er   an' near - er,   aye my __ Lord.

Sweet Jesus

Sweet Jesus, Sweet Jesus;
He's de Lilly of de Vally,
De bright and mornin' star.
Sweet Jesus, Sweet Jesus;
He's de ruler of all Nations,
Praise His name.

Can you trust Him, can you trust Him;
He's de Lilly of de Valley,
De bright and mornin' star.
Can you trust Him, can you trust Him;
He's de ruler of all nations,
Praise His name.

Sweet Jesus, Sweet Jesus (etc. same as first verse)

Sweet Jesus

Sung by Mrs. Rachel Ponder
at Fort Valley, Ga.
Spiritual

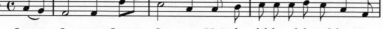

Sweet _ Je - sus, Sweet _ Je - sus; He's de   lil-ly of de val-ley, De

bright an' __ morn-in' star. Sweet _   Je - sus,   Sweet _

Je - sus; He's de   rul-er of all na-tions, Praise his name.

Get in Union

Get in union,
Jesus is lis-a-nin,
Oh, get in union,
Jesus died.

Church in union (etc.)

I'm in union (etc.)

Stay in union (etc.)

Get in Union

Three Tone Spiritual

Get in un - ion, Je - sus is lis - a - nin; Oh,

D.C.

get in un - ion, Je - sus died.

I Stand an' Fol' My Arms

Here is a deep, moving song that shows the Negro's ability to put drama into a few simple words and notes. It is a sorrow spiritual born of the feeling that the singer at times becomes weak in his religious faith and tires of wearing the yoke of Jesus and bearing his burden. Yet the singer weeps at the very thought of spiritual frailty, so much so that he gathers his troubled breast in his arms and wrings his hands in total anguish, weeping aloud.

> Sometime I feel dat I never been born ag'in.
> Oh, sometime I feel dat I never been born ag'in.
> Oh, sometime I feel dat I never been born ag'in.
> Den I stand an' fol' my arms an' I cry, cry, cry.
> Den I stand an' fol' my arms an' I cry.

> Sometime I feel dat I jes can't bear my load.
> Oh, sometime I feel dat I jes can't bear my load.
> Oh, sometime I feel dat I jes can't bear my load.
> Den I stand an' wring my hands an' I cry, cry, cry.
> Den I stand an' wring my hands an' I cry.

I Stand an' Fol' My Arms

Spiritual

Some-time I feel dat I nev-er been born _ a - g'in. Oh,

some-time I feel dat I nev-er been born _ a - g'in. Oh,

some-time I feel dat I nev-er been born _ a - g'in. Den I

stand an' fol' _ my _ arms an' I cry, cry, cry. ____ Den I

stand an' fol' __ my __ arms an' I cry.

Don't God's Chillun Have a Hard Time

De wind may blow on me,
De worl' may use me hard,
I'll put my trust in Jesus,
An' keep my faith in God.

My friends may turn on me,
My family use me hard,
I'll put my trust in Jesus,
An' keep my faith in God.

De lighthouse may not be shinin',
My way be long an' hard,
I'll put my trust in Jesus,
An' keep my faith in God.

Don't never be discouraged,
Don't never be down trod,
Jes put your trust in Jesus,
An' keep your faith in God.

Chorus
Don't God's chillun have a hard time,
Hard time, hard time.
Don't God's chillun have a hard time,
Livin' in dis cruel worl'.

Don't God's Chillun Have a Hard Time

CHORUS   Spiritual

Don't God's chil-lun have a hard time, _ Hard time, _hard time. _

Don't God's chil-lun have a hard time, _ Liv-in' in dis cru-el worl'.

VERSE

De wind may blow _on me,   De worl' may use me hard,   I'll

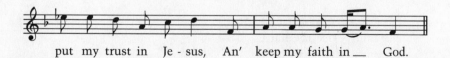

put my trust in   Je - sus,   An'   keep my faith in __ God.

Jesus, Lead Me Thu Dis Troublin' Worl'

Jesus, lead me, lead me thu dis troublin' worl',
Jesus, lead me ev'ywhere ah go.
As ah jernay thu de stawm,
Keep me safe f'om ev'y hawm.
Jesus, lead me, lead me thu dis troublin' worl'.

Jesus, he'p me, he'p me thu dis troublin' worl',
Jesus, he'p me ev'ywhere ah go.
He'p mah stumblin' feet ter stan',
Twell ah view de Promis' Lan'.
Jesus, he'p me, he'p me thu dis troublin' worl'.

Jesus, Lead Me Thu Dis Troublin' Worl'

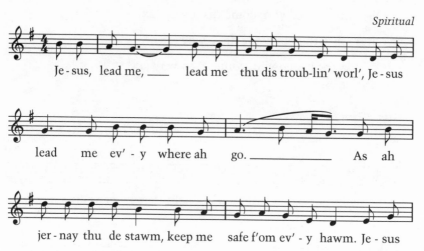

Jesus, Come Dis-a Way

You said you was a-coming,
Come dis-a way,
You said you was a-coming,
Come dis-a way.
Don't come angry,
Come dis-a way,
Don't come angry,
Come dis-a way.

Chorus
Oh! Jesus, come dis-a way,
Oh! Jesus, come dis-a way.

Oh! come in mercy, come dis-a way (2x)

Oh! Lord, I need you, come dis-a way (2x)

Oh! I am afflicted, come dis-a way (2x)

Oh! I know I need you, come dis-a way (2x)

Jesus, Come Dis-a Way

Spiritual

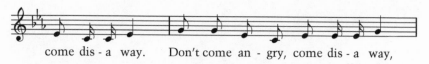

come dis - a way.   Don't come an - gry, come dis - a way,

D.C.

Don't _ come _ an - gry, come dis - a way.

Po' Lil' Jesus

O po' lil' Jesus
Dis worl' gonna break yo' heart,
Dere'll be no place ter lay yo' head, my Lord;
O po' lil' Jesus.

O Mary, she de mother,
O Mary, she bow down an cry,
For dere's no place to lay His head, my Lord;
O po' lil' Jesus.

Come down all you holy angels,
Sing 'round Him wid yo' golden harps,
For some day He goan die to save dis worl', my Lord;
O po' Jesus.

Po' Lil' Jesus

Spiritual

O ___ po' _ lil' _ Je - sus, dis worl' _ gon-na break yo' heart, Dere'll be no place ter lay _ yo' head, _ my Lord; O po' lil' _ Je - sus.

Let Yo' Light Shine

Ef a sinner man sees yo' light,
Let yo' light shine;
He will always try to put it out,
Let yo' light shine.

Ef a lier man sees yo' light (etc.)

Ef a gambling man sees yo' light (etc.)

Ef a hypocrite sees yo' light (etc.)

Chorus
Let yo' light so shine,
Let yo' light so shine,
Let yo' light so shine,
To he'p de wanderin' pilgrim
Fin' de way.

Let Yo' Light Shine

Let _ yo' light so shine, Let _ yo' light so shine, _ Let _ yo'

light so shine, To he'p de wan-derin' pil - grim fin' de way.

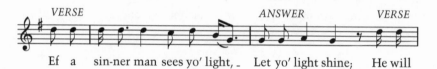

Ef a sin-ner man sees yo' light, _ Let yo' light shine; He will

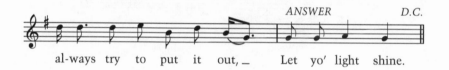

al-ways try to put it out, _ Let yo' light shine.

Anyhow, Anyhow

If your mother treat you wrong,
Let the Holy Ghost be your guide.
At the cross you can bow,
And keep on to Heaven anyhow.

If your sister treat you wrong (etc.)

If your brother treat you wrong (etc.)

If your neighbor treat you wrong (etc.)

If your father treat you wrong (etc.)

If a liar treat you wrong (etc.)

Chorus
Anyhow, anyhow,
Anyhow, anyhow,
At the cross you can bow,
And keep on to Heaven anyhow.

Anyhow, Anyhow

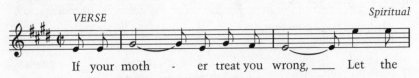

If your moth - er treat you wrong, ___ Let the

Ho - ly Ghost be your   guide, ___   At the   cross   you can

bow, ___   An'   keep on   to heav-en an - y - how.

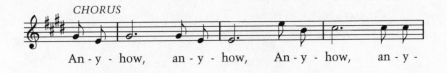

An - y - how,   an - y - how,   An - y - how,   an - y -

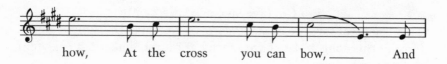

how,   At the   cross   you can   bow, _____   And

keep   on   to   Hea - ven   an - y - how.

I'm Goin' On

I'm on de way to de fiel' of battle,
I'm on de way to de fiel' of battle.
I have no fear for de journey,
I'm goin' on to Canaan lan'.

I'm goin' to stay on de fiel' of battle (etc.)

I am a soldier on de fiel' of battle (etc.)

I'm Goin' On

Spiritual

I'm   on de way _   to de   fiel'   of   bat - tle,

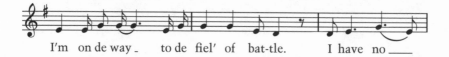

I'm   on de way _   to de   fiel'   of   bat-tle.   I have no _____

fear for   de journ-ey,   I'm   goi'n' on   to   Ca-naan   lan'.

I'm Go' Live So God Can Use Me

This is a great favorite in some parts of Georgia. The simple, direct force of this song, in language as well as music, makes it a true item of Negro creativity.

> I'm go' live so God can use me
> Anywhere, at any time.
> I'm go' live so God can use me
> Anywhere, at any time.
>
> I'm go' serve so God can use me (etc.)
>
> I'm go' pray so God can use me (etc.)
>
> I'm go' work so God can use me (etc.)
>
> I'm go' sing so God can use me (etc.)
>
> I'm go' trust so God can use me (etc.)
>
> I'm go' b'lieve so God can use me (etc.)

I'm Go' Live So God Can Use Me

Spiritual

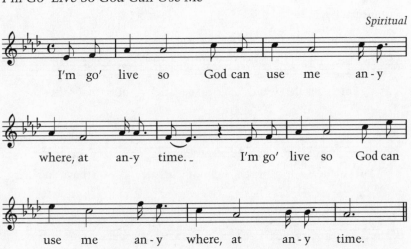

I'm go' live so God can use me an-y where, at an-y time._ I'm go' live so God can use me an-y where, at an-y time.

You Ought to Live So God Can Use You

Obviously these two songs are parent and child. I cannot be certain about which is which, but it seems logical that the one on admonition is older.

> You ought to live so God can use you,
> You ought to live so God can use you,
> You ought to live so God can use you,
> Anywhere, at any time.

> You ought to serve so God can use you (etc.)

> You ought to pray so God can use you (etc.)

> You ought to sing so God can use you (etc.)

> You ought to trust so God can use you (etc.)

> You ought to work so God can use you (etc.)

You Ought to Live So God Can Use You

Spiritual

You ought to   live so   God can use you,   You ought to

live so   God _ can use _ you,   You ought to   live so   God can

use   you,   An - y - where, at   an-y   time. _____

Ah'm Prayin' on Mah Way

Ah'm prayin', ah'm prayin' on mah way,
Ah'm prayin', ah'm prayin' on mah way.
Ah'm prayin', ah'm prayin' on mah way,
Ah'm goin' on dis road to Canaan lan'.

Oh brother, ah'm prayin' on mah way (etc.)

Oh mournah, ah'm prayin' on mah way (etc.)

Oh sister, ah'm prayin' on mah way (etc.)

Oh deacon, ah'm prayin' on mah way (etc.)

Oh elder, ah'm prayin' on mah way (etc.)

Ah'm Prayin' on Mah Way

Spiritual

Ah'm   pray - in', _   Ah'm   pray-in' on mah way, Ah'm

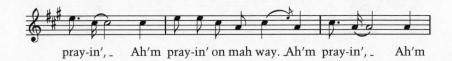

pray-in', _   Ah'm pray-in' on mah way. Ah'm pray-in', _   Ah'm

pray-in' on mah way, Ah'm goin' on dis   road to Ca-naan lan'.

Ah Got Heb'm in Mah View

Ah got Heb'm in mah view,
An' mah jernay ah persue.
Ah'm goin' to dat city,
Lawd, ah got Heb'm in mah view.

Ah Got Heb'm in Mah View

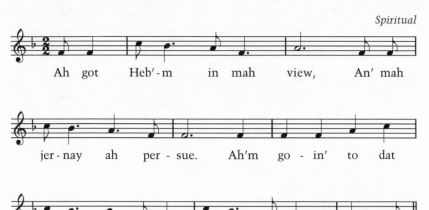

Don' Leave Me, Lord

Don' leave me, Lord,
Don' never leave me, Lord;
Please don' leave me in dis worl' alone.
Don' leave me, Lord,
Don' never leave me, Lord,
Please don' never leave me, Lord.

Don' Leave Me, Lord

leave   me,   Lord, _   Don'   nev-er   leave _ me, Lord,

Please   don'   nev-er   leave me,   Lord. _____

Lord, Have Mercy

Lord, have mercy,
Lord, have mercy,
Lord, have mercy
On my soul.

When I'm troubled,
When I'm troubled,
When I'm troubled
In mah soul.

When I journey,
When I journey,
When I journey
With mah soul.

When I'm cryin',
When I'm cryin',
When I'm cryin'
Through dis worl'.

Lord, Have Mercy

Lord —— have _ mer - cy,   Lord, _ have _ mer - cy,

Lord —— have _ mer - cy   on ____ my __ soul.

Please Don't Drive Me Away

I'm a beggar, don't drive me away,
I'm a beggar, don't drive me away.

I love you, don't drive me away,
I love you, don't drive me away.

I am motherless, don't drive me away,
I am motherless, don't drive me away.

I am afflicted, don't drive me away,
I am afflicted, don't drive me away.

I am needy, don't drive me away,
I am needy, don't drive me away.

Chorus
Lord, you know I am poor,
But don't drive me from your door,
Please don't drive me away.

Please Don't Drive Me Away

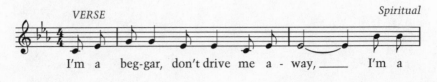

I'm a   beg-gar, don't drive me a - way, ___   I'm a

beg-gar, don't drive me a - way. ___   Lord, you know I am poor,

But don't drive me from your door, Please don't drive me a - way. _

Rock de Cradle, Mary

Mary had but one child,
Born in Bethlehem;
Ev'ry time dat baby cried,
She rocked Him in a wearied land!

Carpenter was Joseph,
Loved de Mary fair;
Journey'd on to Bethlehem,
An' foun' de little Christ chil' dere.

Yonder come old Herod,
Wicked King and bold,
Lookin' for de children
F'om six to eight days old.

Judas was a wicked man,
Wicked man was he,
He betrayed our gracious Lord
An' dey hanged Him on a tree.

Chorus
Rock de cradle, Mary!
Stay all night,
If it's all night long!

Rock de Cradle, Mary

Mar-y had _ but one child, _ Born in Beth - le - hem;

Ev-'ry time _ dat ba-by cried, _ She rocked Him in a

CHORUS

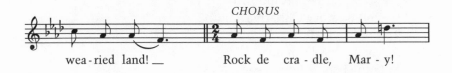

wea-ried land! _ Rock de cra - dle, Mar - y!

Stay all _ night, If it's all night long!

A New Bell

A new bell rang in Glory,
In Glory Christmas mornin'.
It rang in Glory Christmas morn,
To tell ev'ybody
A wonder has been done.
In Bethlehem is born de son,
In Bethlehem, in Bethlehem.

De Angels tol' de story,
De story Christmas mornin'.
Dey tol' de story Christmas morn,
To tell ev'ybody
A wonder has been done.
In Bethlehem is born a son,
In Bethlehem, in Bethlehem.

A star was brightly shinin',
Shinin' Christmas mornin'.
Was brightly shinin' Christmas morn,
To tell ev'ybody
A wonder has been done.
In Bethlehem is born a son,
In Bethlehem, in Bethlehem.

We'll go an' tell de story,
De story Christmas mornin',
Go tell de story Christmas morn,
To tell ev'ybody
A wonder has been done.
In Bethlehem is born a son,
In Bethlehem, in Bethlehem.

A New Bell

A   new   bell   rang   in   Glo - ry, __   In

Glo-ry Chris'-mas morn-in'.   It   rang   in   Glo-ry Chris'-mas

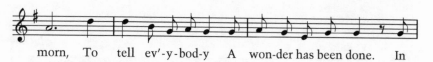

morn,   To   tell   ev'-y-bod-y   A   won-der has been done.   In

Beth-le-hem is born de Son,   In Beth-le-hem,   in Beth-le-hem. —

De Glory Manger

Dey turn 'way Mary an'a Joseph,
'Way f'om de inn!
An' dat's what made de Glory Manger.

Dey laid my pretty li'l' Jesus,
Down in de straw,
An' dat's what made de Glory Manger.

An' all His pretty li'l' fingers,
Played in de straw,
An' dat's what made de Glory Manger.

Chorus
An'a hallelujah!
An'a hallelujah, Lord!
Wasn't dat a bright Bethlehem mornin',
All 'round de Glory Manger.

De Glory Manger

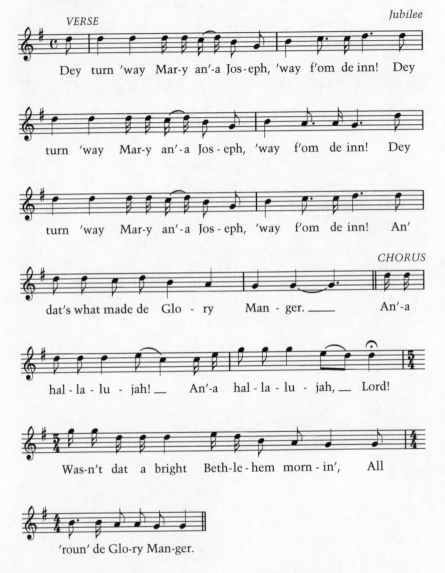

VERSE   *Jubilee*

Dey turn 'way Mar-y an'-a Jos-eph, 'way f'om de inn! Dey

turn 'way Mar-y an'-a Jos-eph, 'way f'om de inn! Dey

turn 'way Mar-y an'-a Jos-eph, 'way f'om de inn! An'

CHORUS

dat's what made de Glo - ry Man - ger. ___ An'-a

hal - la - lu - jah! ___ An'-a hal - la - lu - jah, ___ Lord!

Was-n't dat a bright Beth-le-hem morn - in', All

'roun' de Glo-ry Man-ger.

I Been Tried

Reverend E. R. Carter, pastor of Friendship Baptist Church in Atlanta, Georgia, for more than sixty years, was very fond of Negro religious songs. I was privileged to be in charge of the music celebrating his sixtieth anniversary as pastor, and I used "I Been Tried" as a special token of appreciation for his long and hard service.

> Tried in de fire
> An' tried in de flame,
> My God knows jes what I am.
> I come through in my Jesus name,
> My God knows jes what I am.

> *Chorus*
> I been tried,
> I been tried,
> I been tried, my Lord;
> My God knows jes what I am.

I Been Tried

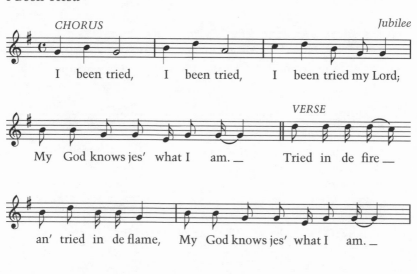

John Wrote

There are now several versions of this song. However, this particular one is rather individual and in my opinion reflects the spirit and singing style of James Craig.

> John wrote my mother a letter,
> When-a he was a-writing.
> John wrote my mother a letter,
> When-a he was a-writing.
> John wrote my mother a letter,
> When he was a-writing.
> Oh! Oh! John, John,
> Seal up de book, John;
> An' don' you write no mo'!
>
> John wrote de seven gospels (etc.)
>
> John wrote on de Isle of Patmos (etc.)

John Wrote

Jubilee

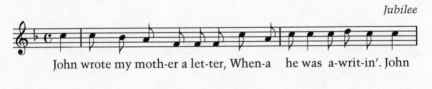

John wrote my moth-er a let-ter, When-a he was a-writin'. John

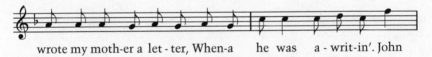

wrote my moth-er a let-ter, When-a he was a-writin'. John

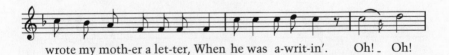

wrote my moth-er a let-ter, When he was a-writin'. Oh!_ Oh!

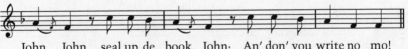

John,_ John, seal up de book,_John; An' don' you write no mo!

Lord, I Done Got Ready
(Version 1)

Lord, I done got ready for travelin';
For travelin',
For travelin'.
Lord, I done got ready for travelin';
Done got on mah travelin' shoes.

Lord, I done got ready for leavin' here (etc.)

Lord, I done got ready for journeyin' (etc.)

Lord, I Done Got Ready
Version I

Jubilee

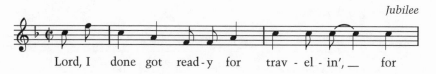

Lord, I done got read-y for trav - el - in', __ for

trav-el-in', _ for trav-el - in'. _ Lord, I done got read-y for

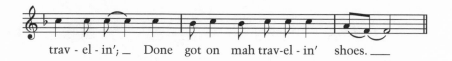

trav - el - in'; _ Done got on mah trav-el-in' shoes. __

I Done Got Ready
(Version 2)
Sung by Cleveland Perry in the Alabama coal mines near Birmingham.
The verse is used for a number of spirituals in this region, as well as in
some parts of Georgia. The chorus is also used often in modified form.

Hear me, Jesus, hear me;
Hear me if you please.

If you won't hear me standin',
I'll fall down on mah knees.

Keep me, Jesus, keep me (etc.)

Guide me, Jesus, guide me (etc.)

Chorus
Lord, I done got ready for trav'lin',
Lord, I done got ready for trav'lin',
Lord, I done got ready for trav'lin',
Lord, I got on mah trav'lin' shoes.

I Done Got Ready
Version II

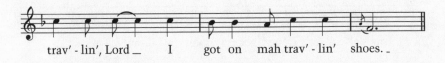

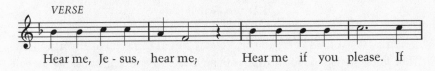

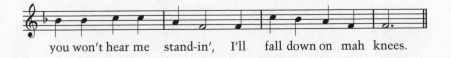

I Got Good News

I would not be a sinner,
I tell yo' de reason why;
I'm 'fraid when my Lord call me,
I could not go on high.

I would not be a hip'crite (etc.)

I would not be a liar (etc.)

I would not be a gambler (etc.)

I would not be a pertender (etc.)

I would not be a back slider (etc.)

Chorus
I got good news to tell you,
I got good news to tell you,
I got good news to tell you,
My soul's done foun' de Lord.

I Got Good News

I got good news __ to tell you, I got good news __ to

tell you, I got good news _ to tell you, My soul's done foun' de Lord.

I would not be a sin-ner, I tell yo' de rea-son

why; I'm 'fraid when my Lord call me, I could not go on high.

I Know I'm Right

I know I'm right,
Because I seen de light;
I know I'm right,
Because I seen de light;
I know I'm right,
Because I seen de light;
I read Gen'sis, Psalms, an' Malachi,
My soul got happy an' it set me on fire;
An' I know I'm right
Instead o' wrong.

I know I'm in,
Because I'm free from sin;
I know I'm in,
Because I'm free from sin;
I know I'm in,
Because I'm free from sin;
I been to de river
An' I been baptize',
My soul's got a home
In Paradise;
An' I know I'm right
Instead o' wrong.

I know I'm blest,
Because I've stood de test;

I know I'm blest,
Because I've stood de test;
I know I'm blest,
Because I've stood de test;
Ol' Satan come
Knocked on mah door,
When he seen my sword
He turned 'roun' to go;
An' I know I'm right
Instead o' wrong.

I Know I'm Right

Jubilee

I know I'm right, Be - cause I seen de light;

I know I'm right, Be - cause I seen de light; _

I know I'm right, Be - cause I seen de light; I read

Gen'-sis, Psalms an' Mal-a - chi, _ My soul got hap-py an' it

set me on fire; _ An' I know I'm right in-stead o' wrong.

Oh, Write Muh Name

I
Write muh name wid a golden pen

II
Write muh name in de Book o' Life

III
Write muh name in de Book o' de Lamb

Chorus
Oh, write muh name,
Oh, write muh name,
Oh, write muh name,
Angels in de heaven go' write muh name.

Refrain
Angels in de heaven go' write muh name.

Oh, Write Muh Name

Over in Zion

I got a new name,
Over in Zion.
I got a new name,
Over in Zion.
I got a new name,
Over in Zion;
It's mine,
It's mine,
It's mine,
I declare it's mine.

I got a mother (etc.)

I got a dear friend (etc.)

I got a Savior (etc.)

Over in Zion

Jubilee

I got a new name, o - ver in Zi - on.
I got a new name, o - ver in Zi - on.
I got a new name, o - ver in Zi - on; It's
mine, it's mine, it's mine, I de-clare it's mine.

Somebody's Here

This two-tone song was heard at the Bethlehem Church of God, on Hunter Street in Atlanta, Georgia. There was only one stanza, which was sung over and over with a steady rise in enthusiasm and a slight increase in tempo.

> Somebody's here
> An' it mus' be Jesus,
> Somebody's here
> An' it mus' be de Lawd.

Somebody's Here

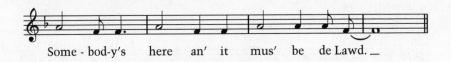

'Til Shiloh Come

> Lord, I got de love of Jesus burnin' in mah heart,
> Lord, I got de love of Jesus burnin' in mah heart,
> Lord, I got de love of Jesus burnin' in mah heart.
> I'm go' stan', I'm go' stan',
> I'm go' stan' 'til Shiloh come.

> Lord, I got de Ten Commandments burnin' in mah heart (etc.)

> Lord, I got de Golden Rule burnin' in mah heart (etc.)

> Lord, I got de Holy Spirit burnin' in mah heart (etc.)

> Oh, I got love for my neighbor burnin' in mah heart (etc.)

'Til Shiloh Come

Jubilee

Lord, I got de love of Je-sus burn-in' in mah heart, Lord, I
got de love of Je-sus burn-in' in mah heart,_ Lord, I
got de love of Je-sus burn-in' in my heart.._ I'm go'
stan' 'till Shi - loh come, I'm go' stan', _____ I'm go'
stan', _____ I'm go' stan' 'till Shi - loh come.

Wonderful Mawnin'

Wasn't dat a wonderful mawnin',
When de angels tol' de good news,
Wasn't dat a wonderful mawnin',
When de angels tol' de good news,
Wasn't dat a wonderful mawnin',
When de angels tol' de good news;
Tol' de good news all 'roun' an' 'roun',
Dat Jesus Christ was born.

Wasn't dat a bright star shinin' (etc.)

Wasn't dat a sweet choir singin' (etc.)

Wasn't dat a day in Glory (etc.)

Wonderful Mawnin'

Jubilee

Was-n't dat a won - der-ful maw-nin', When de

an - gels tol' de good news, Was-n't dat a won - der-ful

maw-nin', When de an - gels tol' de good news, Was-n't dat a

won - der-ful maw-nin', When de an - gels tol' de good news;

Tol' de good news all 'roun' an' 'roun', Dat Je-sus Christ was born.

Mah Good Lord Done Been Yere

Chorus
Mah good Lord done been yere,
He bless mah soul an' gone away.
Mah good Lord done been yere,
He bless mah soul an' gone.

Dig deep ol' warror an' mek no alarm,
Fer ef yo' be anchored in Jesus Chris'
De worl' can do yo' no harm.

Mah Good Lord Done Been Yere

My good Lord done been yere, ___ He bless may soul ___ an'
gone a-way. ___ My good Lord done been yere, ___ He
bless mah soul ___ an' gone. Dig deep ___ ol' ___ war - r'or An'
mek no ___ a - larm, Fer ef yo' be an - chored in
Je - sus Chris', ___ De worl' ___ can do yo' no harm.

Oh, What a Band!

A version of this song appears in *Calhoun Plantation Songs*. This piece has a vigorous, never-ending suggestion of a martial drumbeat. It is one of the few Negro songs that seem to be a direct outgrowth of another type of musical organization.

> I love to hear sweet music
> From dat church above,
> I love to hear sweet music,
> It fills my heart wid love.
>
> I love to hear sweet preachin' (etc.)
>
> I love to hear sweet prayin' (etc.)
>
> I love to hear sweet singin' (etc.)
>
> *Chorus*
> Oh, what a band of music,
> Oh, what a band of music,
> Oh, what a band of music,
> Goes singin' through the land.

Oh, What a Band!

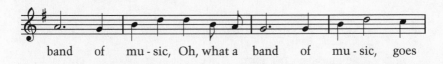

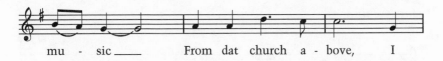

mu - sic ___ From dat church a - bove, I

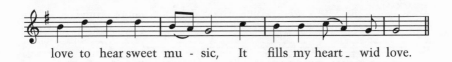

love to hear sweet mu - sic, It fills my heart _ wid love.

Happy Time

(The lines of all verses must be sung before the refrain.)

Great God, I'm gonna put on my golden slippers,
Then I'm gonna walk all around in glory,
Then I'm gonna take up my starry crown,
Then I'm gonna put it a-on my head,
An' then I'm gonna shake hands a-wid King Jesus.

Great God, I'm gonna stand in the Holy number,
Then I'm gonna sit at the welcome table,
Then I'm gonna tell all about my journey,
Then I'm gonna rise and try my wings,
Then I'm gonna fly all around through heaven;
Then I'm gonna come back before the throne,
Then I'm gonna shake hands a-wid King Jesus.

Great God, I'm gonna find my darling mother,
Then I'm gonna find my loving father,
Then I'm gonna know as we are known,
Then I'm gonna come back before the throne,
Then I'm gonna shake hands a-wid King Jesus.

Chorus
Oh Children!
Won't that be one happy time?
Won't that be one happy time?

Refrain
An' won't that be one happy time.

Happy Time

CHORUS   Jubilee

O chil - dren, won't that be one hap-py time? _____

__ Won't that be one hap-py time? _____

VERSE

__ Great God, I'm gon - na put on my gold - en

slip - pers, Then I'm gon - na walk all a - round in

glo - ry, Then I'm gon - na take up my star - ry

crown, __ Then I'm gon - na put it - a on __ my

head, An' then I'm gon-na shake hands a-wid King Je - sus, An'

REFRAIN

won't that be one hap-py time? _____

I Want My Name

I want my name
Written down in heaven;
Lord, I want my name
Written down in de book o' Life.

I know my name (etc.)

I got my crown (etc.)

I Want My Name

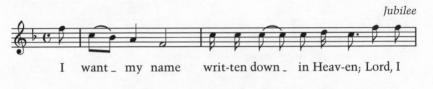

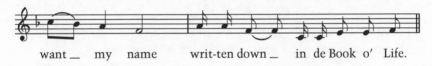

I Saw de Lighthouse

I saw de lighthouse,
Amen.
I saw de lighthouse,
Amen.
I saw de lighthouse,
When I see Jesus,
Trouble be over,
Amen!

I Saw de Lighthouse

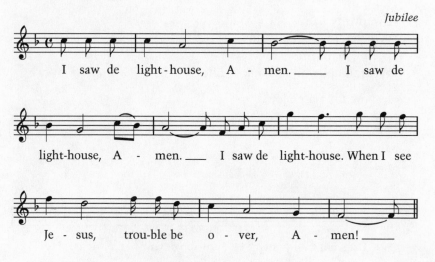

I saw de light-house, A - men. ___ I saw de
light-house, A - men. ___ I saw de light-house. When I see
Je - sus, trou-ble be o - ver, A - men! ___

Jubilee

I Know He'll Bring Me Out

This song was sung for me by a member of the Bryan Baptist Church in Savannah, Georgia. I have never heard it elsewhere.

I know He'll bring me out all right;
Yes, I know He'll bring me out all right.
For He took my feet out de miry clay;
An' I know He'll bring me out all right.

I know He'll lead me all de way (etc.)

I know He'll hold me in de storm (etc.)

I know He'll take me safely home (etc.)

I Know He'll Bring Me Out

Jubilee

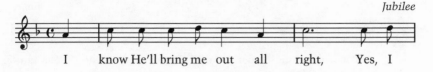

I know He'll bring me out all right, Yes, I

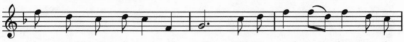

know He'll bring me out all right. For He took my — feet out de

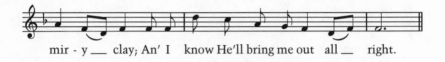

mir - y — clay; An' I know He'll bring me out all — right.

Dat's All Right

The Reverend Zema Hill sang this song in his church in Nashville, Tennessee. That was many years ago. I have never heard it since.

> You can call me ol' pertender,
> But dat's all right.
> You can call me ol' pertender,
> But dat's all right.
> You can call me ol' pertender,
> But dat's all right.
> Jes so ah'm fol'in' Jesus,
> A-dat's all right.

> You can call me ol' backslider (etc.)

> You can call me ol' unbeliever (etc.)

> You can call me ol' sinner man (etc.)

> You can call me unconverted (etc.)

Dat's All Right

You can call me ol' per-ten-der, but dat's all right. _ You can

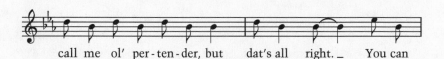

call me ol' per-ten-der, but   dat's all   right. _   You can

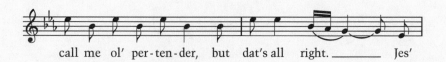

call me ol' per-ten-der, but   dat's all   right. _____   Jes'

so ah'm fol' - in' Je - sus ___   a - dat's all   right. _

Heavenly Dove

This is one of the few Negro songs that seems to demand a deceptive
cadence. The piece seems to end at the eighth measure unless halted
by a VI chord. For imagery and power this song stands high in folk
songs. The picture of the descending dove is one of the great specta-
cles in the Scriptures and lends itself easily to the wings of song. "Oh
for the wings of a dove" is one of the lines that inspired Felix
Mendelssohn and others to write music. The Negro has used the dove
in many songs.

> As I go on my journey here,
> Done come down f'om de tree of life,
> I'll trust in God an' have no fear,
> Done come down f'om de tree of life.

> Ef I was a sinner lis'n what I'd do,
> Done come down f'om de tree of life,

I'd change mah ways an' come along too,
Done come down f'om de tree of life.

Chorus
Oh, de heavenly dove done come down,
De heavenly dove done come down,
Oh, de heavenly dove done come down,
Done come down f'om de tree of life;
Salvation f'om on high.

Heavenly Dove

Oh, de heav-en-ly dove _ done come down, De heav-en-ly dove __

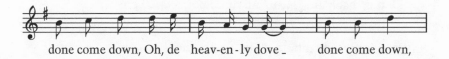

done come down, Oh, de heav-en-ly dove _ done come down,

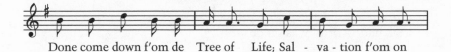

Done come down f'om de Tree of Life; Sal - va - tion f'om on

high. As I go on my jour - ney here, ____

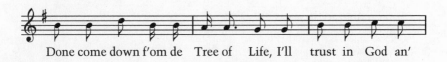

Done come down f'om de Tree of Life, I'll trust in God an'

have no fear, _____ Done come down f'om de Tree of Life.

De Han' Writin' on de Wall

Now God got angry up on His throne,
Angels in heb'm begin to moan,
Dey droop dere wings to hide dere face,
An' Lord have mercy on de human race.
Now, go down angels an' consume de flood,
Blow out de sun an' turn de moon ter blood,
Den go back angels an' a-bolt de do',
Time done been, won' be no mo'.

You read in de Bible an' you understan',
King Belshazzar was a wicked man.
God walked down in Babylon one night,
You never did see such a wonderful sight.
De han' writin' was on de wall,
Go git Daniel, he can read it all.
Ol' Daniel, come an' read de sign,
King Belshazzar den lost his min'.

Well Daniel come an' dere behol',
He read de writin' like a natu'al scroll,
Daniel read upon de wall,
King Belshazzar was about to fall.
Dere de writin' upon de clay,
Was de sign of de reck'nin' day.
King Belshazzar tremble' an' wail',
But he couldn' balance on my God's scale.

Chorus
Oh, what is dat yonder
On de wall?
An can't understan' it—
De han' writin'.
Oh, go an' git Daniel,
He can read it—
De han' writin' on de wall.

De Han' Writin' on de Wall

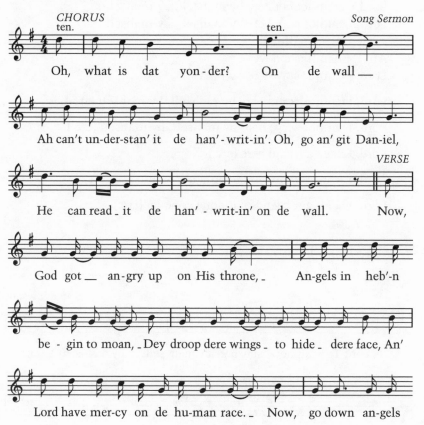

CHORUS   *Song Sermon*

Oh, what is dat yon-der? On de wall —

Ah can't un-der-stan' it de han'-writ-in'. Oh, go an' git Dan-iel,

He can read it de han'-writ-in' on de wall. Now,

God got — an-gry up on His throne, — An-gels in heb'-n

be-gin to moan, — Dey droop dere wings — to hide — dere face, An'

Lord have mer-cy on de hu-man race. — Now, go down an-gels

an' con-sume de flood, Blow out de sun an' turn de moon ter blood, Den

D.C.

go back an-gels an' a bolt de do', Times done been, won' be no mo'.

Here, By Mahself

Lord, I cannot stay here by mahself, by mahself;
Lord, I cannot stay here by mahself, by mahself;
I weep like a willow,
An' I moan like a dove,
Lord, I cannot stay here by mahself.

Lord, I cannot stand here by mahself, by mahself (etc.)

Lord, I cannot serve here by mahself, by mahself (etc.)

Lord, I need a friend here (etc.)

Lord, I want my brother to go wid me (etc.)

Lord, we all got friends dat done gone on (etc.)

Here, By Mahself
Version I

Morality Song

Lord, I can-not stay here by mah-self, _ by mah-self; Lord, I

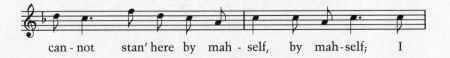

can-not stan' here by mah-self, by mah-self; I

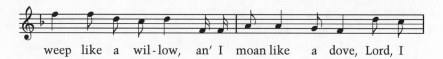

weep like a wil-low, an' I moan like a dove, Lord, I

can - not _____ stay here by mah - self.

Lord, I Cannot Stay Here By Myself

Lord, I cannot stay here by myself, by myself,
Lord, I cannot stay here by myself, by myself.

I want my brother to go with me, go with me,
I want my brother to go with me, go with me.

I'm going away, the Lord knows where, Lord knows where,
I'm going away, the Lord knows where, Lord knows where.

I got a mother done gone on, done gone on,
I got a mother done gone on, done gone on.

Doubting Thomas ain't go' doubt no more, doubt no more,
Doubting Thomas ain't go' doubt no more, doubt no more.

I got a little baby done gone on, done gone on,
I got a little baby done gone on, done gone on.

Chorus
I weep like a willow and I mourn like a dove,
Lord, I cannot stay here by myself.

Lord, I Cannot Stay Here By Myself
Version II

Morality Song

VERSE

Lord, I ___ can - not stay ___ here by my -
self, by my - self, Lord, I can - not stay here by my -

CHORUS

self, by my - self.   I   weep like   a   wil - low   and   I
mourn like   a   dove, Lord, I   can - not stay _ here by my - self.

Bibliography

Allen, William Francis, Charles Pickard Ware, and Lucy McKim Garrison, eds. *Slave Songs of the United States*. New York: A. Simpson, 1867; New York: Peter Smith, 1929.

Ballanta, Nicholas George Julius. *St. Helena Island Spirituals*. New York: G. Schirmer, 1925.

Bolton, Dorothy G., and Harry T. Burleigh. *Old Songs Hymnal*. New York: Century, 1929.

Chappell, Louis W. *John Henry: A Folk-Lore Study*. Jena: Walter Biedermann, 1933.

———. *Songs and Tales from the Dark Continent: Recorded from the Singing and Sayings of C. Kamba Simango and Madikane Cele*. New York: G. Schirmer, 1920.

Curtis-Burlin, Natalie. *Hampton Series Negro Folk-Songs*. New York: G. Schirmer, 1918.

Dett, R. Nathaniel, ed. *Religious Folk-Songs of the Negro as Sung at Hampton Institute*. Hampton, Va.: Hampton Institute Press, 1927.

Diton, Carl R. *Thirty-six South Carolina Spirituals*. New York: G. Schirmer, 1928.

Gellert, Lawrence, and Elie Siegmeister. *Negro Songs of Protest*. New York: Carl Fischer, 1936.

Handy, W. C. *Blues: An Anthology*. New York: Albert and Charles Boni, 1926.

Hare, Maud Cuney. *Six Creole Folk-Songs*. New York: Carl Fischer, 1921.

Hurston, Zora Neale. *Jonah's Gourd Vine*. Philadelphia: Lippincott, 1934.

Johnson, Guy B. *Folk Culture on St. Helena Island, South Carolina*. Chapel Hill: University of North Carolina Press, 1930.

Johnson, J. Rosamond. *Rolling Along in Song*. New York: Viking Press, 1937.

Johnson, James Weldon, and J. Rosamond Johnson. *The Book of American Negro Spirituals*. New York: Viking Press, 1925.

Kennedy, R. Emmet. *Black Cameos*. New York: Albert and Charles Boni, 1924.

————. *Mellows: A Chronicle of Unknown Singers*. New York: Albert and Charles Boni, 1925.

Krehbiel, Henry E. *Afro-American Folksongs*. New York: G. Schirmer, 1914.

Locke, Alain LeRoy. *The Negro and His Music*. Washington, D.C.: Associates in Negro Folk Education, 1936.

Lomax, John A., and Alan Lomax, eds. *American Ballads and Folk Songs*. New York: Macmillan, 1934.

————. *Negro Folk Songs as Sung by Leadbelly*. New York: Macmillan, 1936.

Odum, Howard W. *Rainbow Round My Shoulder: The Blue Trail of Black Ulysses*. Indianapolis: Bobbs-Merrill, 1928.

Odum, Howard W., and Guy B. Johnson. *The Negro and His Songs: A Study of Typical Negro Songs in the South*. Chapel Hill: University of North Carolina Press, 1925.

————. *Negro Workaday Songs*. Chapel Hill: University of North Carolina Press, 1926.

Parrish, Lydia A., ed. *Slave Songs of the Georgia Sea Islands*. New York: Creative Age Press, 1942.

White, Clarence Cameron. *Forty Negro Spirituals*. Philadelphia: Theodore Presser, 1927.

White, Newman I. *American Negro Folk-Songs*. Cambridge, Mass.: Harvard University Press, 1928.

Work, John Wesley, ed. *American Negro Songs: A Comprehensive Collection of 230 Folk Songs, Religious and Secular*. New York: Crown, 1940.

————. *Folk Song of the American Negro*. Nashville, Tenn.: Press of Fisk University, 1915.

Index

Music Index

9654